Rein Müllerson is a professor emeritus at Tallinn University (Estonia). From 2009 to 2017, he was the rector of Tallinn University Nord, later president of the law school and research professor of Tallinn University. Between the years 1994 and 2009, he was professor of international law at King's College London. In 2004–2005, on sabbatical from King's, he worked as the UN regional adviser for Central Asia. During the years 1992 to 1994, he was a visiting centennial professor at the London School of Economics and Political Science.

In 1991–92 Müllerson was first deputy foreign minister of Estonia and in 1988–92 a member of the UN Human Rights Committee. Before that, Müllerson worked as the head of the department of international law at the Institute of State and Law in Moscow and was advisor to President Gorbachev on matters of international law. He is a graduate of the Law Faculty of Moscow University and holds PhD (1979) and doctorate (1985) from that university. Since 1995, he is a Member of the Institut de Droit International (IDI). In 2013, he was elected the president of the IDI, in Tokyo.

To Irina, Jan and George, who have made my life meaningful.

Rein Müllerson

Living in Interesting Times: Curse or Chance?

Recollections of an International
Lawyer – Participant and Observer

AUSTIN MACAULEY PUBLISHERS™
LONDON * CAMBRIDGE * NEW YORK * SHARJAH

Copyright © Rein Müllerson (2021)

The right of Rein Müllerson to be identified as author of this work has been asserted by the author in accordance with section 77 and 78 of the Copyright, Designs and Patents Act 1988.

All rights reserved. No part of this publication may be reproduced, stored in a retrieval system, or transmitted in any form or by any means, electronic, mechanical, photocopying, recording, or otherwise, without the prior permission of the publishers.

Any person who commits any unauthorised act in relation to this publication may be liable to criminal prosecution and civil claims for damages.

All of the events in this memoir are true to the best of author's memory. The views expressed in this memoir are solely those of the author.

A CIP catalogue record for this title is available from the British Library.

ISBN 9781398405097 (Paperback)
ISBN 9781398401945 (ePub e-book)

www.austinmacauley.com

First Published (2021)
Austin Macauley Publishers Ltd
25 Canada Square
Canary Wharf
London
E14 5LQ

I thank all those kindly mentioned in this book. Not only have they made this book possible, but without many of them, I wouldn't have been what I am.

List of Publications

Professor Müllerson is the author of 13 books on international law and politics and more than 300 articles and reviews. His latest books include: *International Law: Rights and Politics* (Routledge 1994), *Human Rights Diplomacy* (Routledge, 1997), *Ordering Anarchy: International Law in International Society* (Kluwer Law International, 2000), *Central Asia: A Chessboard and Player in the New Great Game* (Kegan Paul, 2007, second edition by Routledge in 2012), *Democracy Promotion: Institutions, International Law and Politics* (The Hague Academy of International Law, Recueil des Cours, vol. 333, 2008), Martinus Nijhoff Publishers; *Democracy – A Destiny of Humankind? A Qualified, Contingent and Contextual Case for Democracy Promotion*, (Nova Publishers, New York, 2009), *Regime Change: From Democratic Peace Theories to Forcible Regime Changes*, Brill, Martinus Nijhoff Publishers (Leiden, Boston, 2013), *Dawn of a New Order: Geopolitics and Clash of Ideologies* (London, I.B. Tauris, 2017).

Table of Contents

Preface	11
Introduction	14
1- Childhood and Adolescence in Estonia	19
2- First Years in Russia with Reflections on the Role of Chance in History	29
3- The First Life-Changing Encounter Tunkin in Moscow University	35
4- From Academia to Gorbachev's Advisor	45
5- Advising Michael Gorbachev: the Two Major Cases – The Kuril Islands and The Molotov-Ribbentrop Pact	51
6- The UN Human Rights Committee and Reflections on The Universality of Human Rights	65
7- The Collapse of the Soviet Union and Independence of Estonia	81
8- Another Imperial Capital – London	93
9- My Central Asian Experience	99
10- My Third Coming to Estonia	111
11- From Broken Promises to Cold War II: NATO Coming to Russia	123
12- The 1999 War Over Kosovo a Precursor of a New Cold War?	128
13- Ukraine: Victim of Geopolitics?	137
14- China Has Risen, Russia Is Back, the US is in Relative Decline New Geopolitical Realities	146
15- On Contemporary Revolutionary Situations in the World	168
16- Balance of Powers A Precondition for International Law and Relatively Peaceful World	174
17- Nation-State – A Cradle of Democracy	183
18- Revolution in the Western World: Democracy v. Liberalism	199
19- Instead of Conclusions: Is E Pluribus Unum Indeed Replacing Ex Uno Plures?	214

L'aveuglement est le prix que paient ceux qui croient détenir les clés de l'histoire. (Blindness is the price paid by those who believe that they hold the keys of history).

– J. Lopez, L. Otkhmezuri,
Barbarossa, 1941 (p. 294)

Preface

The manuscript of this book was finished, sent and accepted by the publisher just before the coronavirus pandemic hit the world. Therefore, there was nothing on it in the text. However, reading, watching or listening to the news and comments I, like most of us, had an impression that all other issues, tendencies or events had lost their significance in comparison with this sudden calamity engulfing all the nations of the world. Thus, an itch to peruse the text to see whether modifications would be needed in the light of changing circumstances, to check whether my reflections on geopolitics, the rise of populism, the role of the nation-state and other topics I analysed in the manuscript would need adjustments dictated by shifting perspectives. However, what I found, even with some surprise, was that the pandemic, and particularly the reactions of nations to it, had only accelerated and made more explicit tendencies that had existed before. They hadn't annulled them or created something unprecedented, unheard of. So, the role of the state, whose demise at the beginning of the twentieth century had been prophesised by Marxists-Leninists and at the end of it by liberal democrats, was continuing its comeback. But this had become noticeable already after in 2008 the financial and economic crises had hit the world. The coronavirus made it even more obvious that the efficient and well-run state, no matter whether it is democratic or authoritarian, becomes particularly indispensable in times of crises.

Notwithstanding some cooperation between states on sanitary and health matters in the face of the pandemic, prior contentions between them did not disappear. On the contrary, they intensified, particularly, in the domains such as artificial intelligence or biotechnology. Traditional rivalries over the control of sea-lines, pipelines or natural resources were rejoined by the contest for the control of the human body and mind. Not only the freedom of movement became severely restricted (this may have been understandable, as a temporary sanitary measure), but also the freedom of expression came even under stronger attack, usually under the banner of the fight with 'fake news', suppression of hostile propaganda, or pandering to the devotees of 'political correctness.' And even this was not new. Already for some years, due to the spread of social media and the strengthening of non-Western (particularly Russian, Chinese as well as Arab) channels of information, political, economic and intellectual elites in the Western world had become uncomfortable with the freedom of information.

The virus and measures undertaken to curb its spread have, however, considerably accelerated pre-existing tendencies, including the geopolitical reconfiguration of the world, meaning that when the pandemic ends the world is not reverting to the pre-Covid-19 situation. It will have done a jump ahead in directions, most of which had already been detectable. Similarly, the Covid-19 has also made increasingly obvious and acute pre-exiting divisions between those in Western societies whom David Goodhart has called anywheres and somewheres (or nomads and settlers, according to Alexandre Devecchio), between those, who have hugely benefitted from globalisation and those that have been left behind. As Devecchio writes: 'Nurses, caregivers, policemen, cashiers, truck drivers, delivery boys and garbage collectors, whose work is not appreciated, have taken main risks vis-à-vis the epidemy, while many executives and managers could work from home. These are the disadvantaged who suffer most from the virus and the looming economic and social crises will further amplify existing rifts.[1]

The Covid-19 may have played an important, even crucial, role in the 2020 Presidential elections in the United States. However, as Time magazine headlined one of its articles in the aftermath of the elections, 'Even if Joe Biden Wins, He Will Govern in Donald Trump's America'[2]. Indeed, since Trump's presidency was not a cause but a symptom of divisions existing not only in America, but in many other societies as well. Unfortunately, the election of Joe Biden cannot be a solution to the leadership crisis in the Western world. Rather, his election reminds the final years of the recent American rival, when the gerontocratic Soviet Politburo could not do any better than picking aging Konstantin Chernenko, as a pair of safe hands. Those in power still believed that muddling through as usual would be an option. This paved the way to Gorbachev reforms, leading to the collapse of the Soviet Union and the rebirth of Russia. I

---

[1] 'Karl Marx, Manifeste du Parti Communiste (1848). Les métamorphoses de la lutte des classes' in *Éloge de la Politique: Avec les Grandes Textes (Histoire)*, (Sous la direction de Vincent Trémolet de Villiers) Tallandier/Le Figaro, 2020, p. 225
[2] *Time*, November 4, 2020.

am in no way prophesising the disintegration of the United States; all cases differ. However, the American 2020 choice looks more like kicking the can further down the road instead of taking the bull by the horns. As Daron Acemoglu writes, 'The roots of Trumpism don't begin or end with Trump or even with American politics – they are closely connected to economic and political currents affecting much of the world.'[3]

Instead of following constantly changing numbers of infected persons in different countries and disputes whether wearing masks helps to avoid contamination or not, I found solace in reading or rereading classics. This was not only a remedy, besides good wine and regular exercises, against depression; it also contributed to the better understanding of contemporary challenges. Notwithstanding the obvious technological progress of humankind and acceleration of societal transformations, human nature has not changed much, if at all. And it will remain so at least until the emergence of trans-or post-humans. Our predecessors, at least greatest of them, can still, and probably forever, give us lessons that may be useful for the resolution of today's problems, provided of course, that we creatively use their heritage.

---

[3] D. Acemoglu, 'Trump Won't Be the Last American Populist', *Foreign Affairs*, November 6, 2020.

Introduction

'May you live in interesting times.' This Chinese proverb contains a curse usually addressed to somebody who is likely to lead an adventurous and interesting life, which usually has, as its flipside and necessary concomitant, more than average amount of difficulties, obstacles, 'unknown unknowns' (as per Secretary Rumsfeld) and hurdles to be overcome. Interesting times are usually anything but calm and orderly, when today is very much like yesterday and from tomorrow you don't expect anything radically different. The times, I have lived through, have been anything but dull or predictable, while a reference to the Chinese proverb seems particularly appropriate as I started writing the first lines of my recollections on the times lived through as a lawyer, politician and diplomat, in Xi'an – in a wonderful city that used to be the capital of the ancient Middle Empire, near the tomb of the first Emperor Qin Shi Huang – that is still guarded by more than 7000 Terra Cotta warriors. It was not my first visit either to China or to its ancient capital. Twelve years earlier, being elected Marco Polo fellow of the prestigious Jiaotong University in Xi'an, for having helped build bridges between China and the West, as the certificate says, I had already spent several months in this historic city. I have also visited many other Chinese cities – big and small; small, of course, by Chinese, not by Estonian or even European, standards.

But how did a guy from the Estonian countryside find himself in such far-away places not only geographically, but also in terms of culture and politics? Estonia, though not exactly a micro-state, is nevertheless one of the smallest nations in the world, while China is the most populous country on the Planet Earth? For answering that question, I must go back in history to a recent period that gave an impetuous to radical transformations all over the world. This was not the first of such periods, maybe even not the most crucial one, but, nevertheless, it has been a life-changing experience not only for millions of individuals but also for most nations, big and small.

The rise and the fall of the Roman Empire, the birth, expansion and the long demise of the Genghis Khan's realm, the emergence and collapse of British, French and Portuguese empires and the end of colonialism were all remarkable and revolutionary developments in the world history. However, these were all long processes and their significance, or relative insignificance, became evident much later. Those, who lived during the rise and demise of ancient empires didn't and couldn't realise the significance of these processes since the lifespan of an individual is infinitely shorter than the ascent, duration and death of empires or emergence of nation-states from medieval multi-layered political structures. Conversely, the processes that started and enrolled at the end of the 1980s, and are still going on, have been in historical terms not a marathon but rather a sprinting event. These have been revolutionary transformations, even though at the time of their commencement it was not clear whether it would be a blip in the history of humankind, though crucial in personal lives of millions of individuals, or a beginning of a radical transformation of the world with unforeseeable consequences. Slightly more than thirty years have passed since these processes started, but today we already live in the world that is fundamentally different from that, which existed only a few decades ago. Moreover, it is still changing under the impetus of the forces unleashed three decades ago.

President Macron of France was right when, in summer 2019, he told the French Ambassadors that 'we all live in the world, and you know that better than I do, where the existing order has been propelled in an unprecedented manner and, if I may say, where changes of historical magnitude are occurring almost in all the domains for the first time in the contemporary history. This is, first of all, a geopolitical and strategic transformation and recomposition of the world. Without any doubt we are living through the end of the Western domination of the world.'[4] However, not so long ago many of us believed, together with Francis Fukuyama, in the Westernisation of the whole world and in the advent of the American century. How come that the historical tables have been turned so quickly?

My friends and colleagues, knowing that I had met, written for or advised some important personalities, whose names are associated with crucial changes in the history of their countries or the world, have prompted me to write my

---

[4] *Discours du Président de la République à la conférence des ambassadeurs*. Elysée, 27 août 2019.

memoirs. However, I don't think that many people would find interesting or exiting intimate memoires of a rather insignificant person, even if he happened to be in middle of historical changes, not only as an observer but also as a participant, but never as a top-level decision-maker. However, writing not so much about myself but about the times and events with continuing effects, about the ideas that emerged, circulated, influenced the world history or, on the contrary, turned out to be illusory, like the 'great' idea of the end of history, seems to me to be useful. Having worn in my lifetime different hats and having enjoyed quite a few of them, I believe that the academic writing has been central and most enjoyable for me. This is another reason why I have chosen the genre of personal reflections on personalities, I have met and worked with, times I have lived through, and particularly the continuing role of the ideas that have been influential during those decades and new approaches that have emerged from them.

Since all human beings are subjective and their subjectivity is individual, though conditioned by the communities within which an individual exists and functions, it would be, in my opinion, advisable if a writer declares the nature of his particular subjectivity, as honestly as possible, before touching upon the reality about which he is writing. Notwithstanding such an open declaration of my own subjectivity and my belief that everybody's views are equally tilted, I still think that there is an objective reality that exists independently of our personal subjectivity. In contradistinction to subjective idealists, I believe in subjective realism, i.e., that there is an objective reality that we all subjectively perceive. However, one of the few things, I have become certain of over the years of writing and reflecting, is that our perception of that reality, at least in the areas that are covered by social sciences and humanities, remains always skewed, even if the desire to perceive this reality as objectively as possible is welcome. Therefore, describing and reflecting on my own background, my progress (or regress) over the years and why I think as I do and not otherwise, I can better understand my own subjectivity and its impact on my perception of processes and events I have lived through and going to explain in this book. This, in my opinion, is one of the necessary conditions for approaching objective reality, never of course embracing it in full. The reality is too complicated, too fluid and constantly changing to be caught by an individual mind, and there is no such thing as collective mind (at least until the arrival of so-called trans- or post-humans, if they ever emerge). Even Donald Trump in his 'great and unmatched wisdom' couldn't grasp the objective reality in full.

There is an excellent English saying stating that 'where one stands depends on where one sits.' Following that maxim, I will try to explain why I stand where I stand by taking account of the stumps, chairs or posts I have sat on during my adolescence, mature years and while aging (I like more a nice French term '*viellissement*'). In my life, there have been several such reference points, and they have been rather different. Having had various, often opposing, reference points have made my personal life sometimes quite complicated, has caused frictions with friends and even relatives, but it has also, I believe, given me some advantages in my professional life. One-sidedness is certainly not my weak (or strong, depending on a point of view) point. My dear wife Irina sometimes, when I am bold enough to argue with her, says that I can justify almost everybody's behaviour, including even that of Donald Trump or Boris Johnson, who she intensively dislikes. However, I dare to humbly suggest that she may confuse justification and explanation, though sometimes, indeed, there is no obvious distinction between these notions, since while trying to explain something, one may find oneself also justifying what is being explained. Hence, the choice of a genre that combines personal reflections with the analysis of the times, events and the ideas that accompanied them, seems to me rather appropriate. This helps me, I hope, to see more clearly my own partiality and preferences, to see why I think as I do and not otherwise.

We all have our backgrounds, we are educated and brought up in societies whose values and traditions may hugely vary. Moreover, people cannot be free from their personal interests, interests of their loved ones, interests of the societies they live in. I don't know whether in natural sciences physicists or chemists have their favourite atoms or molecules, whose value or role they exaggerate at the expense of other atoms or molecules. Probably, not. However, in the field of social studies, the opposite – that is, not taking sides – seems to be an exception. Too many social scientists seem to have their preferred 'molecules.' I am not speaking of those journalists who all too often have specific agendas that consist not so much of informing the audience as of mobilising public opinion. They are activists or militants for good, or not so good, causes. In the domain of social sciences, taking sides is widespread, almost automatic and subconscious, even among the best social scientists. For example, Paul Saunders – a clear-minded American analyst of the realist school – once wrote: 'What would a realist foreign-policy strategy look like? It would start with the recognition that maintaining America's international leadership – without incurring costs that neither our political system nor our economy can sustain – is the best way to protect U.S. national interests.'[5] Hence, there is an obvious agenda – to protect the US national interest, to maintain Washington's global leadership, that is, its dominance, in the world. It is a clear agenda that the 'research' has to justify, underpin and promote. And this is so notwithstanding that Paul Saunders, in contradistinction to many other American authors, well understands that without taking account of the positions of other powers, whose interests and visions of the world may not coincide with those of Washington, the United States can neither carry out its leadership, nor can it efficiently protect its national interests. Yet, many of those who call themselves, or by their job-description are, 'researchers' are blatant activists or apologists. Their approaches are almost invariably either, say, pro-Palestinian or pro-Israeli, pro-Ukrainian or pro-Russian, pro-American or anti-American, pro-Serb or pro-Bosniak, pro-Armenian or pro-Azeri and so on and so forth. Moreover, such labels are often used *ad nauseam*, so that they start functioning like self-fulfilling prophecies even if *ab initio* they made little sense. For example, the population of Ukraine was, at the beginning of the conflict, quite artificially divided by the Western mass media into pro-Westerns and pro-Russians. Such an approach contributed to the consolidation of such a division in the Ukrainian society. The intentions of activists may be respectable, and their moral outrages may be often justified or even necessary, but such positions are not those of a researcher. Of course, such activism sometimes helps change the world for the better. Oftentimes, however, it may lead people astray and contribute to the realisation of negative tendencies. I believe that my preference for a researcher's approach, notwithstanding my understanding of its limits, is conditioned, at least partly, by my own background, about which in the following chapters.

---

[5] P.J. Saunders, 'Barack Obama is not a realist', *The National Interest*, 26 August 2014.

1- Childhood and Adolescence in Estonia

My personal life, even before the end of the 1980s, had been rather eventful with several unexpected twists and turns, though they were mainly due to my restless character, desire to try what comes on the way, or resulted from my personal ambitions. The life in the Soviet Union, where I was born and spent my childhood and adolescence, was less exciting than it was in the part of the planet that was called, with some justification and in comparison with the existing alternative, 'the free world'. I have used the inverted commas here partly also because with the disappearance of the largest non-free world in the form of the Soviet Union, the elements and seeds of the non-freedom have sprung up and flourish in the world that was indeed and still is relatively free. However, the disappearance of the erstwhile enemy has done disservice to the triumphant West and has led it to the search of new enemies or making enemies out of those who once hoped to become its friends.

Exceptions to the relatively dull life in the former USSR were the lives of those dissidents who had openly expressed their dissatisfaction with the communist regime and as a result had found themselves in labour camps or GULAGs, as they had become widely known thanks to the works of Aleksander Solzhenitsyn and other dissident writers. Although I was born several years before the death of Comrade Stalin, my childhood and adolescence fell mainly into the years of so-called 'thaw' of Comrade Khrushchev and the 'stagnation' period of Comrade Brezhnev. Therefore, when growing up I knew little about repressions of the Stalin period, though I probably knew a bit more than most of my peers in the former USSR and I knew about a special aspect of them, victims of which had been my fellow Estonians. I had occasionally heard about them here and there in the form of disconnected bits and pieces from adults in Estonia, though, as a rule, they kept silent on such sensitive and unsafe issues. Therefore, as I will explain below, a big and important part of my own family history from my father's side had remained unknown to me until I had already turned sixty; and even then, only by chance.

In 1940, several years before my birth, Estonia had become part of the Soviet Union and already in the summer of the next year tens of thousands of Estonians were sent to Siberia. I am using here a rather neutral term 'became part' leaving for later the complicated questions of 'occupation', 'annexation' and the role of the looming World War II on these fatal events. It is also that the more I learn about those years, the less black and white many aspects of them become in my eyes. Of course, there were millions of others in the former Soviet Union, besides Estonians, who had faced similar journeys to Siberia. But about that, like most Estonians at that time, I knew nothing. I didn't know what Joseph Vissarionovich Dzhugashvili, alias Comrade Stalin, and done to his own nation – the Georgians. I ignored that most Stalin's inmates were Russians, but this, of course, could not and should not justify his crimes against Estonians or any other group of people. With hindsight and personal experience, I must admit that Stalin probably did not commit one major crime against humanity – with a few exceptions at certain periods – he didn't discriminate between his victims on the ground of their ethnicity or religion.

Among those who, in the summer of 1941, left Estonia in cattle wagons against their own will was also my father – an officer of the Estonian army – Avo Laido. His uncle, that is to say my grand-uncle, Artur Lossman had served as general in the same army. Before the Bolshevik revolution of 1917, he, as a graduate of St Petersburg Military-Medical Academy, had been an officer in the Russian Tsarist army taking part in the 1904–1905 war between Japan and Russia. My great-uncle escaped from the Soviets and ended his days in London, where I today live with my family. Indeed, a strange parallel. London – the city at this moment plagued by the coronavirus and in Brexit throws, which I, as Estonian and European, follow also with some personal anxiety. And the Brexit, whose full impact we still cannot foresee, is not unrelated, as I will try to explain below, to those processes that initiated these interesting, promising and worrying times, wrought with unexpected opportunities as well as with serious hazards and dangers.

I first visited to London in December 1991, leading a small Estonian delegation to the Chatham House (the main foreign policy think-tank of the United Kingdom). There we were met, among other dignitaries, by Mrs Nora

Morley-Fletcher – the chairperson of the Estonian community in Great Britain. Only years later I learned that Mrs Morley-Fletcher was born in Estonia as Nora Lossman. She was the daughter of General Artur Lossman – my grand-uncle. I learned this and many other things related to my relatives on my father's side much later – in 2004, when in my UN office of the former Kazakh capital, Almaty, I received an email from two ladies – Heili and Ülle, who had the same surname as my farther – Laido. This was my younger half-sister Heili, who had by chance – once again, a chance helped – learned that they may have one more half-brother, that happened to be me. Then I discovered that not only had I had a grand-uncle in London, who by then was already gone, but also half brothers, sisters and lots of nephews and nieces, all living, with the exception my youngest sister, in the United States. Now I have met all of them, some in their home country and others in my homes either in London or in Tallinn. Meeting them as well as my other relatives, I have learned a lot about my family history and a bit more also about the history of my country – Estonia. In that I have been helped also by two books written by my relatives. General Lossman's memoirs *In the Stormy World* (written and published in Estonian *Rahutus Maailmas*) were printed in Stockholm, though they were obviously written in London. Equally interesting and revealing is a small paperback by my father's second, and I believe his favourite, wife *Johanna's Memoires from Europe 1911-1950*, written in English and published in the United States, where she lived the longest part of her life. The first line of Johanna's book stunned me. She wrote: 'I was born on March 23, 1911, in a hospital in St. Petersburg, the capital of the Russian Empire.' The matter is that my mother gave birth to me in Dudergoff, not far from St. Petersburg, on her way back from Siberia, also on 23 March, only 33 years later. From Johanna's book, I learned also about my father's life in the pre-Second World War Estonia and his deportation to Siberia.

I was brought up by my mother in Tallinn, and my grand-parents and other relatives in the South Estonian countryside, since the war-time love story of my parents didn't last long. I do not remember at all my father. Having returned to Estonia as a major of the Soviet Army, he soon ditched my mom and remarried, living in Tartu and teaching at the local university. Moreover, I didn't know practically anything about my father's family background, and I was, particularly, ignorant of the fact that he had been twice married already before the war. When he returned after the war with the Soviet troops to Estonia, both his wife and ex-wife, together with their children, had escaped from the returning Soviets and eventually, after long peregrinations, found themselves in America. I ignore how much my mother knew about father's pre-war life. I believe not very much, and even less was revealed to me. Therefore, I was truthful when in later years, still in the Soviet Union, I wrote in questionnaires that were necessary, for example, for travelling abroad that I had no relatives living in foreign countries. Otherwise, I certainly wouldn't have been allowed to travel abroad. This means also that the KGB was not omniscient and due to the changes of names and in the absence of computers its officers hadn't discovered the family links with numerous relatives I had in the bourgeois heartlands – Great Britain and the United States.

My father, né also Lossman, had changed his surname according with the trend of Estonianisation of names of mostly German origin in the country that had become independent in 1918, having been a part of the Russian Empire since the times of Peter the Great. However, even under the political rule of the Russian Empire, Baltic Germans had been omnipresent and influential on the territory of current Estonia.

My father, being in one of the labour camps in Siberia when, in June 1941, the Nazi Germany attacked the Soviet Union, was given an option: either to remain in the camps or to join the Red army. I know nothing about the reasons why my farther chose the Red Army, but it was certainly the right choice, especially from the point of view of the world History. Although even today there are quite a few Estonians who, in their belief that the Soviets were worse than the Nazis, would strongly disagree with me. However, in that respect I equally strongly disagree with them. I agree with one of my favourite philosophers – Reinhold Niebuhr, who described the differences between the Nazism and Communism in the following way: if the first was the absolute evil, the second was the corruption of the good.[6] That explains also why the communist movement, notwithstanding the crimes committed on its name, lasted much longer than fascism or Nazism. It was due to the attractiveness of its ideas. Amin Maalouf, member of the *Académie Française*, believes that the communist movement, having generated great hopes among many noble minds, betrayed these ideals and that betrayal has also contributed to the slide of the world to global decay.[7] And he continues: 'when the communist utopia had sunk in the abyss of misery, the triumphant capitalism resulted in the outbreak of obscene

---

[6] R. Niebuhr, *The Irony of American History*, New York 1952; reprint with a new introduction by Andrew J. Bacevich, University of Chicago Press 2008.
[7] A. Maalouf, *Le Naufrage des Civilisations*, Bernard Grasset, 2019. p. 95.

inequalities. What may find justification from the point of view economics, is disastrous in humanitarian terms, in terms of morality as well as in terms of politics.'[8]

Today it has become fashionable, especially in some former communist countries, to equate the crimes of communist and fascist regimes. It is true that communist regimes, be it the USSR under Stalin, China under Mao or Cambodia under Pol Pot, have exterminated more of their own people than fascist regimes, which were in power for far much shorter periods. In practice, both totalitarianisms – fascism and communism – were indeed in some respects similar. However, their ideologies were rather different. If fascism represented moral nihilism and ideas of supremacy of certain races or nations, communism was a utopian creed, which due to its humane ideas had wide attraction. In a way, communist ideology, due namely to its benevolent and compassionate nature and universal appeal, has been more infectious than fascist ideology (the road to hell paved with good intentions). Reinhold Niebuhr concluded that communism as 'the corruption of the good' can be even more dangerous in human history than the 'explicit evil' in the form of fascism.[9] It is easier to recognise the explicit evil.

However, we should not throw away ideas and ideals only because of their association with, or exploitation by, totalitarian regimes. For example, the first draft of the new Russian Constitution under President Yeltsin, which had a chapter dedicated to human rights didn't contain, initially any reference to economic or social rights. Only later, after domestic criticism and critical comments from abroad, did the drafters include economic and social rights as rights protected under the Constitution. And such a draft was prepared under the leadership of Professor Sergei Alekseyev, who in the 1970s had written a lot about the primacy of economic and social rights over civil and political rights. However, in the 1990s, rejecting communist practices, some of which he had earlier praised, Professor Alekseyev together with the bathwater also threw the baby out. Similarly, when Estonia in autumn 1991 ratified, on my initiative, together with many other UN human rights instruments the UN Covenant on Economic, Social and Cultural Rights, I was accused by some of pulling Estonia back to communism. Jumping from one extreme to the opposite one seldom brings positive results in personal lives and even more so in lives of human societies.

---

[8] *Ibid.*, p. 17
[9] Niebuhr, *The Irony of American History*, p. 128.

The Second World War was a war against the 'absolute evil' that threatened the humankind and those who fought the Nazis and their allies were indeed, as it is often said in different contexts either naively or abusively, 'on the right side of the history.' As French historians Jean Lopez and Lasha Otkhmezuri have written in their book on the Nazi plans to attack the Soviet Union (Operation Barbarossa), 'even those who are hostile to the Soviet regime cannot avoid identifying themselves, if only partly, with it in order to save Russia'[10] and the whole world from the Nazi nightmare. As my Israeli friend and colleague Yoram Dinstein, the former President and Rector of Tel Aviv University, once told me in Tallinn: 'The Soviet Union's existence may be justified by its contribution to the defeat of the Nazism.' I am not so sure that this contribution, which indeed was huge and indispensable, can wipe out the atrocities of Lenin, Stalin and their collaborators as well as later repressions, but on this matter, I cannot argue with my Jewish friend. The Holocaust was the most terrible and unique crime in the history of the humankind not only because of the number of the victims, but also due to its unprecedented and extraordinary inhumane ideology and meticulous coldblooded planning. Those who fought to defeat this inhumane regime, that had already subjugated most of the Old Continent, were without doubt on the right side of history, even if many of them may have otherwise been quite unpleasant persons or even criminals.

My mother's story that led her to the Siberia, where my parents met and where I was conceived, was rather different from that of my father, but indicative of the fact that the pre-Second World War Estonian society was no less divided than it is, unfortunately, today, though otherwise and for different reasons, of which more below. A brother of my mother's close friend, Ella, had been a communist in the bourgeois Estonia, an opponent of President Päts' authoritarianism. Obviously, he was not sent to Siberia when the Soviets came; he may have even welcomed them, though later he certainly (and I know it, having spoken to him) regretted his short-sightedness. However, being a communist in Estonia at the end of the 1930s is even more understandable than the communist sympathies of, say, many French or Italian intellectuals before and after the war. So, when the Germans advanced and the Soviet troops withdrew, the brother of my mother's friend not only left with the Soviets, but

---

[10] J. Lopez, L. Otkhmezuri, *Barbarossa 1941. La guerre absolue*, Passes Composes, 2019.
2019.

he also evacuated his mother and sisters further from the wrath of the Nazis. And rightly so, as it soon became clear. The Nazis didn't spare not only Jews or communists, but also their families and sympathisers. My mother, who had moved with her friend from a village in the South of Estonia to Tallinn, left with her for Siberia on her own volition.

The fate of the family – the Korbs, with whom my mother – Erna Müllerson – went to Siberia, is rather symptomatic for Estonia and Estonians. The youngest brother Walter, the communist, spent the war in the Soviet Army. Two older brothers – Jaan and Karl – stayed in Estonia. When the Germans came, Karl, being obviously against all the invaders, was hiding in the forest. The elder – Jaan, who stayed put, was forced by the Nazis to spend the war as a prison-guard in the German concentration camp in Klooga, near Tallinn, though he had never shown any sympathies for the Nazis. When the war ended and Walter returned, he held high posts in the administration of the Soviet Estonia, but only for a while. It was soon discovered that his elder brother had served the Germans in the most hideous place in the Nazi-occupied Estonia. Walter was dismissed from all of his posts and even my mother's friend – Ella, who was working as a waitress in a restaurant, where party bosses used to have their lunches, was sacked. Jaan was lucky to stay alive having spent 10 years in Siberian hard-labour camps. If Jaan Korb may have been a weak and politically ignorant person, there were Estonians who joined the Nazis on their own volition and fought, some even in SS uniforms, against the Soviet troops advancing in 1944. Even if advocates of some of them could use the biblical justification 'for they know not what they do,' others knew or should have known what they were doing. Considering them as freedom-fighters and heroes, as it is still done in Estonia, Latvia or Ukraine is scandalous and disgraceful.

Once, being together with my friend Yoram and seeing in a newspaper a photo of Stepan Bandera, I asked Yoram whether he knew who Bandera was. He gave me a rhetorical and sarcastic answer: 'You ask me, a Jew and Israeli, do I know who Stepan Bandera was?' Indeed, but today Ukrainian nationalists march in major Ukrainian cities honouring Bandera and other fascist collaborators. And no sanctions are imposed against those who do that or who allow it to be done.

Maybe the fact that I was born on the move, or rather on my mother's way back from Siberia to Tallinn, my whole life has also been on the move, sometimes against my own will, every now and then by chance, but often also on my own volition. As an adolescent in Estonia, I became a rather good athlete, excelling particularly in high jump. My first trips outside Estonia, but still within the USSR, were related to my participation in different athletic competitions. As I single-mindedly concentrated on my physical perfection, I often neglected my homework, missed classes and was finally kicked out of the school after only seven years of studies and started earning my living that made the life of our small family a bit more comfortable. Ironically enough, one of the reasons of my expulsion from school was my conflict with my Russian language teacher. Obviously, she didn't like me, and I gave her the taste of the same medicine. Then she told my mom that I was so lazy and so stupid that I would never learn to speak Russian, or any other language for that matter. My mom cried her eyes out and for me this was the final straw. I told the teacher everything I thought of her, including her bowed legs and other physical deficiencies. This was the final straw for the administration, and we went separate ways. The irony consists in the fact that now I speak Russian better than many Russians do, and my first articles and books were all written in the language of Pushkin, whose poetry I admire together with the poetry of many other Russians, including my wife Irina's verses. Moreover, a couple of years later, already in the Soviet Army, I discovered that I had linguistic skills above the average. Although I was certainly wrong when telling my Russian language teacher what I had told her, I believe that educators are often unable to interest young boys and girls and make hastily wrong judgments about them. My own pedagogic experience confirms that. Moreover, at the same school I had also a different experience. A new math teacher, who in his younger years had been a good athlete, treated me, obviously due to my athletic prowess, with undue respect. As I was ashamed to be seen stupid or lazy by him and though caring even less about the math than about the Russian language, I did very well in math, at least when he taught the discipline.

Even if not been at all diligent at school, I was always an avid reader and read whatever I could put my hands on, especially history books. Playing with my neighbour Tõnu, a couple of years junior to me, we found at the bottom of his father's cupboard dozens of history books from the times of the pre-war independent Estonia. Although, as far as I remember, these books were all about ancient and medieval years of European history and there was nothing about the recent controversial periods of Estonian history, Tõnu's father – Paul, reluctantly handing them one by one over to me, warned not to tell or show them to anybody and return them as soon as read.

Much later, already during my university years, or even later, I discovered that I had read in Estonian (the only language I had mastered by then) Victor Hugo, Alexander Dumas, Honoré de Balzac, Aleksander Pushkin and even Charles Dickens. However, the names of the authors I discovered much later. When I read, I didn't pay any attention to what I considered as a secondary factor. Having read in my childhood a voluminous book *The Abay's Way* by famous Kazakh writer Mukhtar Auezov (I was given a book by a small village librarian probably since there wasn't much to choose from), served me, however, well in my diplomatic career. Much later, working for the UN as regional advisor for Central Asia, I met Mukhtar Auezov's son Murat – a Kazakh diplomat, politician, writer and public intellectual. I encountered him for the first time at a huge seventy fifth anniversary party of the most famous Kyrgyz writer – Chingiz Aitmatov, whose short novel *Dzhamilya* Roman Rolland had called the best thing ever written on the love. I certainly had enjoyed reading it. When I mentioned to Murat that, in my childhood, I had read his father's masterpiece in Estonian, many informal channels of communication with important people in the country, where the name of Mukhtar Auezov competed with that of President Nursultan Nazarbayev, opened for me. Through Murat I became acquainted with Kazakh poets such as Olzhas Suleimenov and Bakhydzhan Kanapyanov. Bakhydzhan, who also owns a publishing house, even helped to publish Irina's first book of poetry.

For the time being, the name Auezov has lost in terms of popularity to another Kazakh name. In 2019 even the capital of the country – Astana – was rebaptised after the first name of the former President of Kazakhstan. It is now called Nur-Sultan, having been Astana, when I worked in the region and earlier Akmola. However, I believe that though personality cults of top politicians may overwhelm the veneration of even greatest minds of nations, it is usually a temporary phenomenon. Deep down, in their innermost hearts, most nations remember their scientists, philosophers, writers, poets, composers and other intellectuals, even though nowadays their popularity has become overwhelmed by the fame of football players and pop-singers. However, their fame is even more passing – out of sight, out of mind. And this is so not only in authoritarian countries, but also, and maybe even more so, in Western democracies. Of course, the personality cult of Messi, Ronaldo or Madonna may be more innocuous that the cult of authoritarian presidents, but it may also be an element or sign of banalisation, even degradation, of liberal democracy, but about it later in the book. In my childhood, Valery Brummel – the 1964 Olympic champion and the world record holder – was my hero, though I must confess that my only desire was to become better than him. So, if he was my idol, then only to be overthrown by me, though it never, of course, happened. Today, hardly anybody remembers this name.

I am sure that fate, accidents and chances play role, sometimes crucial, in the lives of individuals as well as in the history of nations, and in our globalised world, of the whole humankind. In my personal life chance has played a much bigger role than in the lives of my childhood friends, fellow-students, or most of the colleagues I have met in my later life. However, I am probably been rather lucky because even bad accidents, or wrong decisions made by me, have usually turned out to have positive outcomes. Certainly, I myself played an active role in turning my bad luck into new adventures, setting goals, the achievement of which turned out to be, at least with hindsight, much more important than lost opportunities. Without these unfortunate turns, I wouldn't be able to accomplish what I have achieved.

The first such accident happened when I was only seventeen and already a promising high jumper. I pulled my Achilles tendon. Although this didn't immediately put an end to my athletic career, it certainly shortened it and prevented me to fully realise my potential. Importantly for my future life and career, instead of pursuing my vocation in Estonia, I was conscripted into the Soviet Army that wasn't at all in my plans. I tried anything imaginable to escape from the clutches of the military. Having heard that the flat feet and high blood-pressure were considered as disabilities exempting from the military service, I tried to rise my blood-pressure by drinking dozens of cups of strongest coffee before going to the medical examination, since it was obvious to me that I didn't have the flat feet. Unfortunately, but with hindsight fortunately, my blood-pressure was considered not to be high enough, notwithstanding that my body was trembling when doctors took their measurements. Without these unfortunate episodes my life would have been very different. At best I could have become an athletic coach in Estonia, maybe even not that.

2- First Years in Russia with Reflections on the Role of Chance in History

Being brought to Russia against my own volition, I returned, so to say, to the country where I was conceived and born. It was also by chance that I made my military service near Moscow. Therefore, after the demobilisation I found myself in the capital of the USSR, now of the Russian Federation. While in the army I had discovered, not yet paying much attention to it, that I had some unused language skills. I quickly started speaking relatively good and correct Russian, without excessively using the army slang peppered with swearwords. Soon I even imitated my fellow conscripts from Latvia and Georgia in their native tongues. Once, having spent fifteen days, for going AWOL (for those not used to military terminology, 'leaving without an official leave' my unit), in a disciplinary cell (this happened to me several times due to my dislike of the military discipline) together with a guy from Ukraine, I became quite fluent in Ukrainian. Of course, it helped that Russian and Ukrainian languages are rather close. As I haven't finished the secondary education before the military service, I couldn't enrol in any establishment of higher education. Therefore, after the three years of service, I enrolled in the School for Athletic Coaches in a town called Malakhovka, near Moscow. There, competing once in decathlon, I was noticed by Yuri Chistyakov – the then chief coach of the Soviet Olympic high jumpers. He believed me to be talented enough to start exercising in his group of high jumpers of the Olympic reserve. There I met also my childhood hero Valery Brummel, who had resumed his training after a tragic traffic accident, which had irrevocably damaged his right leg. At that time, he looked like a disabled person, whose injured leg, due to multiple operations, had become shorter than his left one that he used to jump. Therefore, during the run-up for a jump, he was visibly limping. He had also put on some extra kilos during his stays in various hospitals.

However, even then he jumped higher than quite a few of us – able-bodied athletes, including myself. Three years lost in the military and repercussions of the old injury I had had before my military service, made my professional athletic career rather short. Two years of training with some of the world best athletes brought home to me, what I should have grasped sooner, that I was not gifted enough to become an Olympic champion. I immediately dropped out of the School for Athletic Coaches and spent a year in feverish studies to finish in a year the programme of the secondary education that normally was passed in three years. Differently from my schooling in Estonia that was all done in Estonian, now I studied in Russian. This was my first change of the language of education, work and writing. Later other such changes followed.

With my ambitions intact, though reoriented, and the certificate of the secondary education in the pocket, I went to what I believed (correctly, as it turned out) to be the best university available in the USSR – Moscow University named after Michael Lomonosov. Against all the odds (14 applicants for 1 place), and to the great disbelief of my friends and acquaintances, I was admitted. Surprisingly, I had the highest marks in my foreign language entry exam too – English. The only thing, which my examiners wanted to know, already after the exam, was: who had taught me English. The matter was that I had done this all on my own during a year, having bought some discs to listen and a textbook to read and make grammar exercises. Maybe that is one of the reasons why I still have an idiosyncratic accent in English that even linguists cannot easily pinpoint. It is certainly neither Estonian nor is it Russian.

As Russians would have said, his majesty chance had been favourable to me. Of course, I was ready to see and recognise, usually not by any careful calculation but rather by a mixture of adventurism and intuition, chances that presented to me. Ambition and hard work did the rest. Much later I concluded that chance plays also an important, often crucial and essential, role in the lives of nations and in the history of humankind.

For example, the 1917 Bolshevik revolution, which in the USSR was known under the name of the Great October Revolution, though initially being more like a successful *coup d'état,* was not at all predestined to succeed. It was a confluence of a multitude of objective and subjective factors that led to the Bolshevik's *coup d'état* and to its success. The weakness of the Tsar Nicolas II, the war fatigue, the single-minded ruthlessness of Vladimir Lenin and its co-conspirators, the helping hand given to the Bolsheviks by Kaiser's Germany and other smaller factors converged to make the Bolshevik coup a success. This was a tragedy, first of all for Russia and also for the entire world. However, from a narrower, say, an Estonian or a Finish point of view, it was indeed the Bolsheviks revolution that made possible their eventual independence. Otherwise, they could well have been satisfied parts of a prosperous and democratic Russian Empire. Maybe not so satisfied, since the national awakening was already underway both in Estonia and in Finland? We see today that, in search of their specific identity, parts of even prosperous and democratic states, like Catalonia in Spain or Quebec in Canada, seek to break away from their mother-nations. To say nothing about the Scots in the post-Brexit United Kingdom. Therefore, who knows? There is no uchrony (alternative history), only alternative historiography.

The Bolshevik revolution was a tragedy also in the sense that some noble ideas of Marxism and quite correct criticism of capitalist societies became discredited by the attempts to put into practice a theory with significant utopian elements, without 'pulling any bricks out of the edifice,' as Lenin had put it, since otherwise the whole structure would collapse. Although Lenin was quite disingenuous and was ready to distort even Marx, whenever it benefitted his political aims. For example, according to Marx's dogma, a socialist revolution would have chances of success only in a highly developed industrial, i.e. bourgeois, society and not in a relatively backward country that was Russia at the beginning of the twentieth century. To circumvent this theoretical obstacle and remaining within the frames of Marxism, Lenin developed an incomprehensible theory, according to which there had been, in February 1917, a bourgeois revolution that had paved the way, i.e. created necessary preconditions, for the socialist revolution in October of the same year. In six months from feudalism to a developed bourgeois society and then successfully to socialism? Unbelievable, but we know that many people believe even in more incredible and weird things like the virgin birth of Jesus, his resurrection after the crucifixion or even that seventy-two virgins in the heavens are waiting for martyrs to arrive. Gullibility and naivety are all too human. Whatever the strong points of Marxist theories, and there were such, no social theory can be put into practice without constant assessment of changing circumstances and respective modifications.

There seems to be, at least in social sciences, a kind of sliding scale: the more rigorous is a theory the more it leaves unexplained, and the more comprehensive is a theory the less rigorous it becomes, and therefore also less valuable in practical terms. Bertrand Russell analysed a somewhat similar problem in philosophy: 'No one has yet succeeded in inventing a philosophy at once credible and self-consistent. Locke aimed at credibility and achieved it at the expense of consistency. Most of the great philosophers have done the opposite. A philosophy that is not self-consistent cannot be wholly true, but a philosophy which is self-consistent can very well be wholly false. The most fruitful philosophies have contained glaring inconsistencies, but for that very reason have been partially true.'[11] This assessment applies also to Marx's social theory. There is no comprehensive social theory that could be put into practice, as such, without violence. The social practices are always full of controversies and unexpected challenges or 'unknown unknowns', using a self-serving but nevertheless precise definition of the former US Secretary of Defence Donald Rumsfeld. Therefore, there is no society that can be successfully and peacefully squeezed into a Procrustean bed of some philosophical, theoretical, ideological or political doctrine and long-term societal changes are much less predictable than weather forecasts.

There are basically two ways of explaining societal changes – deterministic and voluntarist. The two Karls, Marx and Popper, may be two social thinkers whose views on this matter seem to be diametrically opposed. However, it is necessary to emphasise that critics often tend to simplify the views of those whom they criticise. Karl Marx, in my opinion, is not at all such a primitive determinist, as it is sometimes depicted by his critics, nor is Popper a pure voluntarist. Nevertheless, the views of these two thinkers seem to express well two contradictory approaches to ideas of change and progress in history.

Concerning the course of history, Marx emphasised: 'Men make their own history, but they do not make it under circumstances chosen by themselves, but under circumstances directly encountered, given and transmitted from the past. The tradition of all the dead generations weighs like a nightmare on the brain of the living.'[12] This is not at all a deterministic or voluntarist utterance. However, writing on the laws of capitalist production Marx sounds, indeed, rather deterministic: 'It is question of these laws themselves, of these tendencies

---

[11] B. Russell, *History of Western Philosophy and its Connection with Political and Social Circumstances from the Earliest Times to the Present Day* (George Allen and Unwin Ltd., 1946), p. 637.

[12] K. Marx, 'The Eighteenth Brumaire of Louise Bonaparte' in *Selected Works*, vol. 1, p. 97.

working with iron necessity (emphasis added) towards inevitable results.'[13] In a more sophisticated and subtle form the idea that there is at least some direction and progress in history is expressed by Robin Collingwood: 'Thus history has value; its teachings are useful for human life; simply because the rhythm of its changes is likely to repeat itself, similar antecedents leading to similar consequences; the history of notable events is worth remembering in order to serve as basis for prognostic judgements, not demonstrable but probable, laying down not what will happen but what is likely to happen, indicating the points of danger in rhythms now going on.'[14]

On the other side of the spectrum is Karl Popper's approach. He passionately criticised 'historicism'–'an approach in social sciences that assumes that historical prediction is their principal aim, and which assumes that this aim is attainable by discovering the "rhythms" or the "patterns", the "laws" or the "trends" that underlie the evolution of history.'[15] Or, as the historian H. A. L. Fisher found in 1935, 'there can be no generalisations, only one safe rule for the historian: that he should recognise in the development of human destinies the play of the contingent and the unforeseen.'[16] At the same time, Popper believed in the power of the free will: 'Although history has no ends, we can impose these ends of ours upon it; and although history has no meaning, we can give it a meaning.'[17] He was convinced that only by means of piecemeal engineering and not through utopian projects can humankind change the world according to its will. In this, it is difficult not to agree with him. However, are we able to impose all desired ends on history, even if only through piecemeal engineering? And equally importantly, are our ends dictated by our sheer whims or are they generally more or less reasonable and determined by various factors related to our nature as human beings? Are not they dependent on our moral evolution and so on? There is a more balanced view, to which I would subscribe, expressed well by Cambridge scholar Philip Allott:

'It is as if an ingenious and inquisitive Creator had chosen to conduct an experiment in one small corner of the universe—an experiment in which a

---

[13] K. Marx, *Capital*, Preface to volume 1 of the German edition, Lawrence and Wishart, 1962, pp. 8 and 10.
[14] R.G. Collingwood, *The Idea of History*, Oxford University Press, 1994, p. 23.
[15] K. Popper, *The Poverty of Historicism*, Routledge and Kegan Paul, 1957, p. 3.
[16] H.A.L. Fisher, *A History of Europe*, Edward Arnold, 1935, p. v.
[17] K. Popper, *The Open Society and its Enemies*, vol.II, Routledge, p. 278.

piece of matter would be given a certain measure of control over its changing states, a living organism would be given a special kind of choice over its own life. But two possibilities of control and choice would be withheld–the possibility of simply submitting entirely to the necessary order of the physical universe and the possibility of acting entirely independently of the necessary order of the physical universe.'[18]

Hence, we neither are submitted entirely to outside (natural or social) forces nor are we completely free from these forces. It seems that in the history of humankind, there are three possible types of forces at play: (1) there are certain patterns, trends, probabilities and regularities as well as sheer impossibilities and improbabilities that human beings can, at least in principle, know and take account of in their activities and behaviour; (2) human beings are, in principle, able to act according to their own will within certain parameters established not only by 'the necessary order of the physical universe,' to use the words of Professor Allott, but established also by the limits of malleability of the social universe; (3) finally, the freedom of action of individuals as well as human societies is limited also by accidents and unpredictable forces that do not have any trends or regularities. Such forces are not only of a physical nature, they may also originate in social life and even be unexpected results ('manufactured uncertainties,' to use the phrase of Anthony Giddens) of our conscious choices.

Accidents, chance encounters, being in the right time in the right place, or in a wrong place at the wrong time, and my own mistakes have performed significant role in my life. My first marriage, at the end of my military service, was a mistake of a young and inexperienced person and by my divorce I caused a lot of suffering to my ex-wife. I have felt guilty for causing this suffering, but at Moscow University I met my future and current wife – Irina – who I fell in love with and who I still dearly love, notwithstanding that our marriage has seen many stormy periods, and not everything has always been sunny. We have two wonderful sons whom we both very much love and care for. Even my mistaken first marriage has had, though probably only for me, a positive side. This was one of the reasons why after my military service I stayed in Moscow; the second being my studies at the School of Coaches and training with some of the world best athletes. Without such happenstances or mistakes, I would not have some life-changing encounters, without which my life would have been rather different.

---

[18] P. Allott, *Eunomia*, Oxford University Press, 1990, p. 55.

3- The First Life-Changing Encounter Tunkin in Moscow University

There have been, in my life, some encounters without which I would have been not only in a different place, but I would have been also a different person. The first such significant encounter took place during my undergraduate years at Moscow University. Professor Grigory Ivanovich Tunkin was not simply a *primus inter pares* among the Soviet international lawyers; he was really a unique figure in the Soviet international law academia and probably the only one, who was accepted as equal by most of his Western colleagues. He regularly lectured in France, in the United Kingdom, in the Netherlands and other countries. Not only was he the founder and the President, until his death in 1993, of the Soviet Association of International Law, but being a member of the then very important UN International Law Commission and the most prestigious *Institut de Droit International*, he combined the pre-eminence in the Soviet academia and acceptance and respect in the West. How did he manage to bring together these almost incompatible qualities? Although his prominence abroad and writings that contained considerably more references (and not always critical) to Western colleagues than to founding fathers of Marxism, created him, from time to time, problems at home while his support and justification of Soviet foreign policy actions occasionally caused frictions with his colleagues in the West, he more or less managed to combine these incompatibles due to the combination of talent, hard work, self-discipline and luck.

Still young, though not any more a teenager, but a man who had already worked as a forester in his home village in the far North of Russia, Tunkin moved to Moscow to study law. Able, hard-working and with impeccable working-class background, he finished his studies, including his PhD, at the end of the terrible purges of the 1930s when the People's Commissariat for Foreign Relations was almost purged clean. Had he come earlier, he may well have found himself in

Siberia or even worse; had he arrived later, it would have been more difficult for him to start a rapid and successful career in diplomacy. This was the timing, chance and luck. The rest was his own doing.

After Grigory Ivanovich's death, his son Volodya found, deciphered and published his personal diary. Nobody, even his closest family members, knew that he had kept a small carnet, where he scribbled his inner-most thoughts. This diary, transcribed by Volodya and translated into English and published in the US by Professor Bill Butler, reveal a man of many interests, especially in arts and foreign languages. Almost every other diary entry contains a reference to his visit to museums of different countries; it seems that the Louvre's Venus de Milo may have been to him no less dear than international law. Not only was he fluent in English, French and German, but he also wrote, lectured and even thought in those languages. In his diary Tunkin wrote how he bought books in foreign languages, including Maurice Druon's *Les roi maudits*, which he much later gave me to read. Having returned him the volumes of Druon, Tunkin, during one of our strolls in the park next to his home, suddenly passed from Russian into French, trying probably to test my knowledge of Moliere's language.

The choice of the topic of Tunkin's post-graduate dissertation *Parliamentary Reform of 1832 in England* was rather indicative of the situation in the Soviet academia. It obviously shows his interest in history as well as in foreign languages and countries. However, I don't think that I am simply extrapolating my own experience and reflections (my first undergraduate thesis at Moscow University was on the New Deal of Franklin Delano Roosevelt) back to Tunkin's choice of the topic of his dissertation, but I am pretty sure that quite a few academics in the former USSR concentrated on abstract, theoretical or historical themes, often subconsciously, because, first, it was safer, and secondly, it helped avoid the necessity of making compromises with one's conscience. And though Tunkin often resorted to apology (using Martti Koskenniemi's distinction between apology and utopia in the use of international law) in his use of international law, he sincerely believed in the superiority of the Soviet political system and noble aims of its foreign policy (a few bad apples were due to the distortions of Marxism-Leninism or follies of some leaders, e.g., Gromyko, that I heard him mumbling on rare occasions). He was also a kind of utopian (in Koskenniemi's sense), who sincerely believed in the ability of international law to contribute to the world peace. In his diary he wrote: 'I am writing my works on international law not only with my mind, but with my heart. I am comforted by the thought that I can thereby do something of the greatest importance: the preservation and maintenance of peace.' Knowing him rather well, I have no doubt in the sincerity of these words.

In the Soviet international law academia, there were at that time two major schools. One was centred in the Institute for Foreign Relations under the Foreign Ministry, the other – at Moscow University, where Tunkin since 1965, being forced by Gromyko to leave the Foreign Ministry, chaired, until his death in 1993, the International Law Department. If the first school was overtly and proudly apologetic and ideological, the second one was sometimes accused by the first of so-called 'objectivism', i.e., not always being guided by correct ideology. Although such terminology and practice were used in closed totalitarian societies, like the Soviet Union, it has not been foreign even in some so-called free societies. For example, for some American neo-cons there is a wider truth than the correspondence of one's thoughts and words to facts: it does not matter that there were no WMD in Iraq and Saddam Hussein was not at all allied to Al Qaeda, but it was nevertheless the right thing to invade Iraq and overthrow Saddam, even if democracy is not flourishing there and the country may be on the verge of collapse. Moreover, the so-called Islamic State originated in Iraq when Saddam had gone due to the Western invasion.

As I am writing these lines a day after the funeral of the former French President Jacques Chirac, it is apposite to remark that differently from most countries of the world, the United States reacted without respect to the death of one of the greatest French politicians. Notwithstanding that now even in the United States many experts and politicians have recognised the disastrous consequences of the 2003 Iraqi invasion, they cannot nevertheless forget that France, led by Jacques Chirac, had opposed the invasion and even more that France had been right. Washington accepts only unconditional support of its policies – be they right or wrong. This is only for it to decide what is right and what is wrong. With some discomfort, I observe the sycophancy with which Estonian political elites compete for the place of the most subservient ally of Washington.

How these accusations of 'objectivism' were used against Tunkin in Moscow can be illustrated by an episode, in which I too played a minor role. In 1982, a textbook of international law, edited and co-authored by Tunkin, was published. At that time, as a young researcher I had helped Tunkin to edit and polish the chapters, written by various scholars. Naturally, most important chapters were written by Tunkin and in one of them he had, in a positive way, referred to Hans Morgenthau. Soon Tunkin received a note from the Central Committee of the Communist Party together with an anonymous letter accusing him of having committed serious ideological and political blunders, including depicting a 'well-known Zionist' Hans Morgenthau in the positive light (as far as I remember, Morgenthau had been against the war in Vietnam and this fact was mentioned by Tunkin). As a secretary of the editorial board, I had to spend at least several weeks drafting Tunkin's response to these accusations, explaining, among many other allegations, that if one has a Jewish wife (Tunkin's wife Itta Efimovna was Jewish) and has something good to say about Hans Morgenthau, one is not necessarily a Zionist.

Tunkin belonged to the category of those Soviet intellectuals who enthusiastically welcomed Gorbachev's perestroika and glasnost policies. He, like many others, felt that those distortions of Marxism and occasional follies of Soviet gerontocracy that hadn't allowed the true Marxism in domestic and foreign policy prevail, would be corrected and new foreign policy thinking, based on the primacy of law over politics, would be eventually accepted not only by the Soviet Union but also by the Americans. What he couldn't accept was that the whole Soviet system was not amenable to any meaningful reform and had to be dismantled.

However, even here he was quite prescient. It may have been either at the end of 1989 or beginning of 1990, when on Tunkin's recommendation I had moved to head the International Law Department in the Institute of State and Law of the Academy of Sciences of the USSR, he called me and said that Boris Yeltsin's policies were leading to the dissolution of the Soviet Union (that was a correct analysis, though he may have exaggerated Yeltsin's role). He asked me to join him writing an article that would reveal all the dangers of Yeltsin's anti-Gorbachev policies. By that time, however, I was already under the strong impression that the days of the Soviet Union may be soon over, not so much due to the agitations of Boris Yeltsin but for much deeper reasons. Although I explained myself to my Teacher in rather cautious, polite and circuitous terms, this conversation and my refusal (the first and the only one) to co-author an article with him considerably cooled our relations. It was a serious rift, especially considering that as a supervisor Professor Tunkin didn't impose his views on his students. It was possible to argue and even disagree with him. Only much later, in summer of 1993, shortly before his death in August, in our last telephone conversation (I regularly called him from London), he said such warm words about me that I felt quite embarrassed. He even told me that he was proud of me. This was especially surprising as Grigory Tunkin was by nature a very reserved man, a buttoned-up type of a person, whose character was formed in the country and at the time when remaining silent may have been a means of survival. I didn't know what he knew that this was our last conversation before his death a month later. I am immensely thankful to him also for these words.

Although Tunkin's diary reveals a lot about his attitude to international law, to his colleagues (mostly respectful), his interest in literature, arts and music, reading them I had an impression that he may have written as if somebody was looking over his shoulder. Accepting that Grigory Tunkin was a man of integrity and his private thoughts and personal feelings may have very much conformed to his public image and overt expressions, one would expect to find one's personal diaries also, if not something about his attitude to women, then at least about his views on politics and politicians whom he closely knew. Unfortunately, very little of the latter and nothing of the former. Certainly, he was more complex and even controversial than his diary reveals.

For example, when working in 1977 at the Library of the Hague Academy of International Law on my PhD, I often descended to the cellars of the library. The then junior librarian Ingrid Kost, who until recently worked in the same library in a much senior position, let me sit in the cellars to search and read whatever I wanted. I was afraid of openly ordering up the materials that were not directly necessary for my dissertation and may have even been considered, by some, as anti-Soviet literature. There I found a source where it was written that it had been Tunkin, at that time the Soviet *Chargé d'affairs* in Canada, who, in 1943, on a cargo plane had brought American nuclear secrets to Moscow. Unfortunately, but quite understandably, I didn't write down the source of this information (or misinformation). Much later, already during the years of Perestroika, I asked Grigory Ivanovich about what I had read in the cellars of the Library of the Academy. His dismissed my query by: 'They write whatever comes into their heads.' However, reading in Tunkin's diary what his son Volodya writes about his father's unexpected, and in a hurry, flight to Moscow, while the family was following by boat *via* the Far East, one may believe in such James Bond type of situations in Professor Tunkin's life. Speaking later to Volodya, he confirmed that my information on this episode in his father's career seemed to be correct, though his father had never spoken to him about that.

Tunkin's diary, published in the United States, include his lectures delivered at The Hague Academy of International Law. Brought together in a single volume make them a valuable source for those interested in history of international law of the Cold War period. They reflect the general approach of Tunkin to international law for what Canadian Professor Edward McWhinney dubbed him as 'Mister Peaceful-Coexistence.' One may ask to what extent did Tunkin's understanding of international law, his so-called 'theory of coordination of wills' as the means of creation of norms of international law differs from Western approaches to international law. In my opinion, not much. To summarise and simplifying a bit, I would say that if one were to delete references to Marx, Engels and Lenin, as well as Tunkin's own emphasis that his theory was different from so-called 'bourgeois theories', one could not discover much in his approach to international law that would have been unique. And for me, this is a positive assessment. In my opinion, it was a solid traditional approach to international law, supported by the thorough analysis of views of his Western colleagues. Some peculiarities of his theory were obviously mainly due to the need to squeeze international law theory into the Procrustean bed of doctrinal foundations of Marxism such as the relationship between the basis and superstructure, international law being a specific part of superstructure. Tunkin's strong points were, in my opinion, in his Marxist critical analysis of policies of Western countries, especially that of the United States, in the light of international law, while his weakest points were in discarding the same Marxist critical approach when writing about the Soviet policies and their conformity with international law. Some would take such reading of Tunkin's works as belittling the role of the patriarch of the Soviet doctrine of international law, others may see it as putting him on a par with the greatest international lawyers of the twentieth century.

At the beginning of my lines on my Teacher, I wrote that Tunkin's achievements were due to the combination of talent, hard work, self-discipline, but also chance and luck. Yet, there were significant disadvantages or constraints as well. This was the environment – a closed totalitarian society – within which he lived and worked. To an extent, he certainly understood that. And due to this positive combination of talent, hard work and self-discipline, he was even able to break free of some of these constraints. He travelled abroad more than most Soviet intellectuals, intensively communicated with the brightest and the best in international law doctrine and practice of the twentieth century. Hadn't he felt these constraints imposed by the Soviet realities, he wouldn't so enthusiastically welcomed Gorbachev's policy of openness. But he, like all of us, was mould by the time and space where he lived and worked. He triumphed as one of the best, in his own field as the best, within the confines of the system. His tragedy, in my opinion, was that he could not break free. But that is why he also survived; many didn't.

If chance and luck play a role, often crucial, in the lives of most of the people, in such a closed society as the USSR their role may have been even more significant. Hadn't I not been supervised by Professor Tunkin at Moscow University I wouldn't have read books by Western authors, borrowed from Tunkin's personal library, but unavailable elsewhere even in Moscow, I wouldn't have worked on my PhD in the library of the Hague Academy of International Law. Being a member the Curatorium of the Academy, he once pulled out of his pocket a *cart blanche* invitation to the Academy with an offer of a generous doctoral scholarship. Then he wrote my name on it. Without spending fruitful months in The Hague, I certainly would have had much narrower vision of the world. Later, sitting often next to him during meetings of various academic councils where somebody was proudly reporting that this or that was done for the first time in the Soviet legal scholarship, I heard him mumbling almost inaudibly 'It is not important whether it is done for the first time in the Soviet Union; what matters is whether this is done for the first time in the world.' So, this was a man without whom not only my career and but also my life would have been quite different. He gave me, probably, more than to anybody else among his countless students. He rarely co-authored articles with his colleagues, but we published quite a few works together and co-edited and co-authored first volume of the seven volume Soviet course of international law. Most of the volumes of the course were published already after the collapse of the Union. I often recall his pieces of advice he sometimes, as if in passing, gave me: 'Rein, don't do something that somebody else could do. Rein, don't waste time by standing in queues.' I well remember these casual utterances. Of course, like all maxims, these pieces of advice cannot be absolute. I queued in Moscow, for example, for baby-milk for both of our sons, as well as for other less important things. But even still now, where there is a long queue, I usually turn around and don't waste my precious time. Obviously, I have done also quite a few things that somebody else could have done instead of me or even better than me, but most of the times in my professional life, I have concentrated on issues and problems that, in my opinion, nobody else in the world can understand better than me. And of course, as somebody without useful connections whatsoever, without an 'hairy hand', as the Russians say, or friends on high places, I wouldn't have become a PhD student at Moscow University, I wouldn't have had a job in that prestigious university and I wouldn't have started publishing in most influential journals.

Naturally, there are many other people, whose friendship I treasure and who have had a deep positive impact on me. About some of them, related to my professional career I would like to say a few words later, especially since these encounters also characterise the times when they occurred. At the Faculty of Law of Moscow University there were, besides Professor Tunkin, many other interesting people. One of them was colourful Professor August Alekseyevich Mishin. When Nazi hordes in 1941 were approaching Moscow, young, even too young to be called to the army, August forged his documents, pretending to be a year older than he really was, being therefore able to participate in the battles for Moscow. Unfortunately, he was soon wounded, losing his left arm. However, he survived and this tragedy helped him continue his education and become, by the time I entered the University, a constitutional law professor. With long reddish beard, stick glasses, with only one arm and obligatory pipe, he presented a colourful figure.

However, it was not only his appearance that distinguished him; equally distinctive were his views that he quite often, sometimes being emboldened by half a bottle of cognac, expressed even outside a narrow circle of close friends. Already as a student I heard from him sarcastic comments about the Soviet political gerontocracy and local communist party hierarchy. He actively despised those who built their academic careers climbing political ladders, who were 'politically correct', i.e., who spoke, behaved, and quite a few, probably, even thought, according to the Party line. Even if they sometimes had vacillations, they always vacillated together with the party line, praising, for example, the greatness of comrade Khrushchev instead of comrade Stalin, or suddenly recognising the bright future in comrade Brezhnev's speeches. In the Soviet Union, whenever we travelled abroad, which didn't happen often, or expected a promotion, we needed to have a so-called character reference from a respective Party instance. These documents had to contain, among a list of other positive features and achievements of an applicant, also a magic formula: *morally stable and politically correct*. These features were partly interlinked. Let me explain.

At the beginning of the 1980s one of my friends and a colleague at Moscow University was lucky to spend ten months at King's College, London, where, by a strange coincidence, more than a decade later I started to chair the Department of International Law. On his return to Moscow, a letter from the Soviet KGB residency in London (where at that period worked famous/infamous double agent Oleg Gordievsky) followed. As it turned out, my friend had had 'sexual relations' with a 'bourgeois girl', i.e. being not only morally unstable but also politically incorrect. During the discussion of his doubly reprehensible behaviour, the party bosses wanted him to be sacked from the University and only the interference of Professor Mishin saved him from the worst. Condemning, first, the behaviour of my friend in exaggeratingly and grotesquely strongest terms, Mishin then blamed everybody, including the party hierarchy, for not properly preparing this young man for the long stay in the 'lair of imperialism', for not warning him of the 'treacherous and lecherous' nature of 'bourgeois' women, and specifically not providing him with medication that would have suppressed young man's sexual urges. He specifically mentioned that he excluded castration, as too extreme measure, of ensuring the moral stability and politically correct behaviour of Soviet citizens abroad. Making farce out of the KGB accusations, Professor Mishin saved the career of my friend.

Since then, all forms of political correctness are for me a *prima facie* sign of stupidity and a certain inferiority complex. Moreover, I believe that the Western world, starting from the United States, has unleashed a process of self-destruction by undermining, even destroying talents, who happen to have characteristics that do not correspond to the canons of what is currently considered in the West as politically correct. Just an hour before I sat down to start working on this manuscript, I read in the news that Placido Domingo was forced to quit his post as the Director-General of the Los Angeles Opera because of the allegations of sexual harassment and his forthcoming performances with the Philadelphia and San Francisco Operas had been cancelled. The only consolation for us, none obviously for one of the greatest musicians of the twentieth and twenty first centuries, is that the whole world has enjoyed his performances for many decades. Many, if not most, great men, and women too, have had their darker side, irresistible impulses or weaknesses. President John Kennedy, suffering probably from priapism (constant erection) had sex with thousands of women, even in the White House. This makes Bill Clinton look like a choir boy. Not only Franklin Delano Roosevelt had love affairs, so did his wife, equally a formidable woman, Eleanor Roosevelt. And Winston Churchill was not only a chain-smoker but also a heavy drinker of strong alcohol. Often greatness in laudable domains has it opposite in the same person; like madness and creativity, they are parts of human nature (see, e.g., Daniel Nettle, *Strong Imagination: Madness, Creativity and Human Nature*). No one has put it better Leonard Cohen in his Anthem: 'There is a crack in everything. That's how the light gets in.' In no way want I justify crimes against women or the abuse of position of power, but political correctness running amok in Western societies is not socially innocuous.

Only his short but valiant military career, brilliant lectures and support of many colleagues (though there were also those who envied and hated him because of these very characteristics), enjoyed by students, saved Professor Mishin from being expelled from the University. He was one of those about whom the English say that they don't gladly suffer fools. Therefore, his good will towards me, which certainly was at least partly due to his high respect for my Teacher Professor Tunkin, is particularly dare for me. When I defended my doctoral theses and was attacked not so much on professional grounds, but for being too young and having just a few years earlier defended my PhD, Professor Mishin put his only hand on my theses, as on the Bible, and solemnly declared: I will vote for, and call you (i.e. members of the Council) to do the same. In that respect, I cherish particularly my friendship also with Yoram Dinstein, of whom I wrote above. Although we often disagree, and have even publicly criticised each other more than once, we retain mutual respect and his tolerance towards me is a kind of quality test since Yoram too doesn't easily suffer fools and does not conceal it from them behind a 'politically correct' verbiage.

4- From Academia to Gorbachev's Advisor

After the graduation from Moscow University in 1976, my career, until the beginning of Gorbachev's perestroika and glasnost era in the mid-nineteen eighties, was relatively uneventful. I stayed at the faculty of law of Moscow University, as a PhD student, where I finished a three-year course slightly under two years. I was once again lucky in terms of linguistics. During my undergrad years, the then young linguist Svetlana Kitaigorodskaya – a daughter of a prominent Soviet physicist – was experimenting with teaching foreign languages for non-language students. Then I was one of a few lucky ones, who in parallel with law also studied English language and literature. Consequently, I had two diplomas from Moscow University. Some years after my graduation a linguistic luck once again returned to me. Another experiment – three weeks intensive course of immersion into the French – helped me start my love affair with the French language and literature. These things were not at all regular even at Moscow University, to say nothing about other Soviet universities. Experiments were not particularly encouraged; on the contrary, as a Soviet period adage put it: 'initiatives are punishable.' Initiatives could come only from higher-up to bottom-down and not *vice versa*.

However, both of these linguistic experimentations were essential for my future professional career, especially since in a closed society even for somebody in the elitist Moscow University there were few opportunities for daily practice of foreign languages. The only English-language newspaper available was the British communist party paper *The Morning Star*. Once I had heard from somebody that in the hotel Intercontinental, just around the corner from our law faculty, where mostly foreigners stayed, they sold also *The International Herald Tribune*. Though for a post-grad student, as I was then, its price was almost prohibitive, I nevertheless bought a copy. However, when I made another attempt, I was stopped by two sturdy men of a military stature, but in civilian, asking me who I was and what I was doing in this hotel. Honestly and correctly answering these questions, they told me to never do that again. To their benefit I must add that they let me go and even didn't confiscate my paper that had cost me several lunches in the students' canteen.

However, sometimes confiscated printed materials can be also turned into positive use and serve noble aims. Although maybe it is only me and not everybody that always tries to find something positive in every failure or unavoidable nonsense, especially if it is not in our power to undo the failure or to change the world as it is. In my junior years at the university we had few books in English; only later I could use the library of Professor Tunkin. However, the father of one of my fellow-students, being a senior KGB officer, had confiscated, I guess, some books that would have been prohibited in the country, either from Soviet dissidents or from those foreigners who had tried to smuggle them into the country. As Sasha, this was the name of my friend, didn't read in English and didn't even care to read such books, he sold me some of them for a couple of bottles of beer, warning not to tell anybody. So, I perfected my English skills by reading Orwell's *Animal Farm* and Leonard Shapiro's *History of the Communist Party of the Soviet Union*. I very much regret that during my movements between countries I have lost these two copies with my Russian translations of all unfamiliar words on the margins or between the lines. One wouldn't be surprised to learn that what I read about the history of the CPSU in Shapiro's book differed greatly from what I was taught in my history of the CPSU classes at Moscow University. Much later, already at the London School of Economics and Political Science (LSE), I not only read other books by Leonard Shapiro in the collection of his books at the LSE library; I also discovered that my new friend and colleague at the LSE at that time, later the Legal Adviser of the British Foreign Office, Daniel Bethlehem, being born, brought up and educated in the apartheid South Africa, had read Marx, also under the counter. *O tempora o mores*!

This relatively quiet period of my life ended 14 May 1987 – a memorable date since then our younger son George was born (that is why I never forget also the date of the Independence Day of the State of Israel), when I was elected to become the head of the international law department in the Institute of State and Law of the Soviet Academy of Sciences, though I had had some quite unique for a Soviet citizen's experiences even before.

One of them was my year-long work in Africa. As the youngest and healthiest member of the International Law Department at Moscow University, soon after becoming a member of the staff, I was sent to Guinee-Bissau. Our elder son Jan had just been born, and my wife Irina could not join me in Africa for health reasons. Therefore, I was not at all happy going alone for so long and so far from home. Moreover, I was working already on my doctoral theses (in the Soviet Union, besides the PhD degree, there was also a doctoral degree than almost automatically gave an access to professorship even at Moscow University) and being for long in the middle of the nowhere didn't attract even my adventurous mind. But as the Brits say, every cloud has a silver lining, and during a year I spent in Guinee-Bissau I fine-tuned my theses and also learned Portuguese to an extent that during the last couple of months I lectured in the language of the country. Unfortunately, what comes fast, also goes fast, especially if one does not practice it and today, I don't speak any Portuguese.

The Institute of State and Law of the Academy of Sciences of the USSR, which I joined 14 May 1987, was led by Academician Vladimir Kudryavtsev, who was at the same time also the First Vice-President of the Academy of Sciences of the USSR and soon became also an Assistant to Michael Gorbachev. In the International Law Department, that I was supposed to lead, there were more than twenty professors and Doctors of Law – almost all older than me and whose books I had read as a student. My speedy career elevation was due to Gorbachev's policy of rejuvenation of the academia. Those over 65 had to leave their administrative posts and those already over 60 could not be promoted to high administrative posts. At that time, having just passed 40 years of age, I was the only Doctor of Law in the field of international law who was under 60.

The Institute was then becoming a centre, or as they are known in the West, a 'think tank', for legal reforms, accompanying Gorbachev's policies of 'perestroika and glasnost.' As Gorbachev himself was a graduate of the Faculty of Law of Moscow University and in his speeches constantly referred to law and particularly to international law, we practically didn't do much else, but wrote memo's and drafted proposals of legal reforms in different fields. Often it was done with cooperation with other institutes of the Academy of Sciences as well as of relevant ministries. The International Law Department worked particularly in close contact with the Foreign Ministry of the USSR. With my post soon emerged several additional functions.

So, in summer 1988, I participated in a high-level meeting in the Foreign Ministry, which was chaired by Eduard Shevardnadze – the Minister for Foreign Affairs, a member of the Politburo and one of the three most influential personalities of that period in the country, together with Gorbachev and Aleksandr Yakovlev. I was one of the youngest (maybe even the youngest) and lowest ranking (probably, the lowest) persons present. One of the topics, on which I was supposed to speak (no more than three minutes were allocated), was the question of the ratification of certain human rights instruments, including the Optional Protocol to the International Covenant on Civil and Political Rights, which would have provided the Soviet citizens and all those under the jurisdiction of the state, the right to send complaints (politely called communications) to the Human Rights Committee in Geneva. I was in favour of the ratification and had accordingly drafted my no more than three-minute presentation. As the youngest and the lowest, my turn came up after all the others had already spoken. Wrong practice, but *c'est la vie*. Almost all of the previous speakers had argued, and often quite persuasively, against the ratification of the Protocol. The opinions were between the spectrums that 'all bloody dissidents would go to Geneva to denigrate our country' (such arguments were nevertheless already rare by that time) to the more convincing that 'our legal system and judicial practices are not ready to implement most of the clauses of the Covenant', though the USSR had been bound by it already since 1976 when Covenant had entered into force. The last point was quite valid. It was indeed so that notwithstanding all the words about the superiority of the socialist system over the capitalist one, there had not been, in my opinion, any human rights in the Soviet Union. Even those benefits (the free education, low and stable prices for basic products, free housing etc.) that were real (e.g., without them I couldn't have had, for example, my university degrees) were not rights. They were benefits for hard work and politically correct behaviour.

Listening to speakers, who had presented their arguments before me, I felt like a 'black swan' who is not even a swan and not a black either. I even thought of watering down my arguments in favour of ratification (the main being that such a step would give an additional stimulus for those in favour of reforms and help accelerate the process of perestroika and glasnost), but it was too late. I didn't have time for making any coherent changes. I had only three minutes and my presentation had been drafted exactly to be rapidly made within three minutes limit. So, I said what I had meant to say. Looking at the faces of those closest to me, I understood that my promising career was going to take a downward turn. No one congratulated me on my speech, only pitied.

However, next day or in a couple of days I had a call from the Foreign Ministry. I was invited to meet one of the deputies of the Minister – Anatoly Adamishin. He told me that Eduard Amvrossyevich (i.e. Shevardnadze) had recommended to propose my candidature for the elections of new members of the UN Human Rights Committee. Thus, I became also a member of this most important UN human rights body, though I hadn't said (at least publicly) or written specifically anything about human rights. In the circumstances, this was probably a positive factor since those Soviet citizens, who had been active in this field, were either in prison or in exile (dissidents), or were already in the UN defending the undefendable, i.e. the 'good name' of the Soviet human rights record. However, in the defence of my professional qualifications in the field of human rights I may claim that working on my very theoretical doctoral theses on the relationship between public international law, private international law and domestic laws of different countries, I had analysed, *inter alia*, the implementation of international human rights instruments in various, particularly in Western, societies.

This was how in the USSR of the end of the 1980s careers were made and broken. My predecessor in the UN Human Rights Committee, Anatoly Movchan, who had also been at the meeting and had spoken against the ratification, was very upset and unhappy. I was sorry for him since he was my colleague at the Institute, and we were in quite friendly terms. However, he took the blow stoically and we remained good colleagues. Reflecting with hindsight, I must confess that those who claimed that the Soviet Union was not ready to implement human rights instruments it had signed and ratified, were right. Neither was I completely wrong. However, though it may be true that when states take unfulfillable, at least for the time being, obligations, it may eventually help them fulfil these obligations (this was my hope), we see more often that good intentions may help pave the way to hell. Sometimes reforms that are meant to make societies freer and more prosperous, be they economic or political reforms, have contrary effects. What may work in Estonia, would create chaos in China or some other country.

If inability of the Soviet Union to fulfil its human rights obligations was regrettable, it was not disastrous. However, so-called shock therapy on the economy of Russia under President Boris Yeltsin almost destroyed the country.

For example, Adi Ignatius, the former *Wall Street Journal* bureau chief in Moscow reminisced at the end of 2007 about Yeltsin's Russia of the 1990s: 'I retain three indelible images from that time. The first: the legions of Ivy League – and other Western – educated "experts" who roamed the halls of the Kremlin and the government, offering advice, all ultimately ineffective on everything from conducting free elections to using "shock therapy" to juice the economy to privatising state-owned assets.'[19] And he concluded: it is easy to see why the Russians today are looking for greatness and supporting Vladimir Putin 'after the humiliations of the 1990s, when Harvard M.B.A.s flooded Russia, preaching Western style democracy, only to let a small cabal of criminals bleed the country dry.'[20] If in the West many see Russia in the 1990s as a promising democracy, most people in Russia are not at all nostalgic about those years when oligarchs were running the country.

Membership in the UN Human Rights Committee, of which more below, made me more visible also inside the country, where human right issues, instead of being only a propaganda tool, had acquired practical significance. I participated in numerous commissions, working groups and meetings in the Foreign Ministry and in the Kremlin also on human rights issues. Finally, I was invited to advice the top Soviet leadership on matters of international law.

---

[19] A. Ignatius, 'A Tsar is Born', *Time*, December 3, 2007-January 7, 2008, p. 42.
[20] *Ibid.*, p. 60

5- Advising Michael Gorbachev: the Two Major Cases – The Kuril Islands and The Molotov-Ribbentrop Pact

My work for Soviet leaders, including Michael Gorbachev, consisted mainly in writing short memos on specific questions of international law. It was a good school for learning to be concise and precise. These were the political leaders, particularly Gorbachev, who often practiced logorrhoea (diarrhoea of the mouth). I also wrote speeches, usually only parts of them, for Gorbachev and others. These were usually urgent requests that had to be immediately taken care of, not leaving time for reflection or necessary preparation. However, I led also two relatively large working groups that laboured several months on complicated issues, where deeper analysis and historical research were needed. Both of these themes have not lost their topicality even today. Both tasks stemmed from the events closely related to the Second World War – one in Europe, the other one in the Far East. On both cases I led working groups of prominent experts preparing materials for top politicians of the USSR. The first was the draft of the speech for Aleksander Yakovlev (when we were working on the draft, we didn't know who would deliver it; maybe even Gorbachev) on the so-called Pact of Molotov-Ribbentrop and secret protocols to it. The second was a memorandum for Gorbachev before his 1990 visit to Tokyo on the status of the Kuril Islands, or Northern Territories, as they are known in Japan. Although chronologically it was the Molotov-Ribbentrop Pact speech that came first, I will start with the Kuril Islands, since the work on Yakovlev's speech had repercussions for my future work in the Foreign Ministry of Estonia, of which more below.

It is well known that Japan and Russia have been unable, since the end of the Second World War in 1945, to conclude a peace treaty, notwithstanding all the efforts and even good will from both sides. The stumbling block has been the ownership and status of the Kuril Islands, which in accordance with the Understanding of Yalta in February 1945 between Winston Churchill, Franklin Delano Roosevelt and Joseph Stalin went to the USSR, as a compensation for Moscow entering the war against Japan, after having defeated the Nazi Germany in Europe.[21] It was also considered as a punishment for Japan having attacked allied states, first of all the United States, in East Asia and in the Pacific.

In Gorbachev's favour I would like to mention the fact that when I received this task, the Soviet leader told me that he didn't need the usual gibberish about the eternal Russian (Soviet) territories. I can talk like that myself, he added, and that was certainly true. He could and liked to talk. Gorbachev said that he needed a document where not only strong points of the Soviet side would be emphasised, as had been usually the case, but where also the strong arguments, which the Japanese side may have, would be highlighted. As a result, Gorbachev had a paper where on the left-hand side of every page were both the strengths and the weaknesses of the arguments of the Soviet (now it would be Russian) position and, on the right-hand side, arguments favouring the Japanese position.[22] We particularly highlighted those Soviet arguments that were vulnerable for Japanese counterarguments. We even used a moot court type discussion, partly because one of our proposals, though in a very cautious and tentative manner, related to the possible resolution of the dispute in the International Court of Justice. During that exercise I played a role of the foreign minister of Japan, while my late colleague Professor Igor Lukashuk pretended to be the foreign minister of the Soviet Union. Although I doubt that the Parties would ever go to the ICJ or any other third-party body (arbitration) with this case, it would have one advantage – lowering the level of political sensitivity of the dispute. In bilateral negotiations on such sensitive issues, it is extremely difficult to make any concessions due to domestic pressures on the governments trying to reach a compromise. I well remember that in 2004-2005 while I was working for the UN in Central Asia, domestic critics attacked the then Foreign Minister of

---

[21] In February 2020 the Foreign Ministry of Russia published some secret documents of the February 1945 Yalta conference, including the Agreement signed by Stalin, Roosevelt and Churchill on the Soviet Union joining the war against Japan after 2-3 months after the capitulation of Germany. In para. 3 of this document the signatories agreed that the Kuril Islands should be transferred to the Soviet Union (see the text of the Agreement in Russian in *Международная жизнь* (The International Affairs), 6 February 2020 (https://interaffairs.ru/news/show/25292)

[22] A copy of the Document is in the Archives of the author.

Kazakhstan (today the President of the country) Kassym-Jomart Tokayev, accusing him of the sell-off of Kazakh territories to China, as a result of the delimitation of the border between China and Kazakhstan. There is no doubt that domestic critics, both in Japan and Russia, would use even the minutest compromise on the status and title of the Kuril Islands to attack the political leadership for 'surrendering' national interests.

Our analysis, to make the long story short, showed that the Soviet Union had stronger legal case on the possession of the two biggest islands – Iturup and Kunashir. As to the smaller island Shikotan and a non-inhabited group of small islets called Habomai, Japan had a stronger claim. We also recognised that there certainly was a territorial dispute between the two countries, though until then the Soviet position had been that the territorial question had been resolved and there was even nothing to talk about the non-existing problem. Although historically these islands had belonged to Japan and this had been confirmed by 1855 and 1875 treaties between the two empires, this possession would play no decisive role under international law since it was overrun by subsequent events – the World War II, the Yalta declaration of 1945, the Japanese unconditional capitulation, and particularly by the conclusion of the San Francisco Peace Treaty of 1951 between Japan and its WWII adversaries, with the exception of the Soviet Union that had refused to participate in the Peace conference. In the San Francisco Treaty, Japan had given up all the claims to certain territories that were named in the Treaty, including the Kuril Islands.[23] The fact that the Soviet Union did not participate in the Conference, and is not a party to the San Francisco Treaty, does not play any role in determining the legal title over the Islands. Under the Treaty Japan has renounced all the claims to the Islands; it had solemnly given up the right to raise such pretensions. In territorial disputes it is important to find a critical date that locks the title over a disputed territory. In the case of the Kuril Islands, it is 28 April 1952, when the Treaty that was signed 8 September 1951 in San Francisco, entered into force for its parties, including, of course, Japan. If the Yalta Agreement binds only the United States and Great Britain on this matter, Japan and all other signatories of the San Francisco Peace Treaty are bound to respect Japanese obligation not to make any claims to the Kurils.

---

[23] Article 2 (c) of the Treaty reads: '*Japan renounces all right, title and claim to the Kurile Islands*, and to that portion of Sakhalin and the islands adjacent to it over which Japan acquired sovereignty as a consequence of the Treaty of Portsmouth of 5 September 1905' (emphasis added).

So, why then did we find that Shikotan, as well as the islets of Habomai, should rather belong to Japan. It is not only because the 1956 Declaration between Japan and the Soviet Union that legally put an end to the war between these two states (it is an utter nonsense to assert that since there is no peace treaty between them, Japan and Russia are legally or technically still at war), provides for the handover of these islands to Japan, when the peace treaty would be signed between Japan and the Soviet Union (today the Russian Federation, as its successor). The reason being that Kunashir and Habomai don't really belong to the category of the Kuril Islands, mentioned in the Treaty of San Francisco. Historically and administratively, they had always (until 1945) been parts of the Japanese island Hokkaido. One should only look at the map to see that they are out of the range of islands that start in the north from the Kamchatka peninsula and end in the south close to Hokkaido, i.e. the Kuril Islands. If there were an impartial tribunal resolving the matter, I believe that Japan would have much stronger case as to the title over Shikotan and Habomai. However, I have my doubts about the impartiality of international tribunals and even more about the Japanese satisfaction for having back these two relatively insignificant territories. Russia may be more ready to go for that, but in that case even Putin's rating in Russia would suffer. Ultra-nationalists would unleash all the hounds on the President and his Foreign Minister, while so-called liberals, in any case, would not appreciate whatever the President does.

Notwithstanding statements and quite intensive high-level contacts between Japanese and Russian politicians and experts, I am sceptical about the possibility of resolving this territorial dispute in the nearest future. Besides domestic pressure on both sides that make the achievement of any compromise, and a compromise it must be whatever the legal arguments, very difficult, there are also sensitive geopolitical and security issues on which the parties hold opposing positions. However, when the geopolitical configuration of the world will change, and it is already rather rapidly changing, of which more below, the dispute of the Kuril Islands may also find its solution.

But, now about my second important job for the Soviet leadership – the work on the speech for Aleksander Yakovlev on the Molotov-Ribbentrop Pact and its secret protocols. If the issue of the possession of the Kuril Islands has been always a bone of contention between Japan and Russia, the interest to the Molotov-Ribbentrop Pact was revived by the 80th anniversary of the signing of the document 23 August 1939 and the beginning of the Second World War on 1

September 1939. Of course, these two events were interlinked but their relationship is very often distorted depending on political interest or ideological preferences.

There is nothing ominous in the Pact itself. An analogous document named *The German-Polish Non-Aggression Pact* was signed in January 1934. Estonia and Latvia signed such Pacts with the Nazi Germany in June 1939. As Estonian I had heard about the existence of the German-Soviet Pact already in my childhood, though as somebody who was interested at that time in becoming an Olympian, I had paid no attention to it. It was quite different with my Russian wife Irina, who was born and brought up in Moscow, in the family of a well-known Russian journalist. She had never heard about such document either at school or from her parents or friends. At the beginning of September 2019 Irina, reading somewhere about the Pact, asked me whether I had known anything about it. She was surprised, and even felt hurt, when I told her that thirty years earlier, i.e. at the end of the 1980s, I had spent several months of my life in archives in Moscow and in hot discussions not only on the content of secret protocols to the Pact, but on their very existence. She had probably forgotten that I was the main author of Mr Yakovlev's speech. What I had forgotten was that, based on my work on the speech, I had also published, in 1989, an article on the matter in the main Soviet legal journal.[24] I found this article and photocopied it. So, Irina read it with great interest while admonishing me for not telling her about it earlier.

However, my first direct encounter with the matter occurred even earlier than that. As a student interested in international law, and with Professor Tunkin's advice and permission, I had an access to what in Russian was called Spetshran, i.e. a special collection of materials that may have had, from the point of view of Soviet censorship, anti-Soviet or anti-Socialist character. Although I mostly read, as I was supposed to do, what was strictly necessary for my coursework or theses, I often tried to break the rules and have a glimpse also on materials that were supposed to be none of my business. In Moscow's Lenin's library, close to our Law Faculty, were I sometimes in the 1970s – during the flourishing of Brezhnev's 'stagnation' period as it was widely known and secretly called – worked I came across of Viacheslav Molotov's speech of 31 October 1939

---

[24] Р. Мюллерсон, Советско-германские договоренности 1939 г. в аспекте международного права, Сов. государство и право, 1989, N 9 (R. Müllerson, Soviet-German arrangements of 1939 and international law, Soviet State & Law, 1989, n. 9).

before the Supreme Soviet of the USSR on the foreign policy of the Soviet Union, published in *Pravda*. What I read there shouldn't have been, in my opinion, and probably was even not meant to be, even in Spetshran. After Hitler's invasion of the Soviet Union on 22 June 1941, saying something positive about Nazi Germany and recalling deals done with the Nazis, would have been anathema and should have been cut, in accordance with the Soviet tradition, from all the sources. I thought then, and I still believe, that this had been somebody's oversight. I was reading, naturally, in Russian and I have remembered almost by verbatim the following paragraph that I am now reproducing in English:

> 'The ruling circles of Poland boasted quite a lot about the 'stability' of their state and the 'might' of their army. However, one swift blow at Poland, first by the German army and then by the Red Army, and nothing was left of this ugly offspring of the Versailles Treaty, which had existed by oppressing the non-Polish nationalities. The 'traditional policy' of unprincipled manoeuvring between Germany and the USSR and of playing off one against the other has proved unsound and has suffered complete bankruptcy.'

Naturally, there were positive things said about the Soviet-German Non-Aggression Pact, signed a couple of months earlier, but of course, there was nothing about the secret protocols to that document. So, this was the context in which at the end of the 1980s I was tasked to lead a working group to draft a speech on the topic of the Pact and its secret protocols. The impetus for that had come from the Baltic republics of the Soviet Union claiming that they had been unlawfully occupied according to the Pact, and particularly its protocols, and therefore they had the right to leave the Union unilaterally. This would be an end to their illegal occupation, not the exercise of the right to self-determination – the slogan under which some other Soviet republics had already started claiming their independence from the Union.

In parallel, I was also involved in another working group of the Supreme Soviet, which was working on a draft law on the right to leave the Soviet Union. The problem was that while the Constitution of the USSR of 1978 had declared that the constituent republics of the Union were sovereign (they all had their own Foreign Ministries) and provided for their right to leave the Union, there was no procedure foreseen to implement this right. As a member of this working group, I was invited in spring 1990 to Amsterdam to participate in a conference and to speak on that draft. Instead, I spoke on legal problems that could rise in a case when the Soviet Union may disintegrate, or if some of the republics may leave without any law. By then I already had a feeling that process of disintegration was underway, though I wasn't, and of course I couldn't be, sure of that. Hence, my presentation in Amsterdam was devoted to the issues such as recognition of new states and legal problems related to the issues of state succession. Such a speech had, naturally, hostile reactions in Moscow and this was the beginning of my move from Moscow back to Tallinn.

But *revenon à nos moutons*, to the German-Soviet Pact of 1939 and my work on the speech for Yakovlev and whether now, after thirty years of experience in different countries and posts, my understanding and evaluation of the Pact, reasons for its conclusion and its effects, have changed. My short answer, which I will try to substantiate below, is that not very much. The draft written mostly by me and of which I don't have a copy (Yakovlev's speech was much more emotional, watered down and much less precise than my draft; but this is my lawyer's point of view) and my 1989 article on the *Soviet State and Law Journal*, which I recently reread, show that though my approach now has become more contextual, less lawyerly and more politically, even geopolitically, oriented and more sophisticated, but in substance it remains the same. I was not ashamed to reread the article written by my much younger self.

The working group had its meetings usually in the office of the First Vice-President of the Academy of Sciences of the USSR. Vladimir Kudryavtsev, who had meanwhile become also Gorbachev's assistant (a higher position than an advisor) was rarely present, as he had had a medical operation and was still recovering from it. There were about ten of us, lawyers and historians. I spent also hours in the archives of the Foreign Ministry, where the documents were supposed to be (as it was revealed much later, during the Soviet period they were in the General Division of the Central Committee of the CPSU), but I could find nothing even with the help of the Director of the Department of History and Archives of the Ministry – Felix Kovalyov, whom I had known for some time when he still worked as the Deputy Director of the Legal Department of the Ministry. As none of us had seen the secret protocols and there was only indirect evidence of their existence, what was good enough for me, most of the members of the group simply denied that the protocols had ever existed. The only cautious and qualified support came from the then Director (currently Academic Director) of the Institute of General History of the Academy of Sciences academician

Aleksander Chubaryan. However, even he was mostly sitting on the fence, avoiding actively taking the sides. One historian of Latvian origin, whose name I have forgotten, even called me an 'Estonian nationalist', the label that would have greatly offended all true Estonian nationalists.

Our heated and fruitless, since no compromises seemed possible between opposing opinions (mine being a minority view), discussions within the working group came to an unexpected end. One Sunday evening, I had a call from Vladimir Kudryavtsev, who had been present in our previous meeting in his office, and had spoken, to lower the tension, in favour of a compromise he believed to be possible, though I hadn't seen any. He told me that he had annulled our next meeting that was supposed to take place on Monday. He also informed me that he had dismissed the whole working group. However, having asked me whether I had already drafted something on the matter and having my positive response, he invited me to his place where on the basis of my text we finalised the draft that was then sent to Gorbachev, Yakovlev and possibly to other top leaders of the USSR. In such a way, a minority view became the only view. Some days later, I told the story to my friend and colleague Vladlen Vereschsetin – then a Deputy Director of the Institute of State and Law, later a Judge of the International Court of Justice. I also expressed my annoyance with the behaviour of Vladimir Kudryavtsev who, as it turned out, agreeing with my approach and rejecting the majority view within the group, had nevertheless remained in good terms with everybody, while I had created, if nor enemies, then at least opponents even within my own department. Wise Vladlen responded to that: 'This is why Kudryavtsev is the first Vice-President of the Academy of Sciences and you will never be.' Of course, he was right. Obviously, Kudryavtsev knew in which way the wind was blowing in the upper echelons of the Kremlin and he went with the wind. That the wind was then blowing also my way was accidental as wind's ways are often unpredictable and depend on too many contingent factors. This is probably one of the reasons why, in my lifetime, I have had various jobs in different countries. Winds have blown during these years on different directions and I haven't gone, on main issues, with the wind.

Now, the Russian authorities have found the original version of the protocols. I wonder why it was not possible thirty years ago. Whether they were indeed hidden in such a way that it was impossible to find them, or somebody was interested in not making them public, notwithstanding that in the person of Aleksander Yakovlev – one of the three top politicians of the USSR – the fact that such documents had been signed in August 1939 in Moscow, was recognised. In my article of 1989, I insisted that even if we admit, what would be impossible to admit[25], that there were no written documents, the following behaviour and acts of the Parties showed that there had been at least a tacit understanding (one may say that there was a 'non-gentlemen agreement' between the Parties to the Pact) of the separation of 'spheres of interest', i.e. red lines that they had agreed not to cross.

Being familiar with the matter, I was nevertheless shocked when I read in the Resolution of European Parliament of 19 September 2019 *On the importance of European remembrance for the future of Europe* that 'the Second World War, the most devastating war in Europe's history, was started as an immediate result of the notorious Nazi-Soviet Treaty on Non-Aggression of 23 August 1939, also known as the Molotov-Ribbentrop Pact, and its secret protocols, whereby two totalitarian regimes that shared the goal of world conquest divided Europe into two zones of influence.' As if the Nazi Germany hadn't before August 1939 grabbed territories and annexed countries in Europe and was only looking for the consent of Stalin and Molotov to continue its aggressive foreign policy. The green light to Hitler's expansions in Europa was given much earlier and not by the Soviets.

Hadn't there been another deal, done a year before, between Adolf Hitler, Benito Mussolini, Édouard Daladier and Neville Chamberlain? The Munich betrayal was more shameless deal than the 23 August 1939 Pact (non-aggression pacts with Nazi Germany had signed Poland in 1934, Estonia and Latvia in June 1939), even with its secret protocols. In Munich, Western democracies not only agreed to give to the Nazis what they did not own – a part of Czechoslovakia called Sudetenland. They did it openly, proudly, hoping to have their peace at the expense of a peaceful and democratic country in the centre of Europe and expecting to channel Hitler's aggressiveness to the East. They also remained silent when in March 1939 Germany grabbed the whole Czechoslovakia. It is not a farfetched to presume that without the Munich betrayal there may not have been the Molotov-Ribbentrop Pact with its secret protocols. There wouldn't have been even need for it. Let me quote what Eduard Beneš – the then President of Czechoslovakia – had to say about it:

---

[25] I was in that respect in good company. The farther of international law Hugo Grotius had written that even if there were no God, what would be impossible to believe, natural law would still exist.

'In September 1938, therefore, we were left in military, as well as political, isolation with the Soviet Union to prepare our defence against a Nazi attack. We were also well aware not only of our own moral, political, and military preparedness, but also had a general picture of the condition of Western Europe; as well as of Nazi Germany and Fascist Italy, in regard to these matters. At that moment indeed Europe was in every respect ripe to accept without a fight the orders of the Berchtesgaden corporal. When Czechoslovakia vigorously resisted his dictation in the September negotiations with our German citizens, we first of all received a joint note from the British and French Governments on September 19th, 1938, insisting that we should accept without amendment the draft of a capitulation based essentially on an agreement reached by Hitler and Chamberlain at Berchtesgaden on September 15th. When we refused, there arrived from France and Great Britain on September 21st an ultimatum accompanied by emphatic personal interventions in Prague during the night on the part of the Ministers of both countries and repeated later in writing. We were informed that if we did not accept their plan for the cession of the so-called Sudeten regions, they would leave us to our fate, which, they said, we had brought upon ourselves. They explained that *they certainly would not go to war with Germany just 'to keep the Sudeten Germans in Czechoslovakia'* [emphasis in the original, R.M.]. I felt very keenly the fact that there were at that time so few in France and Great Britain who understood that something much more serious was at stake for Europe than the retention of the so-called Sudeten Germans in Czechoslovakia. The measure of this fearful European development was now full, precipitating Europe into ruin. Through three dreadful years I had watched the whole tragedy unfolding, knowing to the full what was at stake. We had resisted desperately with all our strength. And then, from Munich, during the night of September 30th our state and nation received the stunning blow: Without our participation and in spite of the mobilization of our whole Army, the Munich Agreement – fatal for Europe and the whole world – was concluded and signed by the four Great Powers – and then was forced upon us.'[26]

It is clear that the road to the German-Soviet Non-Aggression Pact as well as to the Second World War was open in autumn 1938 in Munich. Poland, being the

---

[26] *Memoirs of Dr Eduard Beneš: From Munich to New War and New Victory* (Translator Godfrey Lias), George Allen & Unwin Ltd, 1954, pp. 42–43.

first casualty of this war (or maybe it was Czechoslovakia that was the first victim of WWII?), despite having in January 1934 signed *The German-Polish Non-Aggression Pact*, was not an innocent victim, though its guilt doesn't in any way justify German aggression. Nazi Germany, and nobody else, unleashed the Second World War in Europe; full stop.

However, the Polish army, prompted by Hitler, and as a result of the Munich agreement, moved in October 1938 into a part of Czechoslovakia annexing an area of 801.5 km² (309.5 mi²) with a population of 227,399. What the Soviet Union did 17 September 1939, when the Soviet troops moved into the Polish territories that according to secret protocols belonged to the USSR's 'sphere of interest', was not much different from what the Poles had done in occupying and annexing in autumn 1938 a part of Czechoslovakia. As the Poles had taken those parts of the country that was attacked by Germany, which were inhabited mostly by Czech citizens of the Polish ethnic origin, so did the Soviet Union when it took parts of Poland, attacked by Germany that were populated mostly by people of non-Polish origin.

After the Anschluss of Austria in March 1938, the occupation of the Sudetenland and then the whole of Czechoslovakia, coupled with massive rearmament programmes, it had already become clear that Hitler was not going to be satisfied with these annexations. Chamberlain, Daladier and other Western leaders practiced the policy of appeasement, paying a terrible price for it. Stalin knew that the appeasement was not good enough. Concluding the Non-Aggression Pact, accompanied by secret protocols, with Germany, he hoped to delay the inevitable military confrontation with Germany and also to move the Soviet defence lines further to the West. If I may use in a somewhat loose and non-legal way a controversial concept of international law (called also as the Bush doctrine), the Soviet leadership practiced a kind of preventive self-defence. Nevertheless, the Soviet defence was not ready by 22 June 1941, when Germany attacked, and Stalin is to be blamed for this unpreparedness, since in his paranoia of seeing enemies and foreign agents everywhere, he had destroyed the better part of the Red Army and had not heeded to the warnings of his own intelligence (Richard Sorge) about the imminence of the German attack. However, the onslaught of the Nazis would have been much more painful for the USSR, and also for the allies who fought the Nazis, had it been launched even closer to the political, economic and military-industrial centres of the Soviet Union.

The Resolution of European Parliament, by accusing not only Nazi Germany but also the Soviet Union for starting the war, without even mentioning the Munich Agreement of 1938 that had paved the way to the first, amounts to the distortion of history with the purpose of appeasing Russophobic voices in Europe and is further dividing the continent. 30 September, the date of the signing of the Munich agreement in 1938, would better suit to commemorate the European Day of Remembrance. Moreover, it would have been perfectly possible to condemn the crimes committed in the name of communism, be it by Stalin or other dictators, without falsifying the history of the beginning of the Second World War. It is dangerous to build European unity on such falsehoods.

The struggle at the end of the 1980s of Estonians, like Latvians and Lithuanians, for their independence from the Soviet Union was to a great extent led under the banner of the fight for the acknowledgment of the existence of the secret protocols to the Molotov-Ribbentrop Pact, recognition of their illegal, even criminal, nature that would in itself have been sufficient for the restoration of independent statehood, lost in 1940. The Pact and the protocols had become a sacred cow, any doubt in whose existence and their criminal and crucial role in the occupation of these states by the Soviets (not by the Nazis) was considered a crime much more serious than the negationism, i.e. the crime committed by those who either deny the Nazi crimes of the holocaust or belittle their horrific nature and scale. I was considered by many in Estonia as being one of such negationists of sacred cow's character of the Molotov-Ribbentrop Pact. Some even believed and probably still believe, notwithstanding what I have said or written, that I had even doubted the very existence of the protocols. I must, however, confess that for me then as well as now, their role, especially in the occupation and annexation of my country – Estonia – has been greatly exaggerated. Moreover, my critics completely ignore or belittle the role of the Western countries and of Poland in opening the way to Hitler's aggression.

As an Estonian growing up in Estonia, I knew already as a boy that Estonia had not voluntarily joined the Soviet Union. As an athlete, I did think much of it and certainly I did not know any details. Even as an avid reader of history books, notwithstanding not being, to put it mildly, a diligent schoolboy, I read mostly about history of Ancient Greece or Rome and other faraway countries, maybe pits and pieces of my own country but even then, about its ancient, not recent, history. Our dull history textbooks were so unexcited that the pages, which were meant to inform us about the happiness and pride, that the workers and peasants of Estonia had felt, when they able to join the voluntary union of the Soviet people, did not leave any memories. Moreover, what I sometimes overheard from adults, sometimes during their consumption of alcohol and mostly in the countryside, was quite different from what was in the textbooks.

Today I am even more convinced, or I know rather than believe, that Estonia didn't join the USSR on its own volition. Of course, there were those communists and their sympathisers, who like Walter Korb of whom I spoke above, who initially may have indeed been in favour of joining the Soviet Union. However, even for many of them the change of mind came soon, especially after in the massive arrests of summer 1941, followed by the journey in cattle wagons to Siberia. This was Stalin's mistake, but this was also the nature of his regime and doing things differently was not in his character. Pressure exercised on the Baltic governments, the threatening presence of Soviet troops and the formation of left-leaning governments under Kremlin's pressure show that this was not a voluntary reunification with the Soviet Union. Moreover, already since the mid-nineteenth century, there had started the rise of Estonian national self-consciousness, first cultural but later also political. It was not accidental that when an opportunity arrived with the Bolshevik revolution of 1917 and weakening of the Russian Empire, all three Baltic nations, like also Finland, chose independent statehood and fought for it, both against the Bolsheviks as well as German troops. Every year on 23 June, Estonia celebrates its Victory day to commemorate the victory of Estonian and Latvian forces over the German Landwehr in the battle of Cesis in Latvia (known in Estonia, as the battle of Võnnu).

Moreover, having lived and worked in different countries, big and small, I have come to conclusion that it is rare indeed when nations voluntarily renounce their sovereignty and independence. Even when it has happened in history of some nations, it has usually been a choice between the two evils, when a weaker entity chooses a lesser evil by joining one of the two pretenders. For example, one of the three Kazakh zhuses (an amalgamation of nomadic tribes) – the Little Zhuse, having to choose between the Dzhungars pressuring from the South and the Russian Empire in the North, considered the 'White Czar' to be the lesser evil. Therefore, in 1731 the Khan of the Little Zhuse – Abulkhair – swore allegiance to the Russian Empire.[27]

---

[27] M.H. Abuseitova et al., *A History of Kazakhstan and Central Asia*, Almaty, 2001, pp 276–9 (in Russian); I. Yesenberlin, *The Nomads*, Almaty, 1998, p. 354.

At the same time, it seems to me that at the end of the 1930s the Baltic countries did not have much choice. By then, a war in Europe had already become inevitable. Even if it could have been theoretically avoided, there should have been in power in major European countries politicians of the calibre of Winston Churchill or Charles De Gaulle. However, Churchill, calling the Munich deal to be 'a total, unmitigated defeat,' was then only a conservative backbencher, while Charles De Gaulle was a simple general in the French Army that rapidly surrendered to the Nazis. Estonia was occupied and annexed by the Soviet Union not because Joseph Stalin was a dictator and the Bolshevik regime was ruthless. It happened because the war with Nazi Germany had become by 1939, if not inevitable, then at least highly probable. There was no way that states in-between could have remained neutral and stayed away from the coming world-wide conflagration.

Jean Lopez and Lasha Otkhmezuri, in their capital work *Barbarossa: La guerre absolue 1941*, ask: 'Did Stalin, signing in 1939 a deal with Hitler, help the latter to open the door for the war?' Their response, based on detailed study of documents, is: 'No, the German dictator would have attacked Poland even without any agreement with Moscow' (J. Lopez, L. Otkhmezuri, *Barbarossa: La guerre absolue 1941*, Dépôt légal, 2019, p. 98).

6- The UN Human Rights Committee and Reflections on The Universality of Human Rights

Four years (1989-1992) spent in the UN Human Rights Committee plunged me into the field of human rights and their abuses in different parts of the world. I learned a lot from my colleagues, some of them, like Dame Rosalyn Higgins, of whom more below, and Fausto Pocar – later Judge and President of the International Criminal Tribunal for Former Yugoslavia (ICTY), have become my life-long friends. This was a period of high expectations for the future of human rights and the role of international mechanisms in their protection and promotion. An incidence that happened during one of the first sessions of the Committee with my participation deserves to be mentioning. It well illustrates the changes that were taking place in the world.

In summer 1989, in Geneva, the Committee was considering a report on civil and political rights of Vietnam. As a member from the USSR that had been an ally, even a sponsor, of this South-East Asian country, I was given the floor first to question the high-level Vietnamese delegation on the human rights record of their country. Particularly, I asked why so many people were trying to leave the country risking their lives in unseaworthy small boats. By then, the term 'the boat people' had already become well-known all over the world. I don't remember what other problems I raised on the then socialist Vietnam's human rights record, but the repercussions of my questions were stormy. Already many of those who were present, including also some of my colleagues in the Committee, were stunned – the main socialist state was questioning the human rights record of another socialist country, its ally. Of course, it was not the Soviet Union that was questioning it, it was only me who had done that. However, before me no Soviet member of any UN body had acting without instructions from the Government. It hadn't mattered that members of human rights treaty-bodies were acting in their individual capacity as independent experts. All my predecessors from the USSR had acting on precise guidelines. However, I had none and behaved and talked as my conscience and rather limited knowledge of human rights norms and problems told me.

More serious meetings and discussions on my intervention in Geneva happened elsewhere – in Hanoi and in Moscow. The Soviet Ambassador was called to the Foreign Ministry in the Vietnamese capital, where a formal protest on the unfriendly act was presented to the Ambassador. Of course, the latter knew nothing of me or the role of the Committee in Geneva. He informed the Ministry in Moscow and the matter was brought to Shevardnadze's attention. Although the Minister had helped promote me to the post in Geneva, he too knew nothing about procedures of the Committee and of the status of its members. My friend Yuri Reshetov, who then was the Director of the Department of Humanitarian Affairs in the Foreign Ministry and later Russian Ambassador to Iceland, explained to the Big Boss that members of the Committee were acting in their individual capacity and not as representatives of respective states from which they were elected. Shevardnadze saved me once again. With his thick Georgian accent, not comparable with my mild idiosyncratic accent in Russian, the Minister said (as Reshetov later impersonated it for me): 'Tell our Vietnamese friends that what Müllerson said in Geneva was said in his personal capacity, as an independent member of the Committee. But don't tell our Vietnamese friends that he was right in what he was saying.' However, a few days later in Geneva, the Soviet Ambassador invited me to dinner, where the first woman cosmonaut Valentina Tereshkova was also present, to admonish me on my behaviour. But the Ambassador, though being an old school Soviet diplomat, who some years earlier would have sent me back to Moscow for what in his eyes was an inacceptable and scandalous behaviour, was rather cautious in his remarks. All was changing and everything was fluid and as I already had access to those in higher echelons, he refrained from any harsh comments on my address.

From the UN Human Rights Committee started one of my professional trends, both in terms of practice as well as theory. Being still a member of the Committee I published a book (my last one written in Russian) *Human Rights: Theory, Norms and Practice*, that is still often quoted in Russia and in some other countries, where the Russian language is widely used. In London, for many years I gave a course, together with my colleague and friend Lord Raymond Plant, on international protection of human rights. He too is one those whose friendship I very much cherish. One of the most prominent philosophers of the country, member of the House of Lords, and to my great surprise also a good administrator (the former Head of King's College Law School and the Master of St Catherine's College in Oxford), Raymond and his wife and guardian angel Catherine, are both wonderful human beings. Besides teaching and writing on human rights, I practiced them later also in my capacity as the UN Regional Advisor for Central Asia as well as leading or being a member of various human rights missions. Based on this experience, I want to share with the reader my subjective views on human rights generally and especially whether they are indeed all universal and natural. I would also touch upon some contemporary challenges to human rights.

In order to understand the character and the magnitude of new challenges to human rights it is, in my opinion, necessary to shortly clarify some preliminary points. First, a short methodological introduction or comment on the relative weight of ideas and theories, on the one hand, and the past and present of the real world, on the other, seems appropriate. Then I will, to put it somewhat grandiloquently, philosophise a bit on whether human rights as such can be universal and/or natural at all. Finally, I will dwell upon main contemporary challenges to human rights. Of course, these challenges differ depending on countries and regions, and there are places where challenges to human rights, or their virtual absence, have been and are still very much the same as they have been for quite a while. But there are two current general revolutionary changes (of which more in the following chapters) going on in the world that, in my opinion, have a negative impact on many things in the world, including human rights, and not only in the usual trouble spots for human rights, be it the totalitarian North Korea or in the troublesome Middle East and Northern Africa where the promise of the spring has been short-lived and illusory and the following conflagrations seem to be a much more continuing phenomenon. There are serious problems with human rights even in countries that have so far been in the forefront of human rights movements and where, indeed, non-negligible progress has been made in this domain after the Second World War.

The dominant, though not the only, trend in Western social and political philosophy, from at least Emmanuel Kant with his categorical imperative to John Rawls with his veil of ignorance and many others before, in-between and after, has been what one may call abstract (not necessarily in the negative meaning, though in a somewhat limited sense) philosophising or theorising, i.e. an approach that departs from some very general intuitive premises or axioms and from there moves towards more concrete questions and policy recommendations. What such an approach, notwithstanding some great insights of many original thinkers, including the above-mentioned, neglects, is the historical and comparative analyses. Therefore, I am tempted to agree with the Cambridge political philosopher Raymond Geuss when he writes that '…political philosophy must be realist. That means, roughly speaking, that it must start from and be concerned in the first instance not how people ought to ideally (or ought "rationally") act, what they ought to desire, or value, the kind of people they ought to be, etc., but, rather, with the way social, economic, political, etc., institutions actually operate in some society at some given time, and what really moves human beings to act in given circumstances.'[28] Or, as Francis Fukuyama writes (though unfortunately not when prefacing his *End of History and the Last Man*): 'Putting the theory after the history constitutes what I regard as the correct approach to analysis: theories ought to be inferred from facts, and not the other way around. Of course, there is no such thing as pure confrontation with facts, devoid of prior theoretical constructs. Those who think they are empirical in that fashion are deluding themselves. But all too often social science begins with an elegant theory and then searches for facts that will confirm it.'[29] Unfortunately, that has, indeed, been all too often so. Practically all theories concerning the issue of universality of human rights and their naturalness have been, in my opinion, built in such a way.[30] As most of these theories have been elaborated upon by Western (or Western educated) thinkers, it is not at all surprising that practically all of them have supported, or still support, some version of political arrangements based on Western liberal democratic and individualistic values, while belittling the role of communitarian ideas and neglecting responsibility of individuals *vis-à-vis* each other or that of their society.

Differences between various theories of human rights have been so far mainly differences within the same Western worldview (in a way, even the main

---

[28] R. Geuss, *Philosophy and Real Politics*, Princeton University Press, 2008.
[29] F. Fukuyama, *The Origins of Political* Order from Prehuman Times to the French Revolution, Profile Books, 2011, p. 24.
[30] Critique of ahistorical political theorising see, e.g., Raymond Geuss, *Philosophy and Real Politics*, Princeton University Press, 2008 and *Political Philosophy versus History: Contextualism and Real Politics in the Contemporary Political Thought* (eds. J. Floyd, M. Stears), Cambridge University Press, 2011.

twentieth century ideological contradiction between liberal-democratic and communist worldviews was an intra-Western ideological clash into which other peoples were dragged), which has either ignored other worldviews or treated them with a certain condescension and dealt with the classics of Chinese, Indian and Islamic thought as only historically or anthropologically relevant. In order to avoid such theorising without studying concrete societies, which had previously existed or exist today, without the analysis of why some of them had become slave-owning societies while others had evolved into liberal-democracies, why somewhere there had been an Idi Amin or a Saddam Hussein or another notorious strongman, who ruled or still rules, while in other societies democratically elected liberals struggle to find solutions to contemporary challenges, it is necessary to take historical and comparative approaches to all these questions.

Thomas Friedman once put forward a very pertinent question relevant also to the issue of democratisation and liberalisation of societies, though he himself did not give any answers to it, assuming, probably, that the answer was all too obvious. The question stood: 'Was Iraq the way Iraq was because Saddam was the way Saddam was, or was Saddam the way Saddam was because Iraq was the way Iraq was?'[31] A proper, or at least the best in my opinion, answer probably must be that Iraq was ready for Saddam and a person like Saddam Hussein could not have come to power and, even less likely, would not have been able to rule for decades in a society that would have been radically different from the Iraqi society. Rulers usually deserve their societies and societies as a rule, also deserve their leaders, though there may be dictators that turn out to be so bloody, brutal and even mad that no nation deserves them. Idi Amin, Pol Pot, Saddam Hussein or Muammar Gaddafi may have excelled even in their own class.

Only having written these names did I notice that they all had been overthrown due to the external military interference; the main consequential difference being that while the overthrow of the two first – Idi Amin and Pol Pot – brought considerable relief to the peoples over which these dictators had ruled, even though both Uganda and Cambodia remained quite authoritarian, the toppling of the last two throwed the societies they had governed – Iraq and Libya – into chaos. Why so? In my opinion, mainly because in the two first cases the interveners – Tanzania and Vietnam – did not undertake efforts to radically

---

[31] T. L. Friedman, 'The big question', *The International Herald Tribune*, 4–5 March 2006, p. 6.

change the foundations of Ugandan and Cambodian societies, while in Iraq and Libya Western intervenors tried to impose, both naively and hypocritically, ideas of liberal democracy. There is no doubt that the Vietnamese and Tanzanian leaders, being neighbours of societies where interventions took place, knew much better the moods and needs of Cambodian and Ugandan peoples than George W. Bush, Nicolas Sarkozy or David Cameron understood what Iraqi and Libyan societies needed or were able to accept. When on 15 September 2011 I saw on TV David Cameron, the then British Prime-Minister, and President of France Nicolas Sarkozy in the centre of the jubilant crowd in Tripoli celebrating the overthrow of Muammar Gaddafi, I recalled a hilarious French comedy *Tais-toi* (Shut up). In the film two run-away criminals, played by some of the best French actors, have put on women's attire instead of their prison robes. When approaching a shop window, they face their mirror-images. A half-wit Quentin, played by Gérard Depardieu, exclaims: 'Look at those two fags!' To this ruse Ruby, played by Jean Reno, responds: 'You idiot, these are us.' The political leaders of Great Britain and France in September 2011 both reminded me the first of those fictional characters. They indeed did not know and understand what they were doing, what kind of genie they were going to let out of the bottle. French journalist Renaud Girard, writing about the problems and causes of the failure of the 'Arab Spring' and the almost inevitable choice in some Arab countries between military dictatorships and militant Islamists, nevertheless singles out Syria. He emphasises: 'In Syria, the reality is that there is the civil war between the army of the regime and rebels, who in their majority are Islamists. The third way [i.e., between the authoritarian regime and Islamists] exists only as a minute candle at the end of an immense tunnel – as a dream supported by the Westerners.'[32]

Historical and comparative approaches to social and political questions are even more necessary today, at the turn of the XXI century, which seems to mark also a turning point in the history of humankind, as will be discussed below.

My doubts about the universality of human rights and whether they are natural, or on the contrary, even unnatural, result from a rather long way of my personal contact with human rights, attempts to help promote them, observing their violations or even complete absence, in the capacity of a scholar as well as a practitioner. Notwithstanding many disappointments, some of them due to

---

[32] R. Girard, *Le monde en guerre. 50 clefs pour le comprendre* (Carnets Nords, 2016), p. 35.

illusions explained by the absence of necessary knowledge of different and differing societies, of their histories, I still believe in the importance of human rights and in the ability of societies to have progress in their promotion and protection. However, I don't think that declaring human rights to be universal and even natural would help contribute to their protection or improve the world. Probably, on the contrary, ignoring humankind's history as well as cultures of different societies, approaching the topic from abstract philosophical premises, while closing eyes to the history of humanity and to the diversity of today's world, may conceal the roots and reasons of many failings to further advance the cause of human rights. Such approach to the issue of the universality of human rights is to a great extent, though not exclusively, determined by my personal experience of having worked within the United Nations and represented that organisation in countries that are quite different from societies where I have lived most of my life. And I have lived, not simply visited, almost equal thirds of my life in three countries with different sizes and histories. This experience, among other things, has confirmed my doubts as to the universality of human rights and led me to the conclusion that human rights can be neither universal nor natural. Or to qualify such a, shocking for some, conclusion: at least not all human rights are universal and even if some of them may become natural their naturalness results from the long process of evolution of specific societies and not from something called human nature, nor are they God-given.

If we were to claim that human rights all are universal, immutable, natural and not dependent on time and space, we should conclude that, say, the behaviour of members of the Yanomami tribe in the Amazonian rainforest straddling Brazil and Venezuela, whose life-style to a considerable extent resembles that of our ancestors thousands of years back[33], should accord, if not to the *European Convention on the Protection of Human Rights and Fundamental Freedoms,* then at least to the principles of the *Universal Declaration of Human Rights* of 1948. Similarly, it would be necessary to claim that there were human rights, say, in Genghis Khan's empire. Simply neither the Universal Ruler himself nor his subjects had any idea as to their content and even of the very existence of such things. In such a case, human rights would have been like laws of nature (the laws of gravitation or quantum physics), waiting for thousands of years for a Newton or an Einstein of social sciences to discover them. However, the main

---

[33] See, e.g., N.A. Chagnon, *Noble Savages: Mt Life Among Two Dangerous Tribes – the Yanomamo and the Anthropologists* (Simon & Shuster, 2013).

difference between the laws of nature and human rights is that while apples fell even in times of great Mongol warrior notwithstanding the absence of the knowledge of why they did so, the prohibition of torture and other forms of inhumane treatment or punishment, today enshrined, for example, in Article 7 of the International Covenant on Civil and Political Rights and in many other human rights documents (be they international or domestic), had no effect whatsoever either on the minds or the bodies of the Mongol warriors. Differently from laws of nature, human rights are social constructs that cannot exist without human beings being aware of them since they themselves construct them in response to evolving needs, interests and values.

French philosopher Pierre Manent draws attention to another inconsistency in the assertation of the universal character of human rights. He writes that, 'on the one hand, we start from the premise that human rights are universal, applicable to all human beings without exception; on the other hand, we assume that all "cultures", all ways of life are of equal value and denunciation of some of them, or even establishing any hierarchy between them, would be contrary to equality between humans. On the one hand, all human beings are equal; on the other, all cultures deserve equal respect.' [34] And he observes that, 'it is not rare that somebody is outraged by the status of women in Muslim societies, condemning at the same time those who criticise Islam.'[35]

I would admit that today some rights are (or it would be more precise to say, have become) universal, some may arguably be universal, i.e., their universal nature is not yet universally recognised, some may become universal in future, i.e. they are in principle universalizable. But there may be also rights that may never become universal, i.e. they may exist in some societies but be absent in others. And there may be even some rights that exist today but will disappear in future either because of the change of conditions that has made their realisation possible or because a wrong that a specific human right has been called to prevent or remedy has disappeared. The possibility of realisation of human rights, at least in principle, if not necessarily always in practice, is a *sine qua non* of their very existence as rights.[36] It may well be that due, for example, to certain negative effects of globalisation some economic and social rights that may have become natural for people, say, in North European welfare societies will cease to exist

---

[34] P. Manent, *La loi naturelle et les droits de l'homme*, PUF, 2018, p. 4.
[35] Ibid.
[36] See, e.g., R. Plant, 'Rights, Rules and World Order', in *Global Governance: Ethics and Economics of the World Order,* ed. by M. Desai, P. Redfern (Pinter, 1995), p. 207.

even in those societies. Or, on the contrary, though less plausibly, if certain values or fundamental interests of people, which today are guaranteed by means of conceptualising them as human rights, would be completely and irrevocably satisfied, there would be no need to guarantee such values or interests by conceptualising them as human rights. If something comes naturally and cannot be prevented or denied, there is no need to resort to the concept of rights to guarantee naturally existing order of things.

Not only are not all human rights universal but neither are they natural. Or rather, they may be as natural as human wrongs. What we today consider as human wrongs may have been, historically speaking, even more natural than human rights. Practically all existing societies have been, using today's language and mores, for millennia xenophobic; the fear and mistrust of strangers have deeper roots in human societies than openness or even simple curiosity towards foreigners, and as we can observe today, some of our primordial instincts have not yet disappeared for good, if they will ever completely vanish. Whenever life becomes difficult, or something unusual and threatening happens that shakes our quiet and relatively serene flow of life (particularly in Western societies), not only the best, but the worst too, come to the surface in quite a few human beings. Or to put in otherwise, in human beings, though in different degrees, there is something that may be defined as angelic as well as something close to devilish.

Richard Rorty has insightfully observed, and he did it long before the current migration crisis hit the world and particularly Europe, that one's own sense of *security* and *sympathy* towards those who are not like us and are suffering in far-away places go usually hand in hand. He wrote: 'By "security" I mean conditions of life sufficiently risk-free as to make one's difference from others unessential to one's self-respect, one's sense of worth. These conditions have been enjoyed by Americans and Europeans – the people who dreamed up the human rights culture – much more than they have been enjoyed by anyone else.'[37] However, when one's security is threatened, particularly when those far-away and suffering strangers start massively coming to us, our sympathy towards them and towards their suffering becomes undermined. Of course, there are always significant exceptions, but for many it is easier to sympathise with victims of human rights violations from the shores of the *Lac Leman* (in Geneva, where the main UN

---

[37] R. Rorty, 'Human Rights, Rationality, and Sentimentality', in S. Shute and S. Hurley (eds.), On Human Rights. Oxford Amnesty Lectures 1993, Basic Books, 1993, p. 128.

human rights activities take place) than being next to them either in refugee camps in the Middle East or in the streets of some European capitals.

So, both human rights, expressing the good that exists in humans, and human wrongs, reflecting the evil existing in the world and in us, are both equally human, though not necessarily humane. Human rights are social constructs that are called upon to respond to human needs and remedy human wrongs. Alan Dershovitz put it concisely and correctly in the title of his book *Rights from Wrongs*.[38] Had not there been human wrongs, injustices that over time become unacceptable and unjustifiable in the eyes of sufficient number of people, there would not be either human rights; there simply would be no need for them. Historically the emergence of human rights is related also to the advent of centralised nation-states, so called Leviathans, in Europe where even those belonging to the class of nobles needed something that would have justified their claims against the king becoming all-powerful. Therefore, they were the rights of the few, while the majority knew nothing of them and accepted such situation as natural.

Sometimes certain human rights may become even natural in the sense that people in some societies may start considering them as such; they cannot even imagine how they could have lived without them before (say, certain generous welfare rights in welfare states of Northern Europe) or how they could live without them in future, though it may well be that due to various factors, mostly related to processes of globalisation, certain welfare rights, and not only they, may become less comprehensive or even completely extinct. However, even if natural, they are not natural because they are either God-given or stem from something that could be considered as human nature or emerge from behind Rawl's 'veil of ignorance'. Had human rights been natural, it would not have been necessary to constantly struggle for their observance. The compliance with them would come naturally, automatically and almost effortlessly. Rare breaches would be seen as the aberrations of some deranged psychopaths, whose deeds would not be considered as crimes and who therefore should not be behind bars, but in care of medical institutions. Instead of international criminal tribunals in The Hague or elsewhere there would be international medical teams ready to urgently save those poor deranged and erred souls.

---

[38] A. Dershowitz, *Rights from Wrongs: The Origins of Human Rights in the Experience of Injustice*, Basic Books, 2004.

Yuval Noah Harari considers the idea of universality and naturalness of human rights to be a dogma, which may have even contributed to the advancement of human rights, but that nevertheless remains a dogma. He writes: 'Thus article 19 of the United Nations Declaration of Human Rights says that "Everyone has the right to freedom of opinion and expression." If we understand this as a political demand ('everyone should have the right to freedom of opinion') this is perfectly sensible. But if we believe that each and every Sapiens is naturally endowed with a "right to freedom of opinion", and that censorship therefore violates some law of nature, we miss the truth about humanity. As long as you define yourself as "an individual possessing inalienable natural rights", you will not know who you really are, and you will not understand the historical forces that shaped your society and your own mind (including your belief in "natural rights").'[39] And looking into future, Harari observes that 'the dogma of human rights was shaped in previous centuries as a weapon against the Inquisition, the *ancient régime*, the Nazis and the KKK. It is hardly equipped to deal with super humans, cyborgs and super-intelligent computers.'[40]

As can be seen from the history of human rights, even from the very notion of the so-called three generations of human rights – civil and political rights, economic and social rights and so-called solidarity or collective rights (e.g., the right of peoples to self-determination, the right to clean environment, the right to peace, etc., though sometimes the conceptualisation of these or some other values as human rights may be questionable), the emergence and evolution of human rights has been a gradual process. Moreover, it has been a painful process with many setbacks; it has been always necessary to fight not only, and initially not at all, for the observance of human rights, but for conceptualising something as a human right. For example, one of the first written acts that can be qualified as a human rights instrument – the Magna Carta – was a document that King John of England was forced to grant to his barons in 1215 at Runnymede near Windsor. This text that Lord Denning described as 'the greatest constitutional document of all times – the foundation of the freedom of the individual against the arbitrary authority of the despot'[41], was meant to protect only some rights (and they became rights later; before they were demands) of free men, particularly the barons and well as the Church. And the man, who drafted one of

---

[39] Y. N. Harari, *21 Lessons for the 21st Century*, Jonathan Cape, 2018, p. 211.
[40] Ibid., p. 212.
[41] D. Danziger, J.G Gillingham, *1215: The Year of Magna Carta*, Hodder Paperbacks, 2004, p. 268.

the most quoted all over the world phrases 'We hold these truths to be self-evident, that *all men* are created equal, that they are endowed by their Creator with certain unalienable Rights, that among these are Life, Liberty and the Pursuit of Happiness,' was himself a slave-owner. And the struggle for the recognition of rights of women and later rights of people with non-traditional sexual orientation are too recent to believe that human rights are universal and natural. It has always been necessary to fight, first, for recognition even the most important and basic values and fundamental interests as human rights, and then for their observance in practice. What may be obvious for many or even for most human beings today (and I am purposefully not saying 'for everybody and everywhere'), was or may have been heresy for many or for the most people centuries or even decades ago. They were needs and claims that, when first raised, were usually considered by most people irrational, wrong and even absurd.

Let us illustrate this by a useful example from Danish history. In the 1770s, the royal physician of the Danish Court, Johann Friedrich Struensee, by a strange and fatal confluence of circumstances, became very close to the physically feeble and mentally unstable King Christian VII. Using (or abusing) this influence, he became the *de facto* prime minister of the country, issuing laws to effect, among other interesting and wonderful things, the abolition of serfdom and subsidies to unprofitable industries owned by the nobility, while also permitting unrestricting freedom of expression and religious freedoms.[42] Unfortunately, though quite predictably, such laws had little effect in the eighteenth century Denmark, and the only tangible result of the freedom of expression was that shortly everybody started to talk about Struensee's love affair with the Queen. Soon the man, influenced by ideas if the French Enlightenment and being well ahead of his time, was executed and the Queen was sent into exile (back to England where she had come from). As to the serfs, instead of expressing thankfulness for the attempt to liberate them, they started rioting. As a reaction to Struensee's reform attempts, Denmark became even less tolerant than it had been before his attempts to put into practice some radical Enlightenment ideals. It took considerable time before these noble ideas became reality in Europe, including the Kingdom of Denmark.

---

[42] See, P.O. Enquist, *The Visit of the Royal Physician* (New York, Vintage, 2003); A. Ross & O. Espersen, Dansk Statsforfatningsret II (Copenhagen, Nyt Nordisk Forlag, 1980), p. 707.

Even the very idea of the universality of human rights, notwithstanding the good intentions of most of its advocates and regardless of the positive results these ideas have produced, has its dark side. Whether done purposefully to destroy societies that do not conform, or in the sincere belief that what is good and true for us is (or should be) good and true for all, such a forced homogenisation of the world by way of a heterogenisation of individual societies tears apart many countries, destroying societal bonds that had developed during centuries or even millennia and are not amenable to rapid change. Therefore, one could only welcome the statement of the former British Prime Minister Theresa May during her January 2017 US visit that there is no 'return to the failed policies of the past. The days of Britain and America intervening in sovereign countries in an attempt to remake the world in our own image are over.'[43] The Prime Minister vowed never to repeat the 'failed policies of the past' in reference to Western military intervention in Iraq and Afghanistan, breaking from the 'liberal intervention' principle established and promoted by her predecessor Tony Blair. And I would add that not only military interventions have all been failures but intervening in domestic affairs of other countries by means of economic sanctions or political pressure, if not authorised by the UN Security Council, have more often than not made things worse rather than better. Therefore, Hubert Védrine, the former French Foreign Minister, was right in emphasising that 'democracy and human rights will progress in future much less through the prescriptions and interference from the outside by the West than depending on the internal dynamics of individual societies.'[44] It is often, though not always, the case that the less states publicly criticise other states on human rights issues, the better would it be for human rights.

Today, we have some new challenges to human rights that didn't exist only decades ago. There is little doubt that significant migration into the West will be a continuing long-term phenomenon, even if abating in comparison with its 2015 peak. This will bring about increasing nationalistic sentiments, identity problems, greater difficulties of integration (assimilation) of minorities and continuing terrorist threats. The refugee flows to Europe from Syria, Afghanistan, North Africa and elsewhere, though having specific causes, are one

---

[43] Theresa May: US and UK will no longer invade foreign countries "to remake the world in their own image," *The Independent*, 27 January, 2017.
[44] H. Védrine, *Le Monde au Défi* (Fayard, 2016), Empl. 799. See also my article R. Müllerson, 'Democratization through the Supply-Demand Prism', in *Human Rights Review*, November 2009.

of the currents in the ongoing wave of global migration. It is to be expected that even the resolution of the conflicts that have caused them – not an easy task, not at all certain and in any case not a temporary problem – may only slow the general flow of people from developing and poorer countries to more developed and richer ones. Global inequality and the demographic explosion in Africa[45] are the main causes of the current migration wave. Arguably, three grand strategies will be necessary for Europe. First, truly integrating those migrants who are already in Europe and who will inevitably arrive in the future. And by integration, I mean at least partial assimilation (it would be necessary to follow the maxim: when in Rome, do as the Romans do). Secondly, the EU, as well as all its member-states, must make the control and regulation of migration one of their priorities. Thirdly, to fight the Islamist radicalisation and to cooperate with other countries, including China and Russia, in the fight against the threat of political Islam. So far, there have been more double standards in Western approaches to the fight against Islamist extremism than real cooperation with those who also suffer from it. While not being able to adequately fight the scourge of terrorism either at home or in its sources abroad, Western elites condemned Russia when it fought against the Islamic terrorism in Chechnya and are now targeting China over its anti-terrorist policies in the Xinjiang province, claiming that they are the source of the rise of Islamism. Even if some Russian or Chinese anti-terrorist measures may have been either wrong or excessive, open and constant criticism of them is rather adding the fuel to the fire, instead of having any positive effects.

Even if Daesh (ISIS) would be destroyed in the Middle East, its metastases have already reached societies far beyond this region. Moreover, French professor Gilles Kepel – one of the most knowledgeable experts on Islam in the West – has shown that since 2005 when Mustafa Setmariam Nasar, alias Abu Musab al-Suri – a jihadist 'theoretician' – published his *Call for a Global Islamic Resistance*,[46] the main thrust of the movement's efforts, the so-called third wave of jihadism (the first being against the Soviets in Afghanistan in the 1980s, the second being the emergence and terror of al-Qaeda), should be carried out in European countries by dissatisfied young immigrants with the aim of unleashing

---

[45] See, S. Smith, *La Ruée vers L'Europe: La Jeune Afrique en Route pour le Vieux Continent*, Grasset, 2019.
[46] See full text in
https://archive.org/stream/TheGlobalIslamicResistanceCall/The_Global_Islamic_Resistance_Call_-_Chapter_8_sections_5_to_7_LIST_OF_TARGETS_djvu.txt.

a civil war in the West.[47] The ideologies of Wahhabism and Salafism which form the 'scholarly' or ideological background of jihadism are of Sunni origin, emanating primarily from Saudi Arabia, and have been actively, even aggressively, promoted and sponsored by some Gulf monarchies in different parts of the world, including Europe.[48]

If a state fails to take necessary measures to protect the population from terrorist threats, it may, among other things, be in violation of the right to life by omission. However, more often than not even necessary anti-terrorist measures may encroach upon some human rights, like, the freedom of movement, even the prohibition of discrimination and so on. The migration from Muslim, especially Arab, countries has raised the levels of antisemitism in many Western countries, especially and particularly among the migrant communities [49], while Islamophobia has become more widespread than before. At the same time, almost anybody voicing criticism of Islam can be labelled as an Islamophobia[50], not only by some Muslim communities, but also by *bien-pensant* liberal, especially leftist, mass media. After the terror attacks of 22 March 2016 in Brussels – the capital of Belgium as well as of Europe – Alain Destexhe, a senator from Belgium, admitted that 'we have for too long lived in denial. The political correctness has aestheticised the debate.'[51] There are even those in Europe, who believe and write that today's Muslim is yesterday's Jew, that is to say, an innocent scapegoat.[52] There were no voluntary Jewish ghettos in European countries (Jews were forced into them), there were no Jewish terrorist

---

[47] G. Kepel, *Terror dans l'Hexagone: Genèse du Djihad Français* (Gallimard, 2015), pp. 33–66.
[48] See, for example, A. Rashid, *Jihad. The Rise of Militant Islam in Central Asia* (Yale University Press, 2002); O. Roy, *Globalised Islam. The Search for a New Ummah* (Hurst & Company, 2004); R. Müllerson, *Central Asia: A Chessboard and Player in the New Great Game*, 2nd edition (Routledge, 2012); C. Chesnot and G. Malbrunot *Nos très chers émirs: Sont-ils vraiment nos amis ?, Michel Lafon, 2016*.
[49] See, e.g., C. Lamfalussy, J.-P. Martin, *Molenbeek sur Djihad*, Bernard Grasset, 2016.
[50] So, 7th of March 2017 the Paris Criminal Court (*Le Tribunal Correctionnel de Paris*) found historian Georges Bensoussan not guilty of the incitement to racial hatred and islamophobia in the case initiated by organisation called Collective against Islamophobia in France (CCIF). The historian had spoken in a radio programme about widespread antisemitism among French Muslims (*Le Figaro*, 8 mars, 2017).
[51] "'Belgikistan@: comment Bruxelles est devenu un plaque tournante du djihad,' *L'Obs*, 23 March 2016
[52] R. Liogier, Populisme liquide dans les démocraties occidentales, in *Le Retours des Populismes : Etat du monde 2019* (B. Badie, D. Vidal eds), La Découverte, 2018, Loc. 798.

attacks in Paris, Berlin, London or any other European cities before, during or after the Second World War. In my opinion, equating current fears, existing among many Europeans, that mass migration from the Muslim world is threatening not only their identity but also security, with the antisemitism of the 1930s, is disingenuous and even smells of antisemitism. At the same time, the right-wing neo-fascist extremism targeting foreigners is also in rise in many European countries.

Too much is at stake in order to continue in the same vein. One thing is clear, only leaving behind intellectually and politically debilitating political correctness we, notwithstanding whether we are, or consider ourselves to be, populist democrats or elitist liberals, should address these challenges together and with an open mind.

7- The Collapse of the Soviet Union and Independence of Estonia

As I already mentioned above, it was becoming increasingly clear for me since the spring of 1990 that the days of the Soviet Union may not last much longer. Not only were the Baltic republics agitating and claiming their right to go; there had been ethnic clashes in the Azeri capital Baku, the beginning of the conflict between Armenia and Azerbaijan over Nagorno-Karabakh, inter-ethnic disturbances in Kazakhstan and Kyrgyzstan. There emerged with their claims and grievances ethnicities, about whom I had heard nothing. When representatives of the Gagauz, Karaimes and other minorities came to see me in Moscow to speak of their problems I recalled what Woodrow Wilson's Secretary of State Robert Lansing had written about the Versailles Peace Congress and Wilson's advocacy for the right of peoples to self-determination. Lansing wrote that Wilson, being an educated man, a historian, knew that there were Czechs, Poles and Hungarians in Central Europe. But when Ruthenians and Hutzuls in the Carpathian Mountains also started claiming their right to self-determination in the sense of independent statehood, Lansing, who was with Wilson at the Paris Peace Congress, wrote: 'The more I think about the President's declaration as to the right of "self-determination", the more convinced I am of the danger of putting such ideas into the minds of certain races. It is bound to be the basis of impossible demands on the Peace Congress and create troubles in many lands... The phrase is simply loaded with dynamite. It will raise hopes which can never be realised. It will, I fear, cost thousands of lives.'[53] At the end of the 1980s – beginning of the 1990s, in the former USSR, these were not only the 15 so-called constituent republic, that according to the Soviet Constitution had the declared but undefined right to independence, but various ethnic groups within them, who

---

[53] R. Lansing, *Peace Negotiations. A Personal Narrative*, Constable & Company, 1921, p. 87.

had similar claims or who, on the contrary, preferred the continuation of the Soviet Union, instead of being left *vis-à-vis* the majorities of new independent states. These ethnicities, like the Ossetians or Abkhazians in Georgia, saw Moscow as their safeguard against nationalistic majorities of constituent republics.

Being much less requested in Moscow, especially after my 1990 speech in Amsterdam on legal problems that may emerge if the USSR disintegrates and my public criticism of the use of force by Soviet troops in Lithuania in January 1991, and being at the same time invited to Tallinn to discuss constitutional issues with Arnold Rüütel – the then Chairman of the Supreme Soviet of the still Soviet Estonia, later President of the independent Estonia, I started my gradual move back home. Once, in autumn 1990, visiting Tallinn at the invitation of Arnold Rüütel, but still working in the Institute of the Academy of Sciences in Moscow, I met the then Foreign Minister of Estonia (still Soviet) Lennart Meri, who later became President of the Republic. He invited me to become his first Vice-Minister. Although I didn't immediately jump to it, but a germ of the idea started its slow work in my head.

I was used of thinking in global terms, I was professionally more interested in relations between superpowers than in the role of small states in world politics. When I started, at the end of the 1980s, regularly travelling abroad, it was not to Warsaw or Brussels, it was mostly to Washington and New York. I had become used to talk to Americans as equal to equals; learning, yes, but not gladly taking lessons, which I sometimes found incompetent, from my Western counterparts. I may have even acquired a kind of superpower superiority complex. When, for example, the UN Under-Secretary-General was giving a diner for members of the Human Rights Committee, Lady Rosalyn Higgins – the UK member – was sitting on his right, while I was sitting to his left as the Soviet member. I had come used to that when I spoke everybody listened, not because I was so clever but because I either represented or was from a superpower. Therefore, as the Vice-Minister in independent Estonia I was often annoyed when diplomats from small Western countries tried to explain to me the basics of international law and politics. Later, as professor in London and much more experienced in law and politics than during my younger years either in Moscow or Tallinn, I sometimes noticed with certain amusement how relatively insignificant I had become in the eyes of some, who before had been eager to seek my attention. High posts or access to those, who hold them, attract and make even an unremarkable person remarkable. Of course, I retain also many real friends among those with whom I became acquainted during the years when I was remarkable due to my association with important people, who I quite often found unremarkable.

Certainly, my great-power mentality was always somewhat diluted by or mixed with my Estonian background and origin. Still working in Moscow, during various meetings or missions abroad I felt that other representatives of superpowers – both Americans and Russians – were quite often insensitive to problems and approaches of representatives of smaller nations. For them, it was all a small print. However, being used to think, at least professionally, in terms of global politics, I had doubts about joining the Government of Estonia. And I was not alone in those doubts. When I had already started working in the Estonian (not yet independent) Foreign Ministry I had a call from my American friend Thomas Franck – Professor of international law at the New York University (NYU). Tom, who unfortunately is not any more with us, was one of those friends whom I will always warmly remember. He called me from New York, trying to dissuade me from moving from Moscow to Tallinn. I don't remember all the arguments that Tom used, but one is still with me: think, Rein, how much you would do, not only for you personally, but for the world, working in Moscow and what would be your impact, if you move to Estonia. Yes, I had similar doubts, but the die was already cast, and I didn't, and still do not, regret it.

As Estonia was still a part of the USSR, even if doing its best to break away from it, the Foreign Ministry in Tallinn could not perform functions that are traditional for such institutions. During the Soviet period these Ministries, with a small staff, received and organised visits of high-level foreign guests and their representatives worked in some Soviet diplomatic missions abroad. When I joined the Ministry in early spring of 1991, our main mission was to advocate for the end of illegal occupation and for the restoration of our sovereignty lost in 1940. In that respect the Baltic republics distinguished themselves from other 12 constituent republics of the Soviet Union. We did not claim that it would be necessary to dissolve the USSR – let it live long, but without us. As I was at that time also a member of the UN Human Rights Committee, I used my regular visits to New York or Geneva to encourage Western countries to do more to support Estonia's desire to become independent. We were usually listened attentively and promised to do whatever possible to help us. I have still in a drawer of my table in London a badge of a member of the Swiss delegation to the July 1991

OSCE (then still CSCE) meeting in Geneva. This badge gave me a much wider access to delegations of different states and helped bring to their attention our aims, the situation and tendencies in Estonia as well as in the USSR as a whole. These were not only representatives of Western countries with whom I discussed these matters. As I knew personally well many Soviet diplomats who were present in Geneva, I tried to explain also to them our position and I don't remember that I had ever a hostile reaction from their part to my advocacy of the restoration of Estonian independence.

In Geneva, though earlier, I had become close to a young Soviet diplomat Sergey Lavrov. We played football together, drank wine and Sergey played guitar and sang songs, lyrics of some of which was written by him. Sessions of the Human Rights Committee and meetings of the ECOSOC, where Sergey represented the Soviet Union, coincided in time and space and therefore we often spent time together. I came to respect the professionalism and character of the man with great sense of humour, who has by now become the longest serving Foreign Minister of Russia. I believe, Russia has been lucky to have him at the head of its diplomacy. I knew personally, though much less, also Andrei Kozyrev – the first Yeltsin's Foreign Minister of Russia. This lightweight and opportunistic diplomat was a complete opposite to the strong-willed and skilled Lavrov.

In support of this characterisation of Kozyrev, let me reproduce a conversation between the former US President Richard Nixon and Andrei Kozyrev, as written down by Dimitri Simes. This exchange of views also reveals much of what transpired in Russia in the 1990s, and why Russia's foreign policy today appears for some in the West to be too prickly. Dimitri Simes, who was close to ex-President Richard Nixon and is now the President and CEO of *The Centre for the National Interest* in Washington and the publisher of its foreign policy magazine, *The National Interest* writes: 'Nixon asked Kozyrev how his government was defining Russian national interests. Kozyrev…replied that in the past Russia had suffered greatly from focusing too intently on its own interests at the expense of the rest of the world. Now was the time, he added, for Russia 'to think more in terms of universal human values.'

'Well,' Nixon responded wryly, 'That is very commendable sentiment on the Minister's part. But surely there are some particular interests which Russia considers important as an emerging power.' Kozyrev was not persuaded.

'Perhaps, President Nixon, as a friend of Russian democracy you would be willing to help to identify them?' Kozyrev inquired with a shy smile. The former President somehow kept his poker face.

'I would not presume to tell the Minister what Russian national interests should be. I am sure that in due time he will find them on his own. *But I would like to make one point. Russia cannot and should not attempt to walk in lockstep with the United States on all foreign policy issues. As a great country, Russia has its own destiny* [emphasis added]. We want Russia as a friend, and we tremendously appreciate your personal friendship, Mr. Minister, but I know that anyone in Russia who tries to follow foreign advice too closely is bound to get into trouble. And we do not want this to happen to our friends.'[54]

And out of the Foreign Ministry building in Smolenskaya Square, in the centre of Moscow, and in President Nixon's limousine, Dimitri Simes, asked by Nixon what he had thought about the conversation with the Minister, responded that such a blindly pro-Western policy makes Kozyrev vulnerable to public indignation and possibly makes the United States guilty by association. And then comes Nixon's hit: 'This is exactly the point. He is a nice man. He's not enough of a son of a bitch to do the job right, Dimitri. You need to be able to see straight, but also be ruthless to build a new country on the ruins of the empire. I can't see the Russian people respecting wimps like that.'[55] Exactly. I am not too sure about the categorisation of the Minister as a nice man, but a wimp and sycophant certainly. Unfortunately, few American politicians have been able to see international relations in such a clear, straight, and I would also say, maybe surprisingly, in a philosophically profound way. Most are all too content to rely on those foreign diplomats or politicians whom Nixon would have qualified as wimps and lickspittles, though it is difficult do believe that they necessarily respect them. Here, however, I may be wrong since sometimes I have a feeling that top American politicians and diplomats, differently, say, from their British counterparts, having become used to the subservience of their allies, may even have some respect for their own SOBs in high posts in foreign countries.

Sorry for a long digression, but I believe it to be important for the understanding of world politics and relations between Russia and the West as well as relations between Estonia and Russia.

---

[54] D. Simes, *After the Collapse: Russia Seeks its Place as Great Power* (Simon & Schuster, 1999).
[55] Ibid.

Before the August 1991 *coup d'état* attempt in Moscow, after which our frenetic diplomatic activities started, we had time to reflect on possible foreign policy concepts and on other matters that could become important for the future of independent Estonia. One of such issues, usually not within the competence of the Foreign Ministries, was the concept of the citizenship. Who would become automatically citizens of the independent Estonia or acquire otherwise its citizenship? As we considered the newly independent Estonia to be a continuation of the pre-WWII Estonia, and we did not, for example, establish diplomatic relations with most countries but restored them, there were those who claimed that only those, who had been citizens of Estonia before the 1940 occupation and their children and grandchildren could obtain Estonian citizenship automatically; all the rest would have to go through a naturalisation process with the requirement of the knowledge of the language, rather long residency requirement etc. However, the demographic composition of Estonia had been changed radically since 1940. More than one third of the population of Estonia did not correspond to the criteria of automatic citizenship. This would have meant that they would remain, at least for long if not forever, without any citizenship or would be forced to choose the citizenship of some foreign country. Both of these scenarios didn't seem right. I discussed these issues with my direct boss Foreign Minister Lennart Meri and also with Professor Marju Lauristin, who reflected on these matters as a member of the Supreme Soviet. We had almost a consensus that with some exceptions (relatively short residency requirement and exclusion of the serving members of the Soviet military, who were not from Estonia) we should accept the so-called zero version, i.e. every permanent resident, with these few exceptions, of the republic could apply for citizenship and it should be granted. Moreover, such a scenario was foreseen by the Agreement that was signed by the Russian President Boris Yeltsin and Arnold Rüütel in January 1991, when Yeltsin visited Tallinn and expressed its support of the independence strive of Estonia.

However, when on 20 August 1991, our independence was declared and *de jure* restored, moods among the political elites started to change and voices with stronger nationalistic views rapidly gained the upper hand. I thought then, and still believe, that leaving a third of the population without citizenship was not only contrary to basic human rights of those persons, but it was also divisive for the Estonian society and politically dangerous. Moreover, such policies poisoned relations with Russia. Repercussions of this short-sighted nationalistic approach we can still see in Estonian society; it has not become more integrated; the opposite is, probably, true. Today, when I am writing these lines, one of the parties in the coalition Government, called EKRE (Estonian Conservative Peoples' Party) is accused by its political opponents in Estonia as well as by our European counterparts to be too nationalistic. However, their nationalism is nothing else but the same nationalism that in the 1990s left a third of the Estonian population without citizenship. The only difference is that before on the receiving end of this nationalism were mostly ethnic Russians, or other Russian-speaking residents, today's EKRE is less discriminatory. They are not only against Russians, but also against Ukrainian migrants in Estonia and are even sceptical of the European Union and especially its migration policies. This is already an unpardonable sin. Moreover, they are critical of Brussels institutions; they want to have more freedoms from the European Union. This, however, is also taboo. If Russophobia can be tolerated and sometimes even quietly encouraged in Western states, Ukrainians, for example, have become protected species, so far as they are anti-Russian and claim to be part of the West.

My opposition to such citizenship policy and to narrow nationalism was one of the main reasons of my resignation, in spring 1992, from the Foreign Ministry of Estonia. However, there was also another factor. The London School of Economics (LSE), that was going to celebrate its hundredth anniversary, had offered me centenary professorship in international law. It was a great honour and I had always felt to be more academic than practitioner, though I believe that the combination of these two hats has been the best for me and, in my opinion, is generally beneficial for legal practice as well as for academia.

But before moving to my London period, I cannot refrain from mentioning two of my achievements in Estonia, which I am particularly proud of. The first happened at night from 19 to 20 August 1991, when I wrote the text of the Declaration of the restoration of independence of Estonia. The Supreme Council (Parliament), which was sitting at that time at the same building with the Foreign Ministry, had been discussing for hours two different texts on the matter. The leaders of the Peoples Front (Rahvarinne), which had been in the forefront of the independence movement and, and those of a smaller group of more nationalistic Estonian Congress (Eesti Kongress), had been unable to reconcile their differences. It was around midnight, when two young politicians – Jüri Luik, who then worked with me in the Foreign Ministry and is now the Defence Minister of Estonia, and Mart Laar – a future Prime Minister of Estonia, came to see me with those two different versions of the draft Declaration. They asked me whether I could find a compromise between these texts without losing anything vital. I asked them to leave me alone for a while in order to concentrate on the job and soon I went with a new text to the room where the leaders of these two fractions were engaged in the heated discussion. I could feel and still remember the electricity in the air. However, my text was adopted without amendments.

In this context, I would like to mention one small episode of these three days and nights we spent in our offices surrounded by Soviet tanks (remember, it was during a coup d'état attempt). One of those nights I was working in the office of the Minister Meri, as he was on vacation abroad and therefore during these crucial days I was at the head of the Ministry. I overheard the guards, who protected us against a possible attack by the Soviet troops, talking below the windows of the office. They spoke Russian and obviously they were ethnic Russians. Therefore, the choice made by Estonian politicians that left a third of the population, mostly Russian and Russian-speaking residents, without Estonian citizenship, seemed especially insensitive as well as counterproductive to the interest of Estonia.

The second, even more extraordinary, event took place some days later when I flew, together with Arnold Rüütel and the Chairman of the Foreign relations committee of the Supreme Soviet Indrek Toome – the former Prime Minister, whose common sense and sense of humour I always appreciate, to Moscow to seek the recognition of our independence Declaration by whoever was ready to do that. Our first port of call was President of Russia Boris Yeltsin, who after the failed coup attempt against Gorbachev had become the most influential person not only in Russia, but in the whole USSR. Gorbachev was weakened during his days in the captivity in the Crimea while Yeltsin had stood firm against the Putschists in Moscow. It helped that Rüütel and Yeltsin knew each other rather well. Both had been Communist Party bosses and Yeltsin had shortly before visited Estonia, expressing support for the cause of Estonian independence. So, we were rather quickly received by Boris Yeltsin in the White House, then the building of the Russian Supreme Soviet, which was still in barricades, over which we had to climb to reach the building.

As Yeltsin was very busy and was constantly interrupted by other matters, our meeting lasted for hours. Our aim was to have an official and written recognition by Russia of our restored independence. Legally speaking, such a recognition would not be binding under international law; Russia was still a part of the USSR and had no competence to recognise foreign states. However, such a step was politically very significant. As we had expected, recognition of our independence by the Soviet Union followed a couple of weeks after Yeltsin's recognition. His Decree of recognition, though of doubtful legality, played a significant political role in the recognition of our independence by Gorbachev. Yeltsin, being ready to recognise our recently declared independence, however, said that he had no lawyers present, to draft the text. Particularly, his main legal adviser, who later became a deputy Prime Minister of Russia, Sergey Shakhrai, and whom I personally knew well, was absent. Then somebody in Yeltsin's entourage, pointing at me, told the President of Russia: 'Look, there is Rein Müllerson, who until recently drafted documents for Gorbachev, he may serve you as well.' As we had already had some discussion what kind of text we needed, with one of the Yeltsin's aids I went to an adjacent room, where I wrote the draft Decree of the President of Russia on the recognition of Estonia. I doubt that there is any other high-level diplomat, who has written a draft of the act of recognition of his country for the head of a foreign state. But these were extraordinary times. We did things that usually aren't done at all and sometimes simply did them on the hoof.

For example, some weeks after having visited Yeltsin, I exchanged diplomatic notes on the restoration of diplomatic relations between Estonia and the Confederation Helvetique (Switzerland). As it was done in a hurry, we made a mistake in the text; instead of writing that our diplomatic relations shall be governed by the Vienna Convention on diplomatic relations of 1961, it was said in the note that they shall be based on the International Covenant on Civil and Political Rights of 1966. Neither the Swiss Ambassador, who signed the text, nor I saw this error prior to the solemn signing and the exchange of notes before the TV cameras. When it was discovered by the Swiss, I travelled from Geneva, where I attended a meeting of the Human Rights Committee, to Bern and there quietly, without TV cameras, as it had been the case in Tallinn, exchanged the corrected notes.

I retain a soft spot for most of those with whom I participated in the process of restoration of independence of Estonia, and especially for those who during those three days of August 1991 remained in their posts (not everybody was there), even if I don't always share their current views or even if in those days had disagreements on important questions. I have always genuine smile on my face whenever I meet the ex-President Arnold Rüütel. Although my relations with the late Lennart Meri were rather stormy, he once even tried to sack me, our meetings during the last year of his Presidency were always cordial and mutually respectful. He even asked me to become the Chancellor of Justice – one of the highest posts in the Republic of Estonia. As I had shortly before his call published my most voluminous book *Ordering Anarchy*, believing it to be the crown of my academic vocation, I even toyed with the idea of changing once again my career. However, the Estonian media immediately started scandalous attacks not only, and maybe not even so much, against me, but against the President too. Therefore, we decided to bury this idea. And I am happy that it went the way as it did and, in a way, I am even thankful to those who attacked us.

I believe that reading, thinking and writing are the occupations suiting me the best. This, of course, together with some other occupations, less socially useful, but nonetheless no less pleasurable such as drinking good wine, chitchatting with friends, looking at interesting women (my wife being unique), hiking or riding in the horseback in the mountains or swimming in the sea or in the pool. One of the Latin sayings, we had to learn by heart as law students of Moscow University was: *Homo sum humani nihil a me alienum puto* (I am a human being and nothing human is strange to me). As far as I remember, this was said to have been also Karl Marx's favourite aphorism. However, I don't think that it was due to Marx that I too liked this ancient proverb. Moreover, recently I read about a rebuke that Karl Marx father Heinrich had addressed to his son: 'I wonder whether you would ever be able to enjoy simple happiness, simple family pleasures and making happy those who are close to you.'[56] In my life, concentrating too much on my professional career, travelling a lot and even while at home most of the time sitting behind the desk, I have devoted less time than I should have or would have liked to my family. However, I have always loved them and the older I become, the more I miss my dearests. Simple family pleasures, having, for instance, grandchildren, whom we don't yet have, are becoming more and more treasurable.

Coming back from this short personal digression and confession I continue with those personalities I worked closely with while in the Foreign Ministry of Estonia. I feel high respect for Vaino Väljas – the last first Secretary of the Communist Party of Estonia from 1988-1990. In the 1970s, he had already held

---

[56] Quoted and translated from L. Debray, *Fille de révolutionaires* (Editions Stock, 2017) p. 168.

high posts in the Soviet Estonia. However, being considered by Moscow as somebody having nationalistic inclinations, he was removed from Estonia and appointed the Soviet ambassador, first, in 1980 to Venezuela, and then in 1986 to Nicaragua. When, at the end of the 1980s, the independence movement in Estonia gained momentum, Gorbachev recalled Väljas back from Nicaragua and appointed him the First Secretary of the Estonian Communist Party. During the year I worked in the Foreign Ministry of Estonia the Communist Party of Estonia had already disappeared and Väljas chaired the Foreign Relations Commission of the Estonian Parliament. Therefore, we often had opportunities to discuss what kind of foreign policy independent Estonia should have. He was one of the few, maybe even the only one, in Estonia who could professionally, and at the same time with immense erudition, discuss such matters.

Once, in late autumn 1991, I was invited for dinner by Harry Männil – a rich Venezuelan businessman of Estonian origin. Naturally, he was well acquainted with the former Soviet Ambassador to Venezuela. Männil and I discussed Estonian politics and politicians. When I asked him, who, in his opinion, would be the best person to lead the country during those first crucial years of regained independence, Männil didn't hesitate: of course, Väljas. I wondered why this capitalist didn't have any qualms about seeing a former communist leader at the head of the new Estonia and I put the question to Männil. In a way, I regret that I asked him since he may have thought me to be more stupid than I really am. He responded: we are talking about serious things and not about nonsense. Väljas, according to Männil, had never been a real communist, at best (or at worst, depending on one's position) he could have been a social democrat. What matters, he told me, is that he is the most competent person to do the job. And this is what I thought then, and also believe today. Moreover, differently from many other participants in those crucial for Estonia events, Vaino Väljas has never exaggerated his contribution to the restoration of independence of Estonia; if anything, then belittling it.

I worked under two prime ministers of Estonia – Edgar Savisaar and Tiit Vähi. When, as the first Vice-Minister for Foreign Affairs, I participated in the meetings of the Government, Vähi was still the Minister of Transport and communications. As we have remained, or rather have become over the years, close friends, I will say about him more later. Edgar Savisaar, the Prime Minister of Estonia during the most crucial years for the country, has made, in my opinion, the greatest contribution to the restoration of independence of Estonia. First, as the leader of the People's Front – a mass movement that prepared the ground for the coming independence. When the *coup d'état* of 19 August 1991 happened, Savisaar, like Foreign Minister Meri as well as some other high officials, was abroad. However, defying the difficulties, among which the stormy sea was not the only one, he arrived after the midnight when the Government was sitting and took over the reins of power. Not everybody returned to their posts during these uncertain days, not everybody was available. Later Savisaar held several ministerial posts and for long periods was the Chairman of the Centre Party and the mayor of the capital of Estonia – Tallinn. He was one of those rare politicians who didn't hesitate to publicly call for better relations with Russia and worked hard for the integration of ethnic Russians into the Estonian society. Of course, for such a stand he was often criticised as being pro-Kremlin. Some brainless opponents of Savisaar even went so far as accusing him of trying to bring Estonia back to the Russian fold. As idiotic as such accusations were, especially *vis-à-vis* a person who had done everything to separate Estonia from the Soviet Union, they have poisoned, and continue poisoning, the political life in Estonia. However, being inflexible and stubborn even for an Estonian, who are known for their obstinacy and pig-headedness, at the end of his political career Savisaar went a bit off the rails. He obviously believed to be not only indispensable and irreplaceable, but also as someone who never makes mistakes or takes wrong decisions. Unfortunately, not only did he have serious health problems but also lengthy court cases, where he was accused of corruption. This is probably a professional problem for mayors of many cities, big and small. However, for me he remains as somebody who, at the end of the 1980s – at the beginning of the 1990s, was the right man in the right place, and as a strong politician, who in his best days took important and right decisions and carried them through.

During the most uncertain period in August 1991, when tanks were on the streets of Moscow and the most realistic choice was between independence and trip to Siberia, I work in very close contact with the Minister of State Raivo Vare, Andres Kollist – the first Director of the Estonian Nationality and Immigration Office, my Foreign Ministry colleagues Jüri Luik and Tiit Pruuli, then the Press-Secretary of the Ministry and now a successful businessman, adventurous traveller and interesting writer. During the uncertain and dangerous three days of the coup d'état attempt, Tiit hid somewhere in his premises, just in case, one of the two telephones of the Ministry that allowed us to have unhindered contacts with the outside world.

8- Another Imperial Capital – London

In my lifetime I have met several other persons, besides Grigory Ivanovich Tunkin, encounters with whom have had significant influence on my life and even on the lives of my family members. A person, from whom I have not only learned a lot, but meeting who changed my life as well as lives of my family, was Professor Lady (now Dame) Rosalyn Higgins. We first met in 1989, as members of the UN Human Rights Committee, and soon became close friends and some years later, thanks to her, I was selected for the visiting Centennial Professorship at the London School of Economics and Political Science (the LSE celebrated its 100th anniversary), where I spent very stimulating and extremely fruitful two and a half years. After that I was offered the chair of international law at King's College, London, just across the road from the LSE. Friendship with Rosalyn and his husband Terence, now Lord Higgins, earlier a MP (Member of Parliament) and a junior minister in Edward Heath's Government is in itself a precious asset that our family – my wife Irina and our sons Jan and George – cherish, but this friendship has given me a lot also professionally. Rosalyn, being hardworking and busy, whether as Professor at the LSE, arbitrator or barrister (QC), judge and President of the International Court of Justice, always finds time for her friends. When our family, in spring 1992, arrived in London not only was Lady Rosalyn meeting us at Heathrow, but arriving at the small townhouse in London Docklands that the LSE had rented for us, we found a fridge full of everything a family may need for the first days in a foreign country. With Rosalyn, we have discussed and argued, often disagreeing, not only matters of international law, but also internal politics of the United Kingdom, novelties of literature, arts and many other matters. The support of Rosalyn and Terence have accompanied us throughout our life in London. And this is their attitude towards all their numerous friends.

Having been a member (since 1995) of the *Institut de Droit International (IDI)*, whose 130 members are elected for life, and its President from 2013 to

2015, I have been honoured to know well and work closely by most prominent international lawyers of the world. Encounters and contacts with some of them are nevertheless exceptional for me. About one of them, I would like to say more than just mentioning his name. I don't remember whether it was in summer of 1987 or 1988, Oscar Schachter – Hamilton Fish Professor of international law and Professor Emeritus at Columbia University and a former high-level UN diplomat, happened to be with his wife Muriel in Moscow. They had arrived as tourists, interested obviously also in the policies of *perestroika and glasnost*. Oscar had with him also his most voluminous, just published, international law book intended, I guess, as a present for my teacher Professor Tunkin. But it was in midsummer and Tunkin was in his country-house (dacha); it was only me, just being promoted to be head the international law department in the Soviet Academy of Sciences, who he could find in this sweltering day in the city. So, we had our first chat and Oscar gave me his book. After this first meeting, we met often either in New York or in other places; Oscar was also a referee for all my future promotions and thoughtful reader of my books and articles. Often having read something published by me, he wrote me and commented on my writings.

Having met him first in Moscow, I saw Oscar last time in New York several months before his death. I was returning from a conference at the US Naval War College in Newport (RI) *via* New York and Professor Lori Damrosch, also of Columbia University, had invited both of us for lunch. I left Lori's house in Brooklyn together with Oscar under Lori's strict order, coming as if through a chain of command from Muriel, to take a taxi for Manhattan, were the Schachters lived. Only under such conditions had Muriel allowed already rather fragile Oscar to move around in the megapolis. Once on the street, however, Oscar told me: 'Rein, I love so much the smell of New York's subway. I haven't been there for ages. Let's take a tube.' So, I travelled with him to his apartment in Manhattan, promising not to reveal to anybody that we had been so disobedient. Only after Oscar's death I told the story to Lori. Oscar Schachter was one of the greatest international law scholars of the twentieth century and remarkably nice person.

Two and a half years spent at the LSE where academically the most fruitful years of my life. After exciting and frenzied years in Moscow and Tallinn I recharged my batteries in the Library of the LSE or writing in my office. We even lived most of that period at the LSE campus, just around the corner from

Covent Garden. LSE, which ranks among the best universities in the world, is also very international. There I even met Karl Popper, whose seminal *chef d'oeuvre The Open Society and Its Enemies* I had just finished reading (it was gossiped, however, at the LSE, that Popper's students had modified the title of his masterpiece by calling it *The Open Society by its Enemy* since, as professor, Popper hadn't appreciated views that diverted from his own). I listened to Julius Nyerere, who had been the first Tanzanian to have a university degree from Great Britain, and met Henry Kissinger, when his masterpiece *Diplomacy* was published and on display at the LSE bookshop next to my, also just published, *International Law: Rights and Politics* – my first book written in English. At the LSE I took part, as a member of the jury, in an original moot court case against Karl Marx. Marx was impersonated by Professor and a Labour Lord Meghmed Desai, who even looked a bit like Karl Marx, while the procurator, accusing him, was equally prominent conservative academic – Ken Minogue. The role of the jury was performed by the audience – mostly students and professors of the LSE. Marx aka Desai was acquitted of all crimes. The prosecution could not prove before the jury that there were causal links between Marx's teachings and crimes committed by dictators like Lenin, Stalin, Mao, or Pol Pot, who had arrogated for themselves the right to be called only true Marxists.

As a centennial professor I didn't teach much; it was a research professorship. I gave a series of public lectures that were all published in most prestigious journals of the country. Original nomination for two years became two and a half years since I had started to teach also an LLM course on international criminal law and I had to finish the course. The time flew fast and we were already going to return to Estonia, when I was invited to apply for professorship at King's College, London. The College hadn't had the professorial vacancy on international law filled already for many years due to the lack of suitable candidates. I applied and was elected Professor of international law at King's, where among other things, together with Professor James Gow from the War Studies Department of King's, I set up an interdisciplinary course on international peace and security. I started also writing more and more not only on international law, but also on international relations theory and on politics.

Such a change of approach to international phenomena was quite natural for me since I had always wanted to dig to the root causes of various things. Law is, of course, a very important layer of social life. However, it is never an end in itself; it is an instrument of the achievement of certain social, political, economic or other goals; it is a mechanism of protection and promotion of certain values and interests. Although it is possible to be what may be called a 'black-letter lawyer' and often, while practicing law in or before courts or tribunals, it is the only useful way to proceed. One doesn't win cases by speculating at lengths on values protected by legal norms and principles or talking on philosophical foundations of law while addressing the jurors, judges or arbitrators. But sometimes even, when practicing law, it may be necessary to go to the root causes of certain legal principles. These may be so-called 'hard cases', and in international law, due to its relative uncertainty and ambiguity, there a more such cases than in any domestic legal system. They require going beyond the law in order to interpret it in the most appropriate (or useful for the client) manner. My late friend Thomas Franck from the NYU, often using unforgettable colourful descriptions, distinguished between 'sophisticated' norms and 'idiot' norms. In international law, there are very few of those that belong to the latter category.

There was another reason for my intellectual turn towards wider approaches to law or even to purely political or philosophical reflections. At the end of the 1980s and the beginning of the 1990s I had had great expectations for the success of law-based approaches to international relations (of course, I was not the only naïve). I was writing in my articles, and memos I sent to Gorbachev for his speeches, on the primacy of international law over politics. Yet, soon I discovered that things were not at all moving in the direction I had hoped. Hence, attempts to approach international law in its widest context, to deconstruct norms and principles, to carry out *post-mortem* for parts, usually most sensitive and important, of international law. Below, I will reflect on some of those topical issues and try to give my 'subjective' analysis of them.

I enjoyed living and working in London: teaching, research and some practice were exactly the activities I liked though I have found that teaching, even if it is in such research-oriented universities as the LSE or King's, and academic research call for different qualities that are not always present in the same person. British philosopher Brian Magee once wrote about his PhD supervisor in Harvard: 'It was only because he was not creatively original that he was an incomparable teacher.'[57] I have been taught and I have worked with some excellent teachers, who struggled to write an article to pass research assessment exercise (RAE) not to be sacked from the university, and I have met

---

[57] B. Magee, *Confessions of a Philosopher*, W&N, 1998, p. 144.

brilliant researchers, whose lectures have been rather dull and uninspiring (in a way, my Teacher Grigory Tunkin belonged to this category). When teaching, they probably wanted it done as quickly as possible, in order to return to their favourite activity – the research and writing. If a researcher is usually by nature an egoist, who uses public money to satisfy his/her curiosity, a good teacher is usually an altruist giving everything to his/her disciples. Of course, good researchers give to humanity not less than good teachers – often more, but their contribution often comes as collateral, not as the primary purpose of their activities. I probably belong more to the category of researchers. Writing may be frustrating, when satisfactory explanation is not forthcoming or when it is necessary to put in order disorderly reflections, but I feel satisfied and energetic when I spend a day, weeks or months at the desk searching and writing. Of course, a lot of search is done when moving around, especially between the countries and civilisations. On the other hand, many good people, university professors among them, do not like writing. They force themselves to sit down and spend long hours *tête-à-tête* with a laptop and writing, not playing or communicating with friends. At King's, when I saw how some PhD students or even a few of my colleagues struggled to write and to be published, I once said that if one can live without writing, one should not write. However, the Head of the Law School, Professor Robin Morse, told me not to spread heresy, though, between us, he agreed with me. But *noblesse oblige*.

Eighteen years in London past quickly and all good things sooner or later come to an end. In accordance with British legislation and my job contract, I retired at 65. Although I knew well ahead that this was going to happen, I was nevertheless somewhat at a loss. Teaching part-time here and there, some arbitration practice maybe, it would not be enough for me. However, already for some years I had given lectures also in a small private university in Tallinn called Nord. Its Rector, founder and the principal owner Professor Ene Grauberg – a philosopher and public figure in Estonia, had already earlier hinted that she would like me to replace her at the head of the University. Having doubts related to the family situation (our sons were well established in London and Irina didn't want to be away from them for too long) and being spoilt by working in world best universities, going back to my native country didn't seem terribly exciting. However, this looked like the best option available and in autumn 2009 I started a new career in Tallinn. And jumping ahead, I must say that I have no regrets. I am thankful to Professor Ene Grauberg for inviting me and to his son Indrek, who soon became my friend and also my deputy, being extremely helpful, particularly, on matters I hate to waste my time on – administration and finances. However, before I move to the next period of my life, I need to dwell upon a significant experience in my life that started and mostly went on in parallel with my work in London. About it in the following chapter.

9- My Central Asian Experience

My personal connections with Central Asia started in mid-1990s when I did some work for the High Commissioner on National Minorities of the OSCE. Max van der Stoel – the first High Commissioner for Minorities, a former Foreign Minister of The Netherlands, happened to be also a wonderful human being. His personality lacked any signs of haughtiness; he had the same friendly and respectful behaviour *vis-à-vis* presidents, prime-ministers, drivers and cleaners. I was impressed by van der Stoel's personality, so was my wife Irina, who only once met the man. Irina and I were flying to The Hague from London and due to the bad weather, we arrived late for the dinner with the High Commissioner. By chance Irina was seated next to an elderly gentleman with whom she immediately became engaged in a lively conversation. Later, on our way to the hotel, she was shocked when I told her, who this gentleman was. Behaving in the same way with everybody, notwithstanding the rank or the absence of it, Max van der Stoel was firm on matters of minority rights. For example, quite a few Estonian politicians were angered by his criticism of Estonian citizenship legislation and practices that were disrespectful of minority concerns.

As adviser to Max van der Stoel, I regularly travelled between London and The Hague, were Mr van der Stoel had his headquarters. One evening, one of the assistants to the High Commissioner called me and implored me to fly ASAP to Kyrgyzstan since somebody, who should have spoken there about minority rights was either unwell or unable to travel to the region. This was my first visit to Central Asia and many more followed.

However, even before these first trips to Central Asia I had been fascinated by the region. My interest in Central Asia was intrigued by my encounters with two remarkable men. The first encounter, though virtual, had much deeper impact on me. For many years I had been fascinated, both for personal as well as for professional reasons, by a man, who had lived about hundred years before me. This was Friedrich Fromhold (Fyodor Fyodorovich) Martens. We both moved, with century's difference, from an Estonian countryside to the imperial capital. As an orphan, Martens was sent to school to the capital of the Russian Empire, then it was St Petersburg, where he finished his formal education by graduating from the local university. I found myself, after many misadventures and adventures of which I wrote earlier, at Moscow University, then the capital of the Soviet Union. He became a professor of international law in St Petersburg, where he also served the Russian Empire advising the last Emperor Nicolas II and a series of foreign ministers, including the greatest Russia has ever had - Prince Alexander Gorchakov, on matters of international law. I turned out to be a professor of international law at Moscow University, where during the years of perestroika and glasnost I also advised the Soviet leadership, including the first and the last President of the USSR Michael Gorbachev, on issues of international law. Although during my student years, Martens, as somebody who had been in the service of the Russian Empire, was not in the syllabus, I read most of the works, I could put my hands on, of my famous compatriot. I discovered that besides strictly legal texts, like his famous *Law of Civilised Nations*, Martens had taken also keen interest in the Great Game that was playing out at his time between England and Russia in Central Asia. His book, *Russia and England in Central Asia* (St Petersburg, 1880, in Russian), together with another book by another remarkable person, served as one of the stimuli that inspired me to accept an offer to serve as UN regional advisor for Central Asia.

This other remarkable person was Sir Fitzroy MacLean, whom I met personally, though only once, in the Foyles bookshop in Charing cross Road in London. Shortly after my arrival at the LSE, I was invited to a book-launch ceremony for the last book by this legendary British diplomat and spy. This personal encounter together with his fantastic *Eastern Approaches* that I read having met and talked to him, urged me to follow in the footsteps of the man, who being posted in the 1930s in the British Embassy in Moscow (he had preferred Moscow over Paris since the latter seemed much less exciting for him), had chosen to spend his vacation by travelling to Central Asia. During the Second World War he served as Winston Churchill's personal envoy to Josip Bros Tito.

After my first trip to Kyrgyzstan, prompted by my work for Max van der Stoel, I visited all the so-called 'stans', i.e. the former Soviet Republics, whose names end with 'stan' – Kazakhstan, Kyrgyzstan, Tajikistan, Turkmenistan and Uzbekistan. My trips were mostly either so-called UN needs assessment missions, i.e. to find out how the UN could help these countries, or participating in training of judges, lawyers and other law-enforcement personnel, financed and organised by Soros foundation. My first UN mission to Central Asia was to Tajikistan, where the six-year long civil war had just ended. For me, these missions were also interesting and important learning processes. As Russian was, and still is, the *lingua franca* in all these states, I could communicate in equal terms with local people. As always, I did not limit my social life with expats circle, as many foreign diplomats do, and therefore I still have friends in some of these states.

In mid-two-thousands, on an unpaid leave from King's College, I spent a year in the region, working as the UN Regional Advisor. When working in Central Asia, I made some discoveries that no reading could have been able to give me. Western diplomats in non-Western countries, and often also Western NGOs, have contacts typically with leading elites, whom they very often do not respect, and sometimes even hate and despise[58], and with those who are in radical opposition to the authorities, whom they often like and support. In countries that don't belong to the category of liberal democracies, opposition usually claims liberal democratic values (sometimes sincerely, though often naively, every now and then opportunistically) and argues that whenever they come to power, these values would become everyday practice, since it is only incumbent authorities that prevent the people to be free and prosperous. This, however, is rarely true since, as I wrote above, more often than not societies and those in power deserve each other.

In countries where there is a democracy deficit, or where elements of democracy are completely lacking, both categories of people (the governing elite and the opposition) are rarely representative of the majority of the population. Julia Sweig of the US Council on Foreign Relations has identified what she calls the '80/20 problem'[59], meaning that the United States, in its dealings with a particular country, mostly relies on the English-speaking elite – usually not more than 20 percent of the population. In my opinion, this is a very optimistic estimate that may be true in some former British colonies or in Europe but certainly not, say, in Russia or in Central Asia where Russian in still the *lingua franca*, not to mention China. To better understand a country, it is particularly important to communicate with the remaining 80 percent of its population - not only because

---

[58] See, e.g., Craig Murray's *Murder in Samarkand: A British Ambassador's Controversial Defiance of Tyranny in the War on Terror* (Mainstream Publishing, 2006).
[59] J. Sweig, *Friendly Fire: Losing Friends and Making Enemies in the Anti-American Century*, New York, Public Affairs, 2006.

of its numerical weight, but even more so since this majority is more representative of the country than the 20 percent of governing or opposing elites. Talking to people in the marketplace, to a taxi driver, in a barber shop or to those who work out with you in a local gym (and not to those who swim with you in a pool of five-star hotels), often helps more understand the country than spending hours with government officials or members of a radical opposition though, naturally, one cannot and should not ignore them either. While working as UN official in Central Asia I also communicated more than I would have liked with governmental officials and representatives of various NGOs, who were critical of the governments. I always took with a pinch of salt what officials told me. At the beginning of my mission, I was, however, much less critical of representatives of the radical opposition and the NGO people. But soon I discovered that opposition even in authoritarian countries had, as their principal aim, not to change the regime but to come to power and then continue business as usual. Quite a few human right NGOs, though with many and significant exceptions, often made sweeping allegations against governments – some more or less true, others pure inventions – to receive grants for their activities from Western donors or scholarships from Western universities.

Another thing that I discovered while working in Central Asia was that many Westerners took the absence of effective authority for the seeds of democracy. I could hardly agree with those who claimed that democracy and human rights were more developed, for instance, in Kyrgyzstan than in Kazakhstan. However, the *Freedom House* 2006 rating on civil and political rights put Kyrgyzstan above Kazakhstan.[60] Even more astonishing was its following year's assessment. In its 2007 world freedoms' map, this world main democracy watchdog had coloured the whole of Central Asia, with the exception of Kyrgyzstan, as not free.[61] Afghanistan, however, was also coloured as partly free and this notwithstanding that in neighbouring Tajikistan, where there were indeed serious problems with human rights and political freedoms, people, and especially women, felt nevertheless happy knowing that they were not living like their southern neighbours in Afghanistan or even in Pakistan. They would even thank Allah or, depending on which of their historical legacies prevailed, the Communist Party of the Soviet Union, for not living like these nations do. The plight of Afghani women, which has been so well described by Asne Seierstad

---

[60] C. Tilly, *Democracy*, Columbia University Press, 2007, p. 46.
[61] See, *Map of Freedom 2007* (http://www.freedomhouse.org).

in *The Bookseller of Kabul*,[62] would make the hair on Central Asian women's heads stand on end. So-called honour killings, regularly reported in Pakistan and even in some Asian communities in Britain, were unheard of in this region and even forced, though not arranged, marriages are something of rarity, though they are on the increase, especially in rural areas. It indeed defies all logic to consider Afghanistan to be 'a partly free' country – be it in 2006 or in 2020.

When I worked for the UN in Central Asia, the former President of Finland, Martti Ahtisaari, who before his highest post in his native country had worked as Under-Secretary General of the United Nations, had become the personal envoy of the Chairman in Office of the OSCE (Organization on Security and Cooperation in Europe) for Central Asia. We met several times in various capitals of the region and exchanged views on the situation in the countries within our remit since his OSCE and my UN mandates partly overlapped. It also helped that, as representatives of neighbouring Finno-Ugric nations, we could exchange words in languages nobody else understood. So, once, having just spent a couple of weeks in Uzbekistan, I attended a meeting in Bishkek and stayed in the same hotel with President Ahtisaari. During our working breakfast, I informed him about my visit to Uzbekistan and gave my evaluation of the situation in the country. Halfway of my monologue, President Ahtisaari stopped me asking whether I had already written something on my recent trip. Only, he added, don't offer me any of your regular reports to the United Nations. As the former high-level UN official, President Ahtisaari knew better than anybody else the value of such reports. Knowing my academic background, he correctly guessed that I may have written not only UN reports. In a couple of days, having polished my draft chapter on Uzbekistan for my book on Central Asia, I emailed it to President Ahtisaari.

Has anybody thought why various United Nations documents are usually amongst the dullest (this would not have been the most serious problem) and emptiest of writings? There may be many problems with such reports. One is that they must be 'objective', not biased against or in favour of any group of states, and they have also to be politically correct, not offending any interest groups and especially donors. They usually also have too many authors, and therefore the result is reduced to a lowest common denominator.

The same comments apply to many so-called academic writings as well. Quotes replace independent thought and pseudo-scientific language (in the

---

[62] *A. Seierstad, The Bookseller of Kabul, Little*, Brown and Company, 2003.

important UN parlance words such as mainstreaming, streamlining, etc. are excessively used) replaces natural speech. No one has, probably, put it better than the great American writer, Saul Bellow:

> 'After many years of attentive and diligent study, we are left with little more than systems of opinion and formulas that hide reality from us. Personal judgment is disabled, crippled by theoretic borrowing. Abstractions, like the direct rays of the sun, may give us a fine tan and the look of health (or mental mastery) but in the long run we pay for this with premature wrinkles and even cancers of the skin. We are bound, in other words, to be sceptical of learning, too…but in the end a man must master his own experience. He desperately looks for help in books, but it's no good, as Kafka observed, to try to imprison life in a book, "like a songbird in a cage".'[63]

For example, the UN-declared idea that all human rights are universal and of equal value is based on the exaggerated, absolutised and uncritically used Enlightenment ideals of rationality and universality. Societies differ more than individuals do. The current President of Kazakhstan Kassym-Jomart Tokayev, who was the Foreign Minister of Kazakhstan, when I first met him, is also a Sinologue by education. He wrote about Kazakhstan's big neighbour: 'China's strength has traditionally been in its statehood and in discipline. The Chinese have never thought of themselves as separate from the state; it has always been an element of Chinese mentality that they identify themselves as a part of their state. China is strong not because of the strength of individual Chinese but because of the vigour of its people that during centuries have been called to rally for the sake of the state and nation.'[64] I believe Tokayev implicitly extrapolated, to an extent at least, this observation also to Kazakhstan and perhaps to the whole Central Asia as well. He wanted to send a message that it would be the spirit of collectivism, including the respect and concern for the strengthening of the newly found statehood, and not the spirit of individualism that would make Kazakhstan strong and prosperous. Therefore, this observation from one of the top politicians in Central Asia may be, of course, somewhat self-serving but it is not therefore necessarily wrong. It would be disastrous for Central Asian

---

[63] S. Bellow, *The Civilized Barbarian Reader*, New York Times, 8 March 1987.
[64] K. Tokayev, *Overcoming. Diplomatic Essays of a Kazakh Minister* (in Russian: Преодоление. Дипломатические очерки казахстанского министра), Almaty, 2003, p. 286.

countries to try to rapidly introduce, as the Baltic states have done, Western European models of political and social reforms. The result could indeed be chaos, anarchy and possibly even civil wars.

American philosopher Amitai Etzioni, who I had pleasure to meet in the region and with whom I had interesting discussions, *inter alia*, about Central Asia, was right that 'the incontrovertible fact is that those societies that have given up on their strongly "Eastern" sets of beliefs and have moved sharply in the individualistic direction, but have formed few if any new shared sets of beliefs, experience sharp increases in antisocial behaviour.'[65] Or in some countries, as Michael Ignatieff observes, 'pressuring authoritarian regimes to reform may help trigger Islamic revolution.'[66] This observation applies to some Central Asian countries where it is not just an abstract possibility.

As a result of my mission, I wrote and published a book *Central Asia: A Chessboard and Player in the Great Game* (London, Kegan Paul, 2007; second ed. Routledge, 2012), where I analysed, *inter alia*, interests and relative influence of great powers, such as China, Russia and the United States in the region. I remember well how President Nazarbayev of Kazakhstan once said that his country needs Russia in order to balance the growing influence of China, it needs the United States to balance the influence of China and Russia and it needs China against these two other players. In my opinion, this is quite a principled approach to international relations, not camouflaged by talks about universal (or European) values or eternal friendship between nations, particularly if we take account of the geographical and historical realities of the country. This is a Realpolitik approach to international relations that, in my opinion, is one of the most adequate (though not the only one) approaches to the study and practice of these relations. However, the 'real Realpolitik', borrowing the term from John Bew[67], takes account of not only narrow national interests and relative power relations between states, but also the existing distribution of power within societies, their socio-economic structures, the cultural and ideological settings of the time, customs and habits of a people ('even if they appeared atavistic and immoral'), not believing in the unconditional superiority of one political system, but seeing them as reflections of given historical circumstances, and variety of other factors.

---

[65] A. Etzioni, *From Empire to Community. A New Approach to International Relations*, Palgrave, 2004, p. 23.
[66] M. Ignatieff, *The Lesser Evil. Political Ethics in an Age of Terror*, Edinburgh University Press, 2004, p. 100.
[67] See, J. Bew, *Realpolitik: A History*, OUP, 2016, particularly the pp. 300-309.

That is why, one of my favourite philosophers is Reinhold Niebuhr, the author of *Moral Man and Immoral Society*[68], whose chapter entitled *The Morality of Nations* and dealing with relations between nations, reads like a highly moral man writing about an essentially immoral substance. Niebuhr, claiming that 'the selfishness of nations is proverbial,' continues:

> 'Since there can be no ethical action without self-criticism, and no self-criticism without the rational capacity of self-transcendence, it is natural that national attitudes can hardly approximate the ethical...for self-criticism is a kind of inner disunity, which the feeble mind of a nation finds difficulty in distinguishing from dangerous forms of inner conflict. So, nations crucify their moral rebels with their criminals in the same Golgotha...While critical loyalty toward a community is not impossible, it is not easily achieved. It is therefore probably inevitable that every society should regard criticism as a proof of a want of loyalty.'[69]

The reason for this, as Ernst Gellner did put it, is that 'the political effectiveness of national sentiment would be much impaired if nationalists had as fine a sensibility to the wrongs committed by their nation as they have to those committed against it.'[70] I find the thought that the applicability of moral norms, which play an extremely important role in interpersonal relations, declines the further we move from inter-personal relations towards inter-communal relations, while international (interstate) relations are on the vanishing end of the applicability of norms of morality, extremely important. Therefore, the excessive use of moral arguments and justifications in international relations, though not completely excluded, should always be taken with caution. The point is not that the concept of morality is not at all applicable in international relations, but that in this specific field moral arguments are more often than in interpersonal relations used either naïvely or hypocritically.

Moreover, the world is too complicated and colourful to be adequately expressed in black and white colours: democracy versus authoritarianism, absolute evil versus absolute good. In that respect, French philosopher Luc Ferry has made an important observation about some ongoing bloody conflicts:

---

[68] R. Niebuhr, *Moral Man and Immoral Society* (Continuum, 2005).
[69] *Ibid.*, p. 59.
[70] E. Gellner, *Nations and Nationalism* (Basil Blackwell, 1983), p. 2.

'The truth, in contrast to what the majority of small-scale moralists think, is that many bloody conflicts in today's world are tragic in the sense of Greek tragedies where the opposing sides represent not of the good and the evil, the right and the wrong, but quite legitimate, though differing, claims. Had I been a Western Ukrainian of Polish origin, I would have probably wanted my country to join the European Union and even NATO. However, had I been from East Ukraine, from a Russian-speaking family, I would have almost certainly wanted my country to be closely attached to Russia. Had I been a Palestinian boy of fifteen from the occupied territories, I would without doubt be an anti-Semite; by contrast, an Israeli of the same age from Tel-Aviv would almost certainly despise Palestinian organisations.'[71]

Although among the world's rich palette of ideologies, practices and trends are also those that represent so-called absolute evil and deservedly call for moral outrage, most often in today's conflicts, either between or within nations, rare are those where one is absolutely right while the other is absolutely wrong.

Several years after my year-long UN mission in Central Asia, I once again had an official mission to the region. In Southern Kyrgyzstan, in summer 2010, had taken place events that the Kyrgyz Enquiry Commission (KIC), set up by the UN, EU and OSCE, and whose member I was, qualified as *prima facie* crimes against humanity. In three days of inter-ethnic clashes between Kyrgyz and Uzbeks more than 470 people were killed, thousands of properties burned and plundered. More than 110 000 inhabitants of Southern Kyrgyzstan became refugees, mainly in the neighbouring Uzbekistan. These were ethnic Uzbeks, who had suffered the most. What had caused such bloody events in a society that by many was considered as more democratic than its neighbours, or according to the Freedom House, as 'partly free'? A general context of this tragedy was the fact that instead of being 'partly free', the country was anarchic. Inability of the authorities to effectively control the territory was taken for signs of freedom. Or, one may say that in parallel with some positive freedoms (e.g., some newspapers and even TV channels in the country could indeed criticise the Government that was not the case in other Central Asian countries), there were more of what one may call negative freedoms: the freedom to take and give bribes, to traffic in

---

[71] L. Ferry, *La Révolution Transhumaniste: comment la technomédecine et l'uberisation du monde boulverser nos vies* (Plon, 2016), p. 222.

narcotics and human beings, to racketeer and even to kill. But there was also a specific factor that helped trigger the tragedy.

In some ethnically mixed societies, and Kyrgyzstan is a fine example of such a society, parallel launch of market reforms and democratisation may contribute to the danger of inter-ethnic clashes. Amy Chua, though slightly over-generalising, in my opinion, has mapped the negative effects of processes of globalisation in societies characterised by the presence of so-called market-dominant minorities (e.g. Indians in east Africa, Lebanese in west Africa, Ibo in Nigeria, Tutsi in Rwanda, Chinese in several southeast Asian countries). She argues that, 'the global spread of free market democracy has…been a principal, aggravating cause of ethnic instability and violence throughout the non-western world.'[72] This pessimistic conclusion is grounded in the reality that in some developing and post-communist countries there are minorities—perhaps better educated and more entrepreneurial than the majority population—who also may own more land or may otherwise be in a better position to benefit more than the rest of the population from the liberalisation of markets. The simultaneous introduction of democracy can release suppressed discontent that creates a combustible mixture ready to explode in xenophobia, ethnic cleansing or even in acts of genocide. In such cases, there is neither market nor democracy. Amy Chua concludes that 'the United States should not be exporting markets in the unrestrained, laissez-faire form that the west itself has repudiated, just as it should not be promoting unrestrained, overnight majority rule – a form of democracy that the west has repudiated.'[73] Although in the West rule by the majority never came overnight but through sometimes centuries-long processes of trial and error, Amy Chua's warning must be taken seriously. In southern Kyrgyzstan, the difference in lifestyles between sedentary Uzbeks and nomadic Kyrgyz that had exited for centuries, resulted in the situation where the Uzbeks were generally better off than the Kyrgyz. Centuries or even decades ago, this did not really matter because these two communities did not mix much, and in addition, the Soviet (and before the Russian imperial) dominance did not allow any discontent to explode in massacres.[74] However, the migration of Kyrgyz to

---

[72] A. Chua, *World on Fire: How Exporting Free Market Democracy Breeds Ethnic Hatred and Global Instability (Random House, 2002), 187.*
[73] Ibid., 17.
[74] The first such inter-ethnic conflict in Southern Kyrgyzstan took place in 1990. This was also related to Gorbachev's policies of perestroika and glasnost. Then Gorbachev used Soviet troops to quell the riots, though many people were already lost their lives. In

the newly industrialised southern cities, which had commenced already in the 1960s, but increased when Gorbachev initiated his glasnost and perestroika reforms and was further boosted by the establishment of the independent Kyrgyzstan, changed the situation. To simplify a bit, one may say that while the Uzbeks benefited more from the perestroika (economic liberalization), the Kyrgyz benefited from glasnost (political opening). The Uzbeks had more money, while the Kyrgyz acquired political power. Therefore, already in the 1990s, inter-ethnic clashes in southern Kyrgyzstan had as a contributing factor the combined effect of simultaneous introduction of elements of market economy and democracy. Uzbeks were better positioned to benefit more from economic reforms; they had better entrepreneurial skills and, having some start-up capital, though rather meagre by Western standards, they had start-up benefits as well. At the political level, on the contrary, the majority Kyrgyz had the upper hand. Through elections they had secured for themselves all important legislative and executive posts, they dominated the judiciary, law enforcement and military. Using their political, administrative and numerical power, they not only denied the Uzbeks effective access to high administrative posts, law enforcement and judiciary, but they also used these posts as leverage to force Uzbek businessmen to pay up. Racketeering had an ethnic dimension as the membership of criminal networks was primarily Kyrgyz, whereas southern businessmen were mainly Uzbek. Small and medium entrepreneurs were in a particularly vulnerable position. Owners of cafés and car repair shopkeepers suffered the most. The money they were required to pay to criminal groups rose constantly and threatened to make the businesses unviable. Raiding and the forced sale of a profitable business for a token sum, was also widespread. Such a situation could not last indefinitely, and when all the other components for the explosion came together it was a relatively minor incident, or rather a fake news, magnified through social media, that triggered this bloody inter-ethnic clash.

Today, the Central Asia, the land of the ancient Silk Road and the territory where more than a century ago the British and Russian Empire played their Great Game, has become an important part of Xi Jinping's OBOR (One Belt, One Road Initiative). It is also where major players – China, Russia and the West, led by Washington, are playing their new Great Game. It is less hot, at least so far than

---

summer 2010 President of Kyrgyzstan Roza Otunbayeva also asked Russia to help put an end to the conflict. Russia, whose President then was Dmitry Medvedev, prudently in my opinion, declined to intervene.

the previous one, and much more peaceful than their games in the Middle East. Today, the Central Asian countries don't serve as a checkboard for others to play. They are also players and sometimes they even quite skilfully use the rivalry between outside powers in their own interest.

10- My Third Coming to Estonia

Estonia had changed considerably since I had left it for London eighteen years earlier. Lives of most Estonian residents, especially citizens, had greatly improved in comparison with the Soviet period and even more so if compared with the difficult transitional period at the beginning of the 1990s. The economic and financial reforms, the early introduction of Estonian currency – the Krona – instead of the Soviet Rouble – that was carried out well ahead of other former Soviet republics, close links with highly developed neighbouring Finland and the membership in the European Union had changed the country. However, the narrow-minded nationalism, targeting particularly the Russians or Russian speakers in Estonia as well as Russia, could be still felt, particularly within parts of the political elite. Although about fifty percent of the population in Tallinn speaks Russian at home, and on the streets of the capital one can hear Russian almost as often as Estonian, my Russian wife, who is not fluent in Estonian, prefers to express herself in English – the language she perfectly masters. She has had some, though not many, bad experience when she has publicly expressed herself in Russian. However, I often spoil her day, since when she, for example, speaks with a shop-assistant in English and I join her, I address her always in Russian, since this is the language we spoke when we met and fell in love. Often, it turns out that the shop-assistant also prefers to use Russian, instead of English. Even more importantly, I very much do not like to be told, which language I should speak. My only preference has been to address people in their native language, provided I speak it.

Our younger son George, after the graduation from Leeds University, where he had read international relations and diplomacy, worked a year at the Ministry of Defence of Estonia. It was, in 2008, exactly the period when an armed conflict between Georgia and Russia broke out. All the staff of the Ministry were given Georgian flags and with the slogan – 'we all are Georgians' – they all went to demonstrate against the 'Russian aggression.' Such unanimity of thought and action as well as single-mindedness were alien to George, who was brought up in the multicultural London, educated in one of the best British public (i.e. private) schools, where disputes and clashes of opinions were encouraged (Irina often says: you cannot argue with George; he turns out to be right, even when he is obviously wrong). Moreover, if one could find, in Western media, some rare references to the fact that it was Georgia that had invaded South Ossetia, thereby triggering the conflict, there has been nothing like that in the Estonian media. And this notwithstanding that the Independent International Fact-Finding Mission on the Conflict in Georgia (IIFFMCG), set up by the European Union and headed by the Swiss diplomat Heidi Tagliavini, though criticising Russia for its excessive response, nevertheless unequivocally laid the blame of the initiation of the conflict at the door of the regime of President Saakashvili of Georgia.

I recall, how in spring 2003, when the United States had invaded Iraq, George with his friends and thousands of other Londoners demonstrated at the US Embassy in London against this most damaging foreign policy blunder of the Bush Administration. Nobody organised these demonstrators, nobody distributed or carried Iraqi or any other flags. Later, I had to talk to the headmaster of the Eltham College since George had missed, while demonstrating, his classes. However, he was reprimanded not because he was demonstrating against the closest ally of Great Britain, whose Prime Minister Tony Blair, became known for his support of the Iraqi invasion as 'Bush's poodle,' but because he did it while playing truant.

The Americans and their closest allies (subordinates) in Europe constantly complain that Russia is trying to 'drive a wedge' between Europe and the USA, while there are others in Europe who claim that it is Washington who is seeking to break up Europe. In January 2003, Donald Rumsfeld, the then-US Secretary of Defence, referred to France and Germany, who were against the invasion of Iraq, as 'the Old Europe,' in distinction to 'the New Europe' aligned with the United States. How this alliance functioned is well illustrated in the following diplomatic episode-turned-embarrassment. In the run-up to the 2003 American invasion of Iraq, the leaders of the CEE (Central and Eastern European) countries addressed a letter to President George W. Bush where they, contrary to France and Germany, wholeheartedly supported the American policy against Iraq. Later it became known that the letter originated from the State Department in Washington, was written by a junior clerk and sent to the CEE leaders for signature. The Estonian Ambassador to NATO, Harri Tiido, in response to the question form the then-Prime Minister Siim Kallas, how should one react to such an offer (or rather order?), answered: 'If we don't sign, a big hammer will immediately hit us. If we sign and it becomes known, small hammers may hit us later, but we would survive.'[75] Instead of being destroyed right-away, Estonia, like the other CEE countries, opted for its moment of shame.

When one of the greatest presidents in the post-De Gaulle France – Jacques Chirac died in the autumn of 2019, I saw in *Le Figaro* of the 29 September, a questionnaire where there were indicated 11 achievements that Chirac had initiated and carried through during his years in the highest post in France. Trying to find out how well I may understand the French mentality, I decided to take part in the online voting and clicked on the icon indicating one of these achievements. In my opinion, this was the refusal to participate in the 2003 war in Iraq. I wasn't surprised that most of the readers of *Le Figaro* had pushed on the same icon, but I was nevertheless shocked that 55% of them were of the same opinion, while on the second place was an achievement that gathered no more than 10% of votes. In that respect, I recalled not only Dominique de Villepin's, then the Foreign Minister of France, 14 February 2003 speech in the UN Security Council, where he warned against the war in Iraq (in my opinion, to be studied by all those interested in international politics), but also that Charles de Gaulle had once revealed that one of the qualities, he expected from those who would succeed him, was the ability to say 'no' to Washington.[76] In that respect, I recall how the former UK spy-master Sir Richard Dearlove, being one of those who had dragged Britain, in March 2003, into the American military adventure, would have done better by keeping his mouth shut when common decency would have required it. Only days after the death of Jacques Chirac, he stated to *The Mail on Sunday* that the French President had received, for his elections campaign, millions of pounds from Saddam Hussein and that is why France had been against the war in Iraq. Of course, there was no evidence provided, as had been also the case in 2003 when the Americans and British claimed that Saddam had weapons of mass destruction. Or rather, the 'evidence' presented in the UN Security Council by unhappy Secretary of State Colin Powell, being misled by Anglo-Saxon spy-agencies, was fake.

---

[75] H. Tiido, 'The Estonian Letter of Support for Washington was written in Washington', *Postimees*, 22 March 2013 (in Estonian).
[76] G. Matzneff, *Venus et Junon* (La Table Ronde, 1999), p. 50.

Naturally, I wouldn't expect from Estonian politicians this kind of freethinking going against the will of Washington, but it would have been more dignified not to always follow blindly the Big Brother across the Atlantic. Here the example of our northern neighbour across the Finish Gulf would be useful. I believe that such obsequiousness before Washington may be due not only to the Russophobic mentality among a part of the political elite of Estonia and elsewhere in Eastern Europe, but also to the habit of docility and obedience, acquired during the Soviet period. Simply, instead of Moscow, now it is Washington towards whom it is necessary to kowtow.

There was, and still is, in Estonia such narrow-minded picking on Russia. Even if something positive is happening in that country and it is reported in Estonian media, it has to be accompanied by a proverbial fly in the anointment. For example, when Islam Karimov – a life-long President of Uzbekistan – died, one of the headlines in the main Estonian newspaper red: 'Islam Karimov – dictator and friend of Putin – is dead.' It is not only that Russia and Uzbekistan under Karimov had rather strained relationship and it is under the new President Shavkat Mirziyoyev that Russian-Uzbek relations seem to have gained momentum; there aren't and cannot be, in my opinion, any facts evidencing the friendship between Putin and Karimov. However, this doesn't matter; no opportunity to bark at Russia should be missed. And whenever there are signs that Europe or the United States may try to improve relations with Russia, there are always some Estonia politicians and media available to warn against it. Speaking and writing constantly about the Russian threat to the Baltic countries, they behave as if they themselves really do not believe in this threat. If such a threat would indeed exist, it would be counter-productive to provoke Russia, to irritate the Bear. Or maybe simply they hate Russia more than they love Estonia. Hatred makes some humans even blinder than love. This may, indeed, be true in the case of some most vociferous and mindless critics of Russia.

Of course, there are in Estonia many business leaders, intellectuals and ordinary people who well understand that trying to be in the forefront of verbal attacks against Russia, to be holier that the Pope, or more royalist that the King, i.e. Washington and Brussels, is counter-productive to economic interests of Estonia and may be dangerous in terms of national security. Among them I would single out two individuals, who have become my good friends – the former Prime Minister of Estonia Tiit Vähi and the most prominent Estonian poet and writer Jaan Kaplinski. They both have made significant contributions to the restoration of independence of Estonia. Jaan was a critic of the Soviet regime already then, when many praised it. He was also a member of the first convocation of the Riigikogu (Parliament) of independent Estonia. Tiit was at the head of the Government in the first half of the 1990s, when most important decisions, including the introduction of the Estonian currency – Krona in June 1992, for the country were taken. Both of them have publicly criticised mindless verbal attacks on Russia and alienation of Estonian Russians. There are quite a few others, but their voices are lost in the loud and constant cacophony of Russophobic utterances.

On the one hand, this shows that Estonia is not the former Soviet Union and the criticism of the Government or the President can be regularly heard and seen. Even some of my books have been translated into Estonian (already for thirty years I write mostly in English), though I was told by one of the Estonian students of the *Baltic Defence College* that their library had refused to obtain for their collection my latest book; probably to avoid corrupting young and fragile minds. The student had to buy it on the Amazon. The sacred cows are NATO, Estonia's membership in it, and significant financial contributions to NATO (this made even Donald Trump happy) and the alignment with Washington, with its anti-Russian elements and tendencies. At the same time, the criticism of the European Union, from which Estonia has tangibly benefitted, in contradistinction of NATO, is quite widespread. In Estonia, like in other Baltic states, for some people there are still only two main reference points – the Soviet past that they vehemently reject and the 'American dream' that they wish and admire. This gives one a black and white, quite simplified, vision of the world.

The life in Estonia was certainly more exciting than I could have imagined while in London, where people say: if you are tired of London, you are tired of life. One of the most recorded conductors in the world – Neeme Järvi, and his sons Kristjan and Paavo, regularly perform also in their motherland, particularly in their hometown Pärnu. Thanks to my sister Ülle Laido, though living in Florida, but regularly returning to Estonia, I became acquainted with another well-known and original musician – Andres Mustonen. Ülle, in her younger days, was a leading singer in Mustonen's *Hortus Musicus*, specialising in performing tunes of past centuries, including 8th-15th century European religious music. I tried to enjoy in full this abundance of musical life in Tallinn and beyond. The same year as I retired from King's College, our friends Agnes Oaks and Toomas Edur – the principal dancers of the English National Ballet, whose performances Irina and I had for years enjoyed in London, also retired. The professional life-expectancy of ballet dancers, like professional athletes, is shorter than that of law professors. Toomas, or Tom as he is known, became the artistic director of the ballet in Tallinn's theatre of opera and ballet – *Estonia*. Not only did we see many performances directed by Tom; Irina wrote the librettos for two ballets – *Modigliani – the Cursed Artist* and *Catherine*, both directed by Tom and accompanied by the beautiful music of the talented Estonian composer Tauno Aints.

If it is clear, even without elucidating it, about whom was the first ballet, but the second requires some explanation. The ballet *Catherine* is about the second wife of Peter the Great – the Czar and Emperor or Russia. After the death of her husband, she became the Empress of Russia, known as Catherine I. Her ethnic origins are not firmly established and therefore contested; what is known is that she was found by Peter's officers somewhere close to Tartu – today the second largest city in Estonia. She was moving through the ranks until becoming a lover of Peter's right-hand man Prince Aleksander Danilovich Menshikov. From there, higher up was only Peter the Great (in Russia he is more often called Peter the First). She was obviously in many ways very able person, not being – to charge from her portraits – a stunning beauty, though the standards of what is beautiful and what is not change over time. In Tallinn, our apartment is in the park called Kadriorg – named after Catherine the First (Catherine the Great being the Second). The park was created by the orders of Peter the Great and there is still a small edifice called Peter's house, where the Emperor used to stay when in Tallinn. Irina's storyline, that I very much liked, was to show how a poor, a peasant girl, arguably of Estonian origin, can become an Empress of Russia. To express this idea in the ballet, there was a small bird – her guardian angel, who constantly hovered over Catherine's head while she was dancing. At the very last moment of the ballet, when Catherine, after the death of Peter, was crowned the Empress of Russia, the bird should have turned into a big and powerful double-headed eagle similar to one on Russia's coat of arms. However, such an end would have been too bold for some in the direction of the theatre. It could have been seen as an expression of an indissoluble link between Estonia and Russia, where an Estonian could thrive and achieve the highest posts, even becoming Emperor (or President) of Russia. Without the bird turning into the double-headed eagle of the Russian coat of arms over Catherine's head, the ballet lost somewhat in its symbolic strength.

In January 2019 the ballet *Modigliani – The Cursed Artist* was successfully performed in the Bolshoi in Moscow. This is only one of the examples of Estonian dancers, musicians and artists being warmly welcomed in Russia and vice versa. During my stay in Tallinn together with hundreds of lucky Estonians I enjoyed, for example, Valery Gergiev conducting the St Petersburg's Mariinsky symphony orchestra and the *Virtuosos of Moscow* chamber orchestra of Vladimir Spivakov performing in Tallinn. Intensive cultural exchanges between the two nations show that notwithstanding efforts of the most vociferous parts of the Estonian political elites, with the accompaniment of the significant part of media, trying to drive a wedge between the two peoples, have borne fruit mainly at the political level and damaged Estonian economy. Of course, Estonia has many good journalists, though as to the covering international relations, most of them follow not only the spirit, but also the letter of Anglo-Saxon media. There a few exceptions. For example, Ahto Lobjakas, a columnist and political analyst, is one of the few critically minded and globally thinking journalists, what hasn't made, due also to his sharp tongue, his professional life in Estonia easier.

As a former athlete, I have always followed with great interests the ups and downs of Estonian sports. I found some of my former colleagues in sport with whom I like to reminisce about the times, when we exercised or competed together. A famous Estonian wrestler Tõnu Lume, whom I initiated to wrestling, is one of them. I meet from time to time a former decathlete Toomas Suurväli, who now coaches new generations of decathletes. Multiple Olympic medallist in hammer throwing, Jüri Tamm, has become my friend since the time, when he, being in 2000 a member of the Estonian Parliament, supported my candidature for the post of the Chancellor of Justice against the position of his party. I immensely enjoy and are always looking forward my rare meetings and sauna with my childhood friend Heiki Krimm, with whom, in our youth, we started training and competing and who later used his medical skills helping Estonian athletes to win Olympic medals.

Sometimes I wonder, why my homeland has had so many talented musicians, conductors and composers, artists, discus throwers and decathletes, but remains rather poor as to the politicians, especially in the field of international relations. It may have something to do, of course, with the smallness of the country. Any foreign minister of Estonia has very little say in the world affairs, while our ministers of defence, to meet the expectations of NATO generals, have to lower their intellectual capacities; critical reflections are not appreciated. Jaak Aaviksoo, the former Rector of the Tallinn Technological University and the Tartu University, having previously held also the posts of the Minister of Defence and Education, is the only ex-minister of defence in Estonia, whose intellectual capacities weren't hurt by holding the post of the Minister of Defence of Estonia. I have personally known some of them, who, having been quite intelligent persons before, became 'Yes, Sir' men while heading this Ministry. Obviously, within NATO's command hierarchy Estonian Minister of Defence is at the level of a platoon commander, who has to suppress any ability of critical thinking (better, of course, if he doesn't have it at all).

However, the dearth of politicians who could play more independent role is also due, I believe, to the historical grievances, especially recent ones, the Estonian people have been forced to live through. The mentality of victimhood, that has been artificially kept alive and enhanced, and directed almost exclusively against our eastern neighbour (all other invasions have been forgotten and forgiven), is not the best adviser in politics. However, it would be too much, in any case, to expect every nation having its own Nelson Mandela.

Working in the field of higher education in Estonia, I saw more clearly the advantages of the British system of higher education. Of course, these advantages are to a great extent due to the fact that the native language of Great Britain, like that of the United States, has become the *lingua franca* of the whole world. If in Estonia, it is important to encourage foreign students and professors to come to study or work in Estonia, to make the process of the higher education more international, in Britain such efforts were not needed. All the best of the world is, in any case, interested in coming and often even settling in the British academia (though the Brexit may change that, but in my opinion only to an extent). Of course, the traditions that are centuries long also play an important role. However, there is something that is not due to the language of education, maybe somewhat more to the historical traditions, that has made British higher education one of the bests in the world. It was the tradition of the academic freedom, which today unfortunately is suffering also in Britain. The main reason of this decline is the bureaucratisation and formalisation of teaching and particularly of academic research.

In Estonia, and I am sure, in many other Western countries as well, it has become more important to report well than to write or teach well. The more one publishes in journals that belong to specific categories, the more money one brings to his/her faculty, institute or the university. At my time at King's College, London, it was not yet so. Every seven years there took place what was called RAE (research assessment exercise). Every academic member of the staff had to present four pieces of work, no more. It was quality, not quantity that mattered. These works were anonymously assessed for their quality. Today, in Estonia, like in many other places – the more, the better. Some academics even cut their articles into two, in order to have more pieces that count. In research the rule that more is better is not at all applicable.

Then, there is a scramble for the grants in order to survive. Grant-based financing of the research has its benefits – it may contribute to the fulfilment of concrete short-term social and economic programmes, underpin certain political objectives, bring ideological support or justification for ends that governments or political parties want to achieve. However, new original concepts, trends or theories can hardly emerge from grant-based research. Moreover, the time spent for applying for grants and if and when they have been granted, which is not always the case, reporting on their implementation, is prohibitively high.

In my life, either being at the receiving end of the bureaucracy or holding bureaucratic posts myself, I never actively fought against it, believing it to be too time-consuming and in most cases simply useless or even counterproductive. I simply avoided or evaded it as much as possible. Meetings chaired by me were always also the shortest. This started already in Moscow under the Soviet rule, when bureaucracy was omnipresent and omnipotent, and in that respect too, I learned something from my Teacher Tunkin.

As the head of the international law department at Moscow University, he once received an honorary diploma of the University for the successful military-patriotic education of students. He was stunned; in his opinion, he hadn't done anything in this field. Neither had I or any other staff member. Then Tunkin invited Katya, who was then an active young postgrad, to his office. It turned out that Tunkin had asked her to prepare reports on behalf of the whole department, as well as of any member of the department, on all kinds of activities going on in the department, as requested by bureaucrats in higher echelons. Katya, not particularly excelling in the academic field, turned out to be an excellent writer of reports. Not only did she meticulously fix everything done by the staff; in reporting she disclosed the creativity that she was lacking in her academic research. For example, Tunkin's lectures on international law before WWII, then after WWII, my seminars on the use of force and state responsibility and lots of other things contained, in Katya's view, elements of military-patriotic-education of students.

Even King's College, London rose in the university ranking when a special service, responsible for reporting, was created. Two conclusions follow from this. First, those who cannot do well in research, usually report well; let them do that and those who excel in research should be exempt from reporting. Secondly, bureaucratic procedures don't give a genuine picture of the situation in higher education.

The intrusion of political correctness that has been already for some time ravaging the academia in the United States, has now spilled over to European campuses. When in France, for example, in October 2019, groups of leftist students, supporters of the LGBT and marriage for all groups, of the Montaigne University forced to cancel a lecture by prominent philosopher Sylviane Agancinski (the spouse of the former French Socialist Prime-Minister Lionel Jospin), whose views differ from those of these students, journalist Eugénie Bastié wrote: 'The censorship does not come anymore, as it was at the times of McCarthyism, from the academic administration, but from the students themselves.'[77] Censorship in the form of political correctness (Mathieu Bock-Coté is justified in defining it as 'postmodern censorship'[78]), even if not as dangerous as the McCarthyism in the US or the persecution of dissidents in the former USSR, since people don't (yet) go to prison, they are only forced to leave their jobs and their right to freedom of expression is suppressed, is nevertheless having debilitating effect not only inside the academia but on Western societies as a whole.

To my own surprise, I worked in Estonia eight rather productive years travelling regularly between Tallinn and London. Besides Professor Ene Grauberg, who generously invited me to Tallinn to succeed her as Rector of University Nord, I had pleasure to know and work closely with several leading figures of higher education. Rectors of Tallinn University Rein Raud and Tiit Land, though very different personalities, gave everything to betterment of teaching and research and achieved what was achievable in difficult circumstances (lack of resources, diminishing numbers of students etc.). I appreciate my friendship with the former Rector of Tallinn Technological

---

[77] E. Bastié, 'Sylviane Agancinski censurée, jusqu'où ira le maccarthysme universitaire ?' Le Figaro, 25 Octobre 2019.
[78] M. Bock-Coté, *Le multiculturalisme comme une religion politique*, Les Editions du Serf, 2019, p. 219

University Andres Keevallik. Although I was not working in his University, he was very helpful in organising the session of the *Institut de Droit International* in Tallinn. Under his able leadership the Technological University had become one of the best in the region. The two rectors of Tartu University, whom I had pleasure to know – Jaak Aaviksoo and Alar Karis – are both high-level professionals and scientists.

Only a year was I at the head of the University Nord. The tendency of the merger of universities is not only an Estonian phenomenon, but in a small country, where the number of potential students is falling, our Nord was forced by the Government to join one of the three public universities. We chose the Tallinn University and instead of being the Rector, I became the President of the Academy of Law within Tallinn University. This left me more time for writing. I also travelled a lot, especially when, in 2013, I was elected the President of the *Institut de Droit International*. In that post I replaced a prominent Japanese diplomat and international lawyer – former President of the International Court of Justice and the Japanese Ambassador to the UN in New York – Hisashi Owada, who happens to be also the father-in-law of the new Emperor of Japan Naruhito. We retain cordial relations and we talk naturally, among other things, about the Kuril Islands – a topic that is close to every Japanese.

Although in Estonia, there is no obligatory retirement age and I could have continued working as professor in Tallinn University, I felt that I needed more freedom to think and write. I have since given some shorter courses in Tallinn as well as in Helsinki, but I like to spend more time with the family in London, from time to time travelling for conferences, brain-storming meetings, like recent and forthcoming in Charlottesville, Virginia; or like now in China, lecturing and discussing with Chinese scholars and practitioners how this rising superpower is dealing with multiple internal and external challenges.

This was my third coming to Estonia, the first being the trip with my Mom from Siberia to Tallinn, followed by my childhood and adolescence in Estonia; the second from Moscow to the Foreign Ministry of Estonia; the third, from London to Tallinn to become the Rector of Nord University and professor at Tallinn University. In Tallinn I published dozens of articles in academic journals and even more columns in media; I authored two more books. *Regime Change: From Theories of Democratic Peace to Forcible Regime Change* was published in 2013 by Brill, while *Dawn of a New Order: Geopolitics and the Clash of Ideologies* in 2017 by I.B. Taurus. In these books and articles, even more than during my London period, I tried to explore underlying causes of the changes in the world, including the fundamental reasons why high expectations that many, including myself, had for the coming of an era when not force, but law would govern the behaviour of states, didn't materialised. My reflections on these matters are in the following chapters.

11- From Broken Promises to Cold War II: NATO Coming to Russia

NATO's expansion to the borders of Russia started already under President Clinton and has continued under all his successors. The existence and expansion of this relic of the Cold War, which should have lost its *raison d'être* after the disappearance of its erstwhile opponent – the Warsaw Pact and the Soviet Union, reveals more than anything else about the imperial ambitions of Washington. If the Soviet communists' slogan of equating Lenin with the Communist Party (when we say Lenin, we mean the Party; when we say the Party, we mean Lenin) was quite vacuous and devoid of any meaning, equating NATO with the US has been more than appropriate. It has always been Washington's arm in Europe.

In December 2017, the US National Security Archive published 30 documents[79] that unequivocally testify that during the 1990 negotiations between Soviet and Western leaders, the highest officials of leading NATO countries had indeed promised that while a unified Germany would be in NATO, the alliance will not move an inch closer to Soviet (now Russian) borders. These newly-revealed documents, about which the mainstream media has remained silent, debunk numerous allegations made by many Western politicians, diplomats and experts (with some prominent exceptions such as the former Washington Ambassador to Moscow Jack F. Matlock, or the former US Secretary of Defence Robert McNamara) that any promises, given to the Soviet leaders, that NATO would not move eastward, are simply myths. For the sake of brevity let's refer to just a few of them.

So, in response to those few in the West who had different recollections of those crucial days in 1990, Mark Kramer writes: 'These assertions were sharply challenged at the time by other observers, including former U.S. policymakers

---

[79] https://nsarchive.gwu.edu/briefing-book/russia-programs/2017-12-12/nato-expansion-what-gorbachev-hea...

who played a direct role in the German reunification process. George H. W. Bush, Brent Scowcroft, and James A. Baker, who served as president, national security adviser, and secretary of state in 1990 respectively, all firmly denied that the topic of extending NATO membership to former Warsaw Pact countries (other than East Germany) even came up during the negotiations with Moscow on German reunification, much less that the United States made a 'pledge' not to pursue it. In 1997, Philip Zelikow, who in 1990 was a senior official on the National Security Council (NSC) staff, responsible for German reunification issues, maintained that the United States made no commitment at all about the future shape of NATO, apart from some specific points about eastern Germany that were codified in the Treaty on the Final Settlement with Respect to Germany signed in September 1990. 'The option of adding new members to NATO,' Zelikow wrote, was 'not foreclosed by the deal actually made in 1990.'[80] Echoes Steven Pifer from Brookings Institution: 'Western leaders never pledged not to enlarge NATO, a point that several analysts have demonstrated.'[81] Mary Elise Sarotte asserts that 'contrary to Russian allegations, Gorbachev never got the West to promise that it would freeze NATO's borders. Rather, Bush's senior advisers had a spell of internal disagreement in early February 1990, which they displayed to Gorbachev. By the time of the Camp David summit, however, all members of Bush's team, along with Kohl, had united behind an offer in which Gorbachev would receive financial assistance from West Germany – and little else – in exchange for allowing Germany to reunify and for allowing a united Germany to be part of NATO.'[82]

And one may go on and on. However, in newly-revealed documents we can see that, for example, on 9 February of 1990 the then US Secretary of State James Baker communicated to the Soviet Foreign Minister Eduard Shevardnadze: 'There would, of course, have to be iron-clad guarantees that NATO's jurisdiction or forces would not move eastward' (U.S. Department of State, FOIA 199504567 (National Security Archive Flashpoints Collection, Box 38). The same day he states to Mikhail Gorbachev: 'We understand the need for

---

[80] M. Kramer, 'TWQ: The Myth of a No-NATO-Enlargement Pledge to Russia,' Centre for Strategic & International Studies, Spring 2009 (https://www.csis.org/analysis/twq-myth-no-nato-enlargement-pledge-russia-spring-2009, April 1, 2009).
[81] https://www.brookings.edu/blog/up-front/2014/11/06/did-nato-promise-not-to-enlarge-gorbachev-says-no...
[82] M. E. Sarotte, 'A Broken Promise? What the West Really Told Moscow About NATO Expansion,' Foreign Affairs, September/October 2014.

assurances to the countries in the East. If we maintain a presence in a Germany that is a part of NATO, there would be no extension of NATO's jurisdiction or forces of NATO one inch to the east (Ibid).'

I refrain from quoting from the memos from various negotiations with the participation of other political leaders such as Helmuth Kohl, Francois Mitterrand and Vaclav Havel on the matter. They can all be found in the published documents, which allowed Svetlana Savranskaya and Tom Blanton to conclude: 'The documents show that multiple national leaders were considering and rejecting Central and Eastern European membership in NATO as of early 1990 and through 1991, that discussions of NATO in the context of German unification negotiations in 1990 were not at all narrowly limited to the status of East German territory, and that subsequent Soviet and Russian complaints about being misled about NATO expansion *were founded in written contemporaneous memcons and telcons at the highest levels'* (emphasis added).[83]

In reading all these documents there remains no doubt that those who have denied that such promises were made, but were or should have been in the know, were consciously spreading fake news, while various commentators, to use Harry Frankfurt's philosophical definition[84], were simply disseminating bullshit. But as international lawyer, I would like to make also some legal comments. Yes, there were no solemn treaties signed or ratified on these issues. Therefore, there is some truth in claims that Gorbachev and Shevardnadze may have been simply naïve in believing in such oral promises, though fixed in different written memos. But there is no truth in claims that oral promises do not have political or even legal consequences. The matter is that international law knows so-called gentlemen agreements in oral form, as well as unilateral statements that create legal obligations.

The UN International Law Commission (ILC), whose task is the codification and progressive development of international law, having studied state practice and the judgements of the International Court of Justice (ICJ), has adopted the Guiding Principles on unilateral declarations capable of creating legal obligations, which provide: 'Just as every state possesses capacity to conclude treaties, every state can commit itself through acts whereby it unilaterally undertakes legal obligations under the conditions indicated in these Guiding

---

[83] https://nsarchive.gwu.edu/briefing-book/russia-programs/2017-12-12/nato-expansion-what-gorbachev-hea...
[84] H. Frankfurt, *On Bullshit*, Princeton University Press, 2005.

Principles. This capacity has been acknowledged by the International Court of Justice.' It is also generally acknowledged that the heads of state, heads of governments and ministers for foreign affairs are competent to formulate such declarations *ex officio*, i.e. without special credentials called full powers. The ILC confirms that 'while written declarations prevail, it is not unusual for states to commit themselves by simple oral statements. The binding character of such declarations is based on the principle of good faith.' The states concerned, in this case the Soviet Union and the Russian Federation, as the state continuation of the USSR, may take them into consideration and rely on them. This is what the Soviet Union did in 1990 and 1991. The ILC also emphasises that 'such states are entitled to require that such obligations be respected.'[85] Therefore, NATO expansion to the East, the continuation of this major Cold War institution, whose very *raison d'être* had been the containment of an enemy that had disappeared, was not only the greatest geopolitical tragedy of the end of the twentieth and beginning of the twenty-first century, the greatest missed opportunity to change the world for the better; it has also been contrary to international law and significantly contributed to the weakening its core principles.

It is undeniable that during the Cold War NATO played a counter-balancing and crucial role in guaranteeing the security of Washington's European allies *vis-à-vis* Moscow's missionary strive. However, in the post-Cold War world, NATO has become not only an anti-Russian, but an anti-European organisation, in the sense that by means of the Atlantic Alliance, Washington has deprived Europe of any independent foreign policy decision-making power, particularly on matters of European and international security.

Moreover, as military might and political levelheadedness are often at odds, and what may be enjoyable for Uncle Sam may not necessarily satisfy Marianne or Germania, such an outsourcing of European security has become dangerous for the Old Continent. Therefore, it is natural that many in Europe, particularly in Rumsfeld's 'Old Europe', consider the current tension between Russia and the West to be one of the greatest follies of the century, one that is mainly due to the short-sighted policies of Western political elites. French journalist Renaud Girard has written that 'we definitely lack a serious policy on Russia' and 'it is

---

[85] *Yearbook of the International Law Commission*, 2006, vol. II, Part Two, pp. 368-381.

urgent that France become closer to Russia' ('que la France se rapproche de la Russie').[86]

Already in 1998, George Kennan, the father of the containment policy *vis-à-vis* the Soviet Union, warned against moving NATO closer to Russian borders: 'I think it is the beginning of a new cold war. I think the Russians will gradually react quite adversely and it will affect their policies. I think it is a tragic mistake. There was no reason for this whatsoever. No one was threatening anybody else. This expansion would make the Founding Fathers of this country turn over in their graves. We have signed up to protect a whole series of countries, even though we have neither the resources nor the intention to do so in any serious way. [NATO expansion] was simply a light-hearted action by a Senate that has no real interest in foreign affairs.'[87] Through the enlargement of NATO, Washington extended its 'sphere of interest', to use the terminology of the secret protocols to the Molotov-Ribbentrop Pact, to the borders of Russia. At the end, 'NATO's existence became justified,' as Richard Sakwa observed, 'by the need to manage the security threats provoked by its enlargements.'[88]

And here we are. And there is no way back to those 1990s, which were so promising but failed to deliver. What has been light-heartedly done cannot be undone in the same way. The hardest thing for politicians to do is to admit their own mistakes or mistakes made by their states (my country, right or wrong). Therefore, I don't expect any apologies or that somebody would start sprinkling ash onto his/her head. I am writing these words in the hope that there are those, especially among younger generations, who may learn from the mistakes made by their predecessors and think more in terms of collective security than in terms of military alliances. Security against others has always been temporary, usually short-lived and often illusory. It is more difficult to create durable and effective collective security arrangements than collective self-defence organisations, that is to say, military alliances. Yet, the logic of military alliances is confrontational logic that, as history of international relations testifies, usually ends with a military confrontation.

---

[86] R. Girard, 'La diplomatie française doit en finir avec le néo-conservatisme', *Le Figaro*, Vox Monde, 29 March 2016.
[87] T.L. Friedman, 'Foreign Affairs; Now a Word From X', *New York Times*, 2 May 1998.
[88] R. Sakwa, *Frontline Ukraine: Crisis in the Borderlands* (I.B.Tauris, 2015), p. 4.

12- The 1999 War Over Kosovo a Precursor of a New Cold War?

One of the first serious cracks between the West and Russia emerged with NATO's 1999 war against Serbia over Kosovo. Yet, Washington's behaviour *vis-à-vis* Russia as if the latter wouldn't matter (though, it is necessary to note that Yeltsin's and particularly his Foreign Minister Kozyrev's behaviour could have indeed given grounds for such attitude), had antagonised many in Russia even before. I was at that time not only teaching at King's in London and working on my most voluminous book *Ordering Anarchy: International Law in International Society*, that was published the following year, when I followed with unease the run-up to a new war in the Balkans. Being, however, directly within this propaganda bubble and not having access to the materials I found only later, I must confess that I was also inclined to believe that maybe it was indeed necessary to use military force to save the lives of innocent Kosovar civilians, even if it would be done in violation of international law. However, when NATO's high-altitude aerial bombardment started hitting bridges, TV towers and other civilian object and civilians, it became clear that humanitarian concerns were only a pretext and once again geopolitics reigned in the Balkans.

It has become a commonplace assertion that the first victim of every war is the truth. The truth being the first victim of war may have had relatively little impact before the era of mass media. Today, however, the CNN phenomenon and then the Internet have increased the importance of this, one may say pre-emptive, 'killing' of the truth. Psychological warfare and propaganda wars have become necessary concomitants of all military conflicts; they precede, accompany and follow them. The run-up and build up to the 1999 Kosovo war was exemplary in that respect.

There are indeed situations where impartial and detached reporting may seem almost impossible, even immoral. For example, Christiane Amanpour, one of the most famous, and probably also one of the best journalists in the world, once claimed: 'When you're neutral in a situation like Bosnia, you are an accomplice – an accomplice to genocide.'[89] Of course, from the standpoint of the law she was completely wrong, but from a more humane point of view one may understand her indignation. At the same time, as it has been observed by some of her colleagues, 'Bosnia is also where she earned the mistrust of some of her colleagues. They complain that she oversteps the traditional bounds of objectivity and takes advantage of the freedom CNN gives her to bash whomever she considers guilty of that day's atrocities – in Bosnia usually the Serbs.'[90] This biased reporting by CNN and other Western media outlets, of what was going on in Kosovo, exceeded the tilted coverage of the earlier Balkan wars.

Indeed, the Yugoslav wars of the 1990s, and especially the run-up to the NATO bombardment of Serbia over Kosovo, were accompanied by one of the most biased media coverages that free press has ever seen; it was like artillery fire in preparation of attack by the tanks and infantry. I do not use quotation marks for the words 'free press', since the best Western European media is still the freest available, which unfortunately does not mean that it is without any bias. Such bias may come either automatically or through careful calculation. Sometimes accusing all sides of a bloody conflict of atrocities, which is more often than not the case, can destroy any mobilising effect. On whose behalf to intervene, who to bomb, if all sides are equally evil? Therefore, it is often felt necessary to single out a particular guilty party, whose crimes are meticulously recorded and reported, sometimes exaggerated, and where any benefit of the doubt is deemphasised for the party who is *a priori* marked as guilty. At the same time, atrocities of the other party are either downplayed or justified as expressions of unavoidable frustration. In Kosovo, there was a propaganda campaign to demonise one party and a concerted victimisation and sometimes even glorification of the other party. And who to single out for condemnation and who to spare often depends on geopolitical calculations. NATO's spokesperson Jamie Shea particularly excelled in this respect, as someone who after the 1999 Kosovo campaign became known as NATO's 'spin doctor'[91] and who today is Deputy Assistant Secretary-General for Emerging Security Challenges in NATO headquarters in Brussels. While the atrocities of the Serbs

---

[89] *Guardian*, 6 July 1996.
[90] S. Kinzer, 'Where There's War There's Amanpour', *New York Times*, 9 October 1994.
[91] See, for example, L. Cooper, M. Pal, 'Lectures from Spin Doctor: A NATO strategist's position at a top British university', *Open Democracy*, 30 June 2011.

were all meticulously reported (and there is no doubt that they did indeed occur), sometimes exaggerated, and any doubts as to the 'who' and 'how' were ignored, similar acts by the Kosovar Albanians, specifically of the KLA (the so-called Kosovo Liberation Army), which mirrored and often exceeded the atrocities of the Serbian side, were often downgraded or received only limited media coverage.

Some years ago, I read Jacques Hogard's excellent book *Europe Died in Pristina*.[92] This highly decorated French colonel, a participant of the 1999 NATO war against Serbia over Kosovo, became utterly disillusioned by double standards of Western countries in the process of this so-called 'humanitarian war.' I do not know whether the damage done to the body, and especially to the soul, of the Old Continent in the 1999 war against the Serbs is indeed mortal, but the wounds inflicted by this cowardly aerial bombardment in alliance with a terrorist organisation (the KLA had been earlier recognised as such by the US State Department) on the ground has indeed left deep scars on the body politic of Europe and beyond.

I am returning to these bygone days not only because it was 20 years ago (the NATO bombardment started 24 March 1999) that for the first time after the Second World War somebody, in complete disrespect of international law, used massive military force in the very centre of Europe. This aggression, covered by the fig leaf of a humanitarian intervention, quite an oxymoron in itself, opened the door wide to further unprincipled uses of force in other places. I am returning to those days also having read recently Dick Marty's book *Une Certaine Idée de la Justice*[93] *(A Particular Idea of Justice)* published in 2019 in Switzerland. This is an excellent, though also disturbing, account of those days. Marty is a prominent Swiss lawyer and politician. In 2011 Carla Del Ponte, the former Procurator of the International Criminal Tribunal for the former Yugoslavia (ICTY), had published her book[94], where she drew attention to the information that in 1999 some 300 kidnapped Serbians had been taken, shortly after the arrival of NATO troops in Kosovo, with trucks from Kosovo to several camps in Albania, where their organs were extracted to be sold in foreign countries. After this publication, the Parliamentary Assembly of the Council of Europe appointed Dick Marty to investigate those alleged horrendous crimes that

---

[92] J. Hogard, *L'Europe est morte à Pristina: Guerre au Kosovo* (Hugo & Cie, 2014).
[93] D. Marty, *Une Certaine Idée de la Justice* (Favre, 2019).
[94] C. Del Ponte, *Madame Prosecutor: Confrontations with Humanity's Worst Criminals and the Culture of Impunity*, Other Press, 2011.

Western leaders and media were eager not to mention. In his report to the Parliamentary Assembly Marty confirmed that 'numerous indications seem to confirm that, during the period immediately after the end of the armed conflict, before international forces had been able to take control of the region and re-establish law and order, organs were removed from some prisoners at a clinic on Albanian territory, near Fushë-Krujë, to be taken abroad for transplantation. Although some concrete evidence of such trafficking already existed at the beginning of the decade, the international authorities in charge of the region did not consider it necessary to conduct a detailed examination of these circumstances or did so incompletely and superficially.'[95]

In his book Dick Marty describes the reluctance of many Western politicians (e.g., former French Foreign Minister Bernard Kushner, a co-founder of *Médecins Sans Frontières* and the UN Representative in Kosovo in 1999-2001), senior diplomats (e.g., former US Ambassador to Kosovo Christopher Dell) and high military commanders (e.g., US Brigadier-General Steven Shook, former commander of the US Camp Bondsteel in Kosovo) even to talk about these crimes and their efforts to prevent the truth to prevail and the justice to be done. Dick Marty concludes: 'I think, and I have always maintained, that the independence of Kosovo was not only achieved by using means of doubtful legality in the light of international law, but it was also poorly carried out and responded to the interests of certain governments, without at all taking account of the interests of the people in the region.'[96]

Let us recall briefly how this act of doubtful legality (an understatement) started. After the collapse of Yugoslavia, encouraged by Western powers, interethnic conflict between Kosovo Albanians (Kosovars) exacerbated in this Serbian province. The UN Security Council became involved and twice in 1998 adopted resolutions (Res. 1199 of 23 September; Res. 1203 of 24 October) condemned the violence in the province by any party, considering it to be a threat to the peace and security in the region, but at the same time reaffirming the sanctity of the territorial integrity of Serbia. Shortly prior to the NATO attack against Serbia, President Bill Clinton's special envoy to the Balkans, Robert Gelbard, had described the KLA as, 'without any questions, a terrorist

---

[95] Report | Doc. 12462 | 07 January 2011 Inhuman treatment of people and illicit trafficking in human organs in Kosovo (http://assembly.coe.int/nw/xml/XRef/Xref-XML2HTML-en.asp?fileid=12608&lang=en).
[96] Marty, *Une Certaine Idée de la Justice*, p. 259.

group.'[97] The KLA had long been engaged in tit-for-tat attacks with Serbian nationalists in Kosovo, using also reprisals against ethnic Albanians who 'collaborated' with the Serbian government, and bombing police stations and cafes known to be frequented by Serb officials, killing innocent civilians in the process. Most of its activities were funded by drug trafficking, though its ties to community groups and Albanian exiles gave it local popularity.[98]

The then UK Foreign Secretary, Robin Cook, told the House of Commons on 18th January 1999, i.e. only a couple of months before the NATO bombing: 'On its part, the Kosovo Liberation Army has committed more breaches of the ceasefire, and until this weekend was responsible for more deaths than the security forces. It must stop undermining the ceasefire and blocking political dialogue.'[99] Later it was revealed by Gabriel Keller, a deputy head of the Kosovo Verification Mission (KVM), that: '…every pullback by the Yugoslav army or the Serbian police was followed by a movement forward by (KLA) forces (…) OSCE's presence compelled Serbian government forces to a certain restraint (…) and UCK (i.e. KLA) took advantage of this to consolidate its positions everywhere, continuing to smuggle arms from Albania, abducting and killing both civilians and military personnel, Albanians and Serbs alike.'[100] However, such revelations from people who knew what was going on the ground were drowned in the sea of misinformation aimed at discrediting the Serbian side.

Another factor confirming that NATO attack had nothing to do with humanitarian concerns is the so-called 'Rambouillet Agreement', presented in February 1999 to Belgrade and to a delegation of Kosovo Albanians in the Chateau Rambouillet in France. The latter expressed their consent with the text of the Agreement while Belgrade rejected it. This rejection was a crucial step leading to the war. However, could anyone have realistically expected Belgrade, or any other sovereign state for that matter, to accept such an agreement? Appendix B of the Agreement, being an integral part of it, provided, inter alia, that 'NATO personnel shall enjoy, together with their vehicles, vessels, aircraft, and equipment, free and unrestricted passage and unimpeded access throughout

---

[97] Council on Foreign Relations. Terrorist Groups and Political Legitimacy. (http://www.cfr.org/terrorism/terrorist-groups-political-legitimacy/p10159).
[98] Ibid.
[99] www.publications.parliament.uk/pa/cm199899/cmhansrd/vo990118/debtext/90118-06.htm
[100] Masters of the Universe? NATO's Balkan crusade (Tariq Ali ed.), Verso Books, 2000, p.163

the FRY [Federal Republic of Yugoslavia that at that time comprised of Serbia and Montenegro] including associated airspace and territorial waters. This shall include, but not be limited to, the right of bivouac, manoeuvre, billet, and utilization of any areas or facilities as required for support, training, and operations.' Furthermore, the authorities in the FRY were obligated to 'facilitate, on a priority basis and with all appropriate means, all movement of personnel, vehicles, vessels, aircraft, equipment, or supplies, through or in the airspace, ports, airports, or roads used.'[101] It was an ultimatum requesting unconditional surrender, something that no state that has not been defeated in a war would have accepted. In a commentary released to the press, the former Secretary of State, Henry Kissinger declared: 'The Rambouillet text, which called on Serbia to admit NATO troops throughout Yugoslavia, was a provocation, an excuse to start bombing. Rambouillet is not a document that an angelic Serb could have accepted. It was a terrible diplomatic document that should never have been presented in that form.'[102] Lord Gilbert stated in the House of Lord of the British Parliament: 'I think the terms put to Milošević at Rambouillet were absolutely intolerable; how could he possibly accept them? It was quite deliberate.'[103]

French journalist Pierre Péan, in his book with an emblematic title '*Kosovo – a 'just' war to create a mafia state'* quotes the former Foreign Minister of France, Hubert Védrine, who participated in the Rambouillet negotiations on Kosovo: 'Robin Cook [then British Foreign Secretary] and I were looking for a political solution, while Tony Blair was for a war. Madeleine Albright [then US Secretary of State] was from the very beginning the most eager to go to war, equating Milošević with Hitler… As to Igor Ivanov [then Foreign Minister of Russia], he constantly repeated: 'I am here to prevent a war,' though he detested Milošević. Joshka Fischer [then Foreign Minister of Germany], was constantly torn between us – Cook and me – and Madeleine Albright, who was accusing the German Foreign Minister, when he was leaning towards finding a political solution, to be a leftist.'[104]

---

[101] US Department of State. Rambouillet Agreement (Interim Agreement for Peace and Self-Government in Kosovo).
[102] *Daily Telegraph*, 28 June 1999.
[103] Select Committee on Defence. Minutes of Evidence, June 2000. http://www.publications.parliament.uk/pa/cm199900/cmselect/cmdfence/347/0062005.htm .
[104] P. Péan, *Kosovo: une guerre 'juste' pour créer un Etat mafieux* (Fayard, 2013). p. 392.

Indeed, a very revealing information. Washington sought a war, no more, no less. Moreover, Dick Marty recalls an episode that took place in 2012 in Prague, where the former US Secretary of State, facing a demonstration in support of victims of NATO bombardment, could not refrain from loudly expressing her hatred: 'Disgusting Serbs, get out.'[105] Professor Bertrand Badie of Science Po-Paris has observed that the Clinton Administration's foreign policy looked very much like a symbolic continuation of the Cold War: 'The first post-bi-polar world American President didn't hesitate to nominate in January 1997 Madeleine Albright as Secretary of State – a person who incarnated the very spirit of the Cold War by her background and family history. The daughter of a Czech diplomate having left the country just after the coup in Prague had worked in the Center for Strategic Studies as one of the specialists on the USSR.'[106] The appointment of Cold War warriors to the top posts in the post-Cold War period was certainly not the wisest move.

John Norris, Strobe Talbott's [the Deputy Secretary of State at that time] Director of Communications during the Kosovo crisis, wrote: 'It was Yugoslavia's resistance to the broader trends of political and economic reform – not the plight of Kosovar Albanians – that best explains NATO's war. Milošević had been a burr in the side of the transatlantic community for so long that the United States felt that he would only respond to military pressure.'[107] Therefore, Kosovo was not at all an operation with humanitarian objectives, but a regime change war with mainly geopolitical purposes and implications, as the creation of the Camp Bondsteel – the largest and the most expensive foreign military base built by the US in Europe, since the Vietnam War – testifies. And like after the destruction of Iraq in 2003, in Kosovo among the major beneficiaries was of the war was Kellogg, Brown and Root (KBR), a former subsidiary of Halliburton, the company where US Vice-President Dick Cheney had been CEO before ascending to the White House. Pierre Péan writes that Washington had been planning the construction of the military base Bondsteel (built by an affiliate of Halliburton) in Kosovo long before NATO's bombs started landing in Serbia. In

---

[105] D. Marty, p. 259.
[106] B. Badie, *Nous ne sommes seuls au monde: un autre regard sur l' ordre international* (La Découverte, 2016), p. 70.
[107] J. Norris, *Collision Course. NATO, Russia, and Kosovo* (Foreword by Strobe Talbott), Praeger, 2005, p. xxiii.

his opinion, 'this confirms the view that the Americans preferred war to peace.'[108]

Finally, an additional fly in Kosovo's anointment came in 2008, after the years of manipulative administration of Kosovo by the so-called international community, including the United Nations and the European Union. This is the recognition of the independence of Kosovo by most Western states, notwithstanding a clause in all Security Council resolutions on Kosovo both before NATO's invasion (Res. 1199, 23 September 1998), (Res. 1203, 24 October 1998) as well as after the invasion (Res. 1244,10 June 1999), that all emphasised the importance of guaranteeing the territorial integrity of Yugoslavia. Notwithstanding all these clauses most NATO and EU member states recognised the independence of Kosovo, which, in turn, made it easier for the Kremlin to recognise later the two Georgian break-away provinces as independent states. This, together with other such *gung-ho* approaches to international law, contributed to the undermining of its foundations.

The Advisory Opinion delivered by the International Court of Justice on 22nd July 2010 stating that Kosovo's declaration of independence 'did not violate general international law', though formally correct, is anodyne in its content, and potentially explosive in its consequences. Even if I were to declare my house with its small plot of land in Tallinn independent from Estonia, I would not be in breach of general international law since international law simply does not deal with such matters. However, if a neighbouring state were to recognise my extravagant declaration, it would certainly violate general international law; this would be a clear-cut interference in the internal affairs of my country.

NATO's Kosovo operation, which many Western politicians and experts refer to as an example to be followed in order to save lives in places like Libya or Syria, serves, however, a different, and much more negative, precedent. German journalist and political scientist Alexander Rar has written that in the aftermath of Kosovo, NATO lost prestige even among many liberally minded people in Russia, and they started to profess doubts in democracy as a form of political regime.[109] Even more disturbing may be another effect of NATO's operation, exposed by Rar: 'Many Russians suddenly lost their antipathy towards use of force by their own country. They sincerely started to believe that if the

---

[108] P. Péan, *Kosovo: une guerre 'juste' pour créer un Etat mafieux* (Fayard, 2013).
[109] A. Rar, *Vladimir Putin - The Best German in the Kremlin*, Moscow, Algoritm, 2012 (Russian translation from German), p. 174.

civilised West is not averse to violence, then Russia with her existential problems simply has to do the same.'[110]

As two books published in 2016 and carrying revealing titles – *Mission Failure: America and the World in the Post-Cold War Era* by American Michael Mandelbaum and *Why We Lose the Wars?* by Frenchman Gérard Chaliand – testify, no Western intervention in the post-Cold War era has achieved its political aims. Professor Mandelbaum writes: 'The United States failed in getting China to protect human rights or constructing smoothly functioning free markets or genuinely representative political institutions in Russia. It did not succeed in installing well-run, widely accepted governments in Somalia, Haiti, Bosnia, or Kosovo. It did not transform Afghanistan or Iraq into tolerant, effectively administered countries. It did not bring democracy to the Middle East or harmony between Israelis and Arabs.'[111] Gérard Chaliand observes that 'the balance sheet of wars waged by the major military power of the XXI century, the United States, often backed up by numerous allies, is without any doubt negative: enormous sums squandered with mediocre military results and politically disastrous consequences.'[112] Concerning the results of the first illegal use of military force in Europe after WWII, French journalist Renaud Gerard concludes that instead of a 'multi-ethnic and peaceful Kosovo' promised by Clinton, 'we have today an entity that is neither multi-ethnic nor pacific, that has become a crime hub and recently also that of Islamism. However, the Americans have managed to benefit from it by establishing a military base called the Bondsteel camp.'[113] It took more than twenty years for the former military leader of the KLA and later the President of Kosovo, Hashim Thaci, together with several of his colleagues (accomplices) – all NATO's allies in the 1999 war against Serbia – to be indicted for war crimes and crimes against humanity by *The Kosovo Specialist Chambers* in The Hague.[114] Although with considerable delay, a small fish get caught while their overmasters, who guided and protected them, have, as always, slipped through the net.

---

[110] Ibid. p. 175.
[111] M. Mandelbaum, *Mission Failure: America and the World in the Post-Cold War Era* (Oxford University Press, 2016), p. 248.
[112] G. Chaliand, *Pourquoi Perd-On La Guerre? Un nouvel art occidental* (Odile Jacob, 2016), p. 17.
[113] R. Girard, 'Il faut européaniser l'Otan,' *Figaro Vox*, 12 novembre 2019.
[114] 'Kosovo leader Thaci in Hague detention over war crime charges,' BBC News, 6 November, 2020.

13- Ukraine: Victim of Geopolitics?

After my retirement from London, during the years in Tallinn, I often visited also Russia. It helped that it is much closer to Estonia than to London. One of my visits was to the Crimea that Russia considers as voluntarily reunited in March 2014with his motherland, but Ukraine and Western countries see as illegally occupied by Russia. This short visit unleashed a barrage of criticism in my address both in Estonia as well as in Ukraine. In Ukraine may name was included in the list of so-called Mirotvorets (Peacekeeper or Peace-enforcer). This is a list of enemies of Ukraine, who would be arrested if they ever visit the country. There I am, however, in a rather good company together with quite a few prominent Western politicians, experts and intellectuals, who have had the temerity to go and see with their own eyes what is going on in the peninsular, be it occupied by, or reunited with, Russia. In Estonia, I was included in the yearbook of the KAPO (the Estonian Defence Police) as somebody, who is undermining Estonian security with his statements and the visit to the Crimea, in other words as being a 'useful idiot' of the Kremlin.

However, long before visiting the Crimea, I had published an article entitled *Ukraine: Victim of Geopolitics*, where I analysed the situation that had emerged after the violent events in Kiev, in Eastern Ukraine and the bundle of controversies over the Crimea. Some months after the publication of the article I happened to be in Mexico City to lecture in several Mexican universities. One evening, however, I had a call from the Foreign Ministry of Mexico and was invited to meet the Minister, Jose Antonio Meade. To put it mildly, I was surprised. I could not have imagined that the Minister could be even aware of the presence of an insignificant professor in the country; to say nothing about the desire to meet me. However, a car from the Ministry soon picked me up and late in the evening I arrived at the building of the *Secretaria des Relaciones Exteriores*, where President of Turkey Erdogan had just finished his lengthy speech. Drinking tea with the Minister and talking on European affairs, I could not suppress my curiosity and asked the Minister what had prompted him to see me. He told me that one of his assistants – an international lawyer by formation – had read my article on Ukraine and having seen on the Internet an announcement of my lecture in the National University of Mexico, had advised the Minister to talk to me on this conflict in Europe. As the Minister a bit jokingly said, he had liked my non-aligned approach. For me it sounded, especially from the mouth of the Foreign Minister of the country that had been one of the leaders of the so-called 'non-alignment' movement, as the highest praise of my professionalism. Neither pro-Russian, nor pro-Western, not even always pro-Estonian, if this would mean to be always in tune with prevailing narrative.

I have often asked myself, why is it so that I am partly at home almost everywhere and at the same time nowhere entirely *chez moi*, as the French say. Maybe it is because being originally from a small country and having imbued with mother's milk something from its suffering and problems, I have become 'spoilt' by long periods in two imperial capitals – Moscow and London. This has, however, given me, so to say, three different vantage points from which to observe and evaluate the world. Maybe due to these long periods of my life in these different societies and being submerged into the lives of the three rather different cultures, I have become also to appreciate and enjoy differences. Or was it an inborn feature, being curious and open to all that is strange and exotic, that has drawn me to different people and societies. I am certainly a hetero in the large sense of the term.

Now, let's take a closer look at the situation in and around the Crimean Peninsula – the situation that is much more complicated than those, who, being guided by 'the correct ideology' know the truth *ex ante*. In the West, it is often emphasised that the annexation of the Crimea has been the first grab of foreign territory since World War II (at least in Europe), and that this makes this act something exceptional, a more aggravated violation of international law than other breaches, be they committed either by Russia or by Western countries. For example, Daniel Treisman writes that 'Russian President Putin's seizure of the Crimean Peninsula from Ukraine in early 2014 was the most consequential decision of his 16 years in power. By annexing a neighbouring country's territory by force, Putin overturned in a single stroke the assumptions on which the post-Cold War European order has rested.'[115] But was it? What about Kosovo? Was

---

[115] D. Treisman, 'Why Putin took Crimea? The Gambler in the Kremlin,' *Foreign Affairs*, 18 April 2016.

it not separated by force from Serbia? In terms of geopolitics the cases of Kosovo and the Crimea are quite similar. The fact that neither the Kosovars nor the Crimeans wanted to stay in Serbia and Ukraine, respectively, also adds to the similarity of these cases.

It may be true that this is the first recent annexation of the territory of another state in Europe, carried out by the threat of use of military force (in the case of Kosovo, it was actual use of force by NATO, which makes an even more aggravated violation), but is it really so exceptional when looked at in the light of ongoing geopolitical processes? Here I am referring neither to historical justifications of Russia's take-over of the Crimea, nor of the desire of the majority of Crimean's to revert to the Russian fold, as was clearly expressed in the referendum of March 2014. I am talking about the geopolitical concerns of Russia. Justifying its annexation (most Russians refer to it as reunification) of the Crimea, Russia has presented a set of emotionally charged arguments: historical (the Peninsular became part of the Russian Empire in 1783, and until Khrushchev's 1954 transfer of it to Ukraine had always been a part of Russia), ethnic (the majority of the population are ethnic Russians) and religious (the christening of Prince Vladimir in 988 took place in Chersonese in the Crimea) factors, and as if an afterthought – military-strategic considerations. However, in my opinion, notwithstanding that President Putin, other Russian leaders and the Russian media have stressed the emotional and historical aspects of the 'reunification', the proximate and most significant reason behind this act was geopolitical. The emotional angle, with its historical, ethnic and justice-based components, made it easier to justify in the eyes of most Russians the reunification of the Crimea (if such justification was at all needed), which was deemed to be necessary for strategic motives.

I would compare the annexation of Crimea (or returning it to the motherland) by Russia, with the attempt of the Soviet Union to install medium range missiles with nuclear warheads in Cuba in 1962, or rather with the American responses to it. As an excellent study of US–Cuban relations by Nigel White of Nottingham University generalises: 'The Cuban missile crisis of 1962, like so many elements of Cuba's relationship with the US, seemed to be conducted outside of the parameters of international law.'[116] Dean Acheson – a distinguished American diplomat and international lawyer, the Secretary of State from 1949 to 1953 –

---

[116] N. White, *The Cuban Embargo under International Law* (El Bloqueo, Routledge, 2015), p. 29.

when commenting on the 1962 crisis, said: 'The power, position and prestige of the United States had been challenged by another state; and law simply does not deal with such questions of ultimate power–power that comes close to sources of sovereignty.'[117] A frank admission. Today, Russian politicians and diplomats could have used the same language in justification of their behaviour *vis-à-vis* Ukraine. And they would not be wrong. As President Putin of Russia said on 18 March 2014, 'You know, I cannot imagine that we will visit NATO marines based in Sebastopol. Though most of them are good guys, we prefer to invite them to visit us in Sebastopol.'[118] For me, if the earlier historical, ethnical and religious reasons were given as main justifications, this somewhat jokingly made statement (for me it is the best geopolitical joke, I have ever heard) was the real explanation for the geopolitical necessity of the annexation (or re-unification) of the Crimea. The Kremlin believed, and not without reason, that if Ukraine were to join the American-led military alliance or even before, the American navy would soon have its base in Sebastopol. For the Americans to better understand the significance of the matter for Russia, it would be necessary to compare the scenario of having an American navy in the Crimea with the scenario of the Russians or the Chinese, separately or together, establishing a naval base, say, at Guantanamo Bay. Therefore, it is difficult to agree with Ivan Krastev and Stephan Holmes when they, without providing any evidence, write: 'What motivated Putin's improvised Ukraine gambit was not so much fear of NATO warships in the Black Sea as fear that disenchanted Muscovites might imitate what he imagined to be remote-controlled street protest in Kiev.'[119] Such a statement could gain credibility only if Vladimir Putin, or somebody else present in their conversation, were to confirm that he, indeed, told it either to Krastev or Holms.

Unfortunately, in the context of today's geopolitical conflicts, legal arguments, due to such slight and even frivolous attitudes to international law (law is how we interpret it, our cause is just therefore what we do has nothing in common what you do etc.) do not carry much weight. At best (or worst), they give verbal ammunition to the current information warfare where the first victim, as always, has been the truth. All sides use it in full; though it is true that if some

---

[117] D. Acheson, 'The Cuban Quarantine – Implications for the Future,' *Proceedings of the American Society of International Law*, 1963, p. 14.

[118] *Statement of the President of the Russian Federation*, 18 March 2014 (official site of the President of Russia, http://eng.kremlin.ru/).

[119] I. Krastev, S. Holmes, *The Light that Failed: Reckoning* (Penguin, 2019) 110.

segments of quality Western media sometimes give voice to the other side, while in the Russian media (at least TV) it is more difficult, though not impossible (especially in social media), to hear any dissenting views. But even in the West you must be somebody of Henry Kissinger's calibre to have one's balanced views on matters of Ukraine expressed in the mainstream media. Only specialists read such quality sources such as *Stratfor* or *The National Interest* where in-depth analysis that goes beyond slogans and name-calling can be found. In general, Western media misinforms rather than informs the people about the developments in and around Ukraine. Western politicians, media and experts, accusing President Putin of living in an unreal world, also inhabit a world that is created by their own brainwashing system. Therefore, Henry Kissinger's warning that, 'for the West, the demonization of Vladimir Putin is not a policy; it is an alibi for the absence of one'[120] hits the nail on the head. The danger is that the clash of the two opposing simplistic virtual visions of the world well exemplified by the mind sets of such firebrands as, say, the late Senator John McCain or member of the Russian Duma Vladimir Zhirinovsky, spill over into the real world. There has been already for some time a rather disturbing undermining of the principles of the non-use of force and non-interference in internal affairs of states. The latter principle seems to have altogether fallen into desuetude. Russia, both then and now, and the Western powers before the fall (well deserved) of President Yanukovych – the thief-in-chief of Ukraine – competed in a rush to intervene in Ukraine, reminiscent of the nineteenth century scramble for Africa by European empires. Russian arguments in defence of its stand on Ukraine are like the justifications used by Western powers when they bend international law. Don't NATO countries understand that in a different context and in other places China, or Russia for that matter, may also resort to all the options if they are on the table? However, this is not the table of international law.

The 16 March 2014 referendum on the status of the Crimea, the string of events that led to it as well as the following decisions of the Crimean authorities and that of Moscow are all of doubtful legality. It is true that international law, though not encouraging secession (the right to self-determination and secession overlap only partly), does not prohibit it either. In that respect the two referenda in Quebec and the Scottish referendum, being authorised by Ottawa and Westminster, didn't violate international law. Even unauthorised by central

---

[120] H. Kissinger, 'How the Ukraine Crisis Ends,' *Washington Post*, 5 March 2014.

authorities referenda, like those in the Spanish Catalonia and in Iraqi Kurdistan, don't breach any norms of international law (it has to be emphasised, however, that any third states' recognition of secessionist outcomes of such referenda would have constituted interference in domestic affairs of Spain and Iraq respectively).

The referendum in the Crimea was marred by the presence of the armed forces of the Russian Federation in the Crimea, even if we assume that only those forces in Sebastopol that were stationed there in accordance with the Agreement between Russia and Ukraine were involved. One should only ask: would the 16 March referendum have been possible without Russian forces being in the Crimea (and not quietly sitting in their bases which would have been a necessary requirement if Russia indeed had done everything to avoid interference in Ukrainian affairs)? In the case of the no answer, and in my opinion, this would be the only possible answer, Russia would be in breach of international law. And this remains so notwithstanding that the huge majority of the Crimeans genuinely chose the reintegration with Russia instead of staying with Ukraine. This does not make the annexation (re-unification) legal but may well legitimise it. There is no doubt that most Crimeans, like most citizens of Russia, welcomed the reunification of the Crimea with Russia. In that respect this all may be even seen as legitimate, though contrary to international law. Here too we see a clear parallel with NATO's military intervention against Serbia over Kosovo in 1999 that the Report of the Independent International Commission on Kosovo headed by Judge Richard Goldstone defined 'illegal but legitimate.' And pay attention, Russia has also started, after 2014, to widely use the term 'legitimacy' instead of 'legality'. Legitimacy – a more elusive and subjective criterion than legality – is usually in the eye of the beholder.

However, Ukraine under President Yushchenko, like Georgia under Saakashvili, was about to sign with NATO a Membership Action Plan (MAP) that would have eventually led to the full membership. Only the opposition of France and Germany in the 2008 Bucharest Summit of NATO didn't allow such a plan to be approved for these two former Soviet republics. NATO, in contradistinction to the EU, is a geopolitical and military alliance and its movement closer to Russian borders serves geopolitical aims. George Friedman writes: 'There are those in the West who dismiss Russia's fears as archaic. No one wishes to invade Russia, and no one can invade Russia. Such views appear sophisticated but are in fact simplistic. Intent means relatively little in terms of assessing threats. They can change very fast. So too can capabilities.'[121] Things that don't change as fast as intents and even capabilities are geography and geopolitics. They are relative constants of world politics and therefore Russia is, and must be, worried by NATO's advance. What is important for Russia, is that Sebastopol remains a Russian naval base, instead of becoming NATO's outpost against Russia. This is a constant that remains, whatever changing intentions and even capabilities.

And the Kremlin is responding to NATO's encroachment. In 2008 it did that in Georgia and in 2014 in Ukraine. This is *in concreto*. But *in grosso modo* Russia is responding to the expansion of the United States and its NATO allies closer and closer to the Russian borders. As John Mearsheimer writes of the Ukrainian crisis, 'Washington played a key role in precipitating this dangerous situation, and Mr. Putin's behaviour is motivated by the same geopolitical considerations that influence all great powers, including the United States.'[122] And Russia, in responding to Washington is also breaching various norms of international law, as we have shown above. In that respect, i.e. bending and breaching international law, Russia has had good teachers.

Ivan Krastev and Stephen Holmes make some important and deep observations studying of the processes of imitation by East and Central European states, as well as by Russia, of democracy and liberal values that are sometimes genuine but often also naïve or hypocritical. However, every now and then they go too far in their fascination with imitation. So, they write that 'to subvert Western hegemony, Russia did not abandon but refashioned, redirected and weaponised its strategy of imitating the West.'[123] Or that 'just as NATO violated the territorial integrity of Serbia in 1999, so Russia violated the territorial integrity of Georgia in 2008.'[124] In their view Russia, or rather Putin's Russia, is simply showing the West, particularly to Washington, its ugly mirror image or parodying 'US foreign policy in order to expose its hypocrisy.'[125] As if Russia has nothing else to worry about but copying Americans even contrary to its self-interest. On the contrary, Moscow is, after the Soviet Union's ideological confrontation with the West and Yeltsin's Russia's awkward attempts to

---

[121] G. Friedman, 'Russia Examines Its Options for Responding to Ukraine,' *Geopolitical Weekly, Stratfor*, 18 March 2014.
[122] J. J. Mearsheimer, 'Getting Ukraine Wrong,' *The New York Times*, 13 March 2014.
[123] I. Krastev, S. Holmes, *Op. Cit.*, pp. 110-111.
[124] *Ibid.*, p. 125.
[125] *Ibid.*, p. 135.

hypocritically imitate the West (in that Krastev and Holmes are right), Putin's Russia is primarily concerned with its national interests, as they are understood, of course, by its political elite. Violations of international law by Western states, be it in 1999 war against Serbia over Kosovo, or 2003 invasion of Iraq, or 2011 destruction of Libya (often claimed as lawful because sanctioned by the UN Security Council; however, the Council authorised to use all necessary means to protect the civilian population, not to help overthrow the government), have indeed given Kremlin the opportunity to refer to these violations as precedents justifying Russia's own behaviour. Claims that Russia goes to war or otherwise breaches norms of international law in order to simply expose West's hypocrisy are too farfetched to be taken seriously. Moreover, there is no evidence given to confirm such conclusions; they are based on the authors' 'reading' of what is in Putin's mind.

One more thing is essential to be mentioned in that respect. The truth of the matter is that Russia is too big to be led by any outside power. This must be understood; otherwise, there would be constant misperceptions and conflicts. British expert Richard Sakwa already some years ago wrote: 'The international system today does not have a mechanism for integrating rising great powers. This applies to China, as well as to Russia and some other countries.'[126] I believe there is a deep truth in this remark, which is not limited to countries as big as Russia or China. Vladimir Putin in his 2012 pre-election article wrote that 'Russia has practically always had the privilege of pursuing an independent foreign policy and this is how it will be in the future.'[127] Such a statement may have been a response to President Yeltsin's failed attempts to have Russia accepted by Washington, and the West in general, as an equal, independent player who may have its own interests, different from those of the United States, but who nevertheless may be a partner of, and on good terms with, Washington and Brussels. This remark also expresses the truth that nations react differently to attempts to 'civilise' them, to induce them to correspond to a dominant trend. Quite a few would happily follow the lead while others do it grudgingly, but some become prickly, and pushing them would be counterproductive. One could have hardly expected from Russia to exercise the politics of bandwagoning that

---

[126] R. Sakwa, 'New Cold War' or twenty years' crisis? *International Affairs* 2008 v. 84, No 2, p. 255.
[127] V. Putin, 'Russia and the Changing World,' *Moscow News*, 27 February 2012.

many smaller states have happily (or not so happily) done and continue doing today.

Jack Matlock Jr., the former Washington's Ambassador to Moscow, writes that Vladimir Putin also 'initially followed a pro-Western orientation. When terrorist attacked the `United States on Sept. 11, 2001, he was the first foreign leader to call and offer support. He cooperated with the United States when it invaded Afghanistan, and it voluntarily removed Russian bases from Cuba and Cam Ranh Bay in Vietnam.'[128] But in return, as Matlock rightly observes, Putin got 'colour revolutions' supported by or instigated from Washington, the invasion of Iraq without Security Council approval, a withdrawal from the Anti-Ballistic Missile Treaty, Kosovo and so on.

---

[128] J. Matlock, 'The U.S. has treated Russia like a loser since the end of the Cold War,' *The Washington Post*, 14 March 2014.

14- China Has Risen, Russia Is Back, the US is in Relative Decline New Geopolitical Realities

As it was in China that I started writing these personal recollections in the context of the times lived, it is only natural that I write more about China than simply referring to it as a rising geopolitical centre, which may soon threaten American dominance not only in East Asia, but much further from its shores. Not being a specialist on China, though having visited it often and sometimes even stayed there for several months in a row, I know Russia much better. Comprehending China without speaking the language is almost an impossible mission. Therefore, I have chosen to compare these two powers that are threatening, though in different ways, the Western dominance. None of them is threatening militarily the West, as it is all too often claimed, but their relative weights and policies are putting an end to the Western hegemonic dominance. These – undermining hegemonic dominance and threatening vital interests, particularly by military means – are two different realities and concepts. If China or Russia, individually or together, were threatening the West, the West must indeed take counter-measures adequate to the threat. However, it is normal and to be expected that these two great nations, and not only they, do not like to be dominated. As smaller and weaker nations may not have much choice but to become followers of a stronger nation or join alliances by practicing bandwagoning, bigger and stronger nations, especially if they have long histories of independent statehood, try to avoid being controlled by outside powers. The worst-case scenario in situations when a hitherto dominant power perceives that there is a threat to its dominance is the so-called 'Thucydides trap'.

Writing about the Peloponnesian war that devastated the two leading city-states of Ancient Greece two and a half millennia ago, Athenian general and historian Thucydides explained: 'It was the rise of Athens and the fear that this instilled in Sparta that made war inevitable.' In his competent opinion, the main cause of the Peloponnesian war of 431-404 BC between Athens and Sparta was the change in the balance of power. The Harvard historian Allison Graham has analysed, in his recent study, sixteen cases of the change of the balance of power, out of which twelve, including the one between Sparta and Athens, ended in a military conflict. He observes: 'China and the United States are currently on a collision course for war — unless both parties take difficult and painful actions to avert it.'[129] Of course, this does not mean that a war between China and the US is inevitable, but today, like in previous changes of balance of power, attempts to artificially prevent the change that usually is based on, and conditioned by, certain long-term social and economic tendencies are wrought with the danger of violent conflicts. Mutual adjustments based on reciprocated compromises help the change be more or less peaceful. And the current change of the balance of power is inevitable since, as I will try to show below, the unipolar moment of the 1990s when there was only one superpower (hyper power, using the term proposed by Hubert Védrine) dominating the whole world, was an aberration in the history of geopolitics.

During last 5-6 years I have regularly participated in the Valdai Discussion Club meetings that had first get-together in 2001 at the lake Valdai, close to Veliky Novgorod. The main purpose of the Club is to promote a dialogue between Russian and international intellectual elites on foreign policy matters. Each year President Putin attends the main event of the Club that now takes place in the mountains near Sochi. There I have met many competent Russian, American, European, Chinese and other experts on international affairs and ex-top politicians such as Hamid Karzai, Dominique de Villepin or Tarja Halonen. Russian experts Sergei Karaganov, Fyodor Lukyanov and many others have become my good friends. Among the participants have always also been top Chinese experts and sometimes also top politicians such as Mrs Fu Ying, the former Chinese ambassador to the United Kingdom and Vice Minister of Foreign Affairs, currently serving as the chairperson of the Foreign Affairs Committee the National People's Congress, and Mr Yang Jiechi, State Councillor and member of the Politburo of the CCP, who formerly also served as Foreign Minister of China. These meetings as well as my frequent visits to China and my life-long interest in great-power relations, notwithstanding my small-country

---

[129] A. Graham, *Destined for War: can America and China escape Thucydides' Trap?* Scribe Publications Pty Ltd, Kindle Edition, 2017 (Kindle Location 45).

origins, have enflamed my curiosity in the current geopolitical restructuring between major poles – Beijing, Moscow, Washington and Europe.

British international relations theorist and diplomat Adam Watson, after studying various international systems over the past 2,500 years, once observed: 'Powers that find themselves able to lay down the law in a system in practice do so.'[130] However, there has been an exception to that rule and this exception was China. During most of its history China has led an isolationist or/and defensive foreign policy. Deng Xiaoping could rely on many wise rulers and philosophers of ancient China when he advised his colleagues to 'keep a low profile' while modernising the country. The construction of the Great Chinese Wall that started during the Qin Dynasty (221–206 BC), and was more or less finished under the Ming Dynasty (1368–1644), was meant to shield China from the raids of the Northern nomads and to protect the Silk Road trade. However, notwithstanding the Great Wall, one of the grandsons of Genghis Khan – Kublai Khan – conquered China and established the first foreign dynasty – the Yuan Dynasty – in the country (the second being the Manchu or Qing Dynasty established by Manchu tribes in 1644 that lasted until the end of imperial China in 1912). It is true that throughout most of its history China exercised some authority over various South-East Asian tributary states (today Vietnam, Korea, Burma etc.) that had pledged allegiance to the Middle Empire. However, according to Professor Brantly Womack of University of Virginia, the main purpose of such relationships was not domination but to guarantee for China peaceful frontiers. He writes about the tributary arrangements:

> 'Both sides want to end the conflict as long as their basic interests can be protected. Those of the larger side are that peace with the smaller side will not harm its security. It wants the smaller side to acknowledge the real power relationship that exists and to behave deferentially. Deference is not obedience—after all, the larger side has failed in its attempt to dominate. Rather, it is the implicit promise of the smaller side not to challenge the overall power relationship. The smaller side, meanwhile, requires recognition of its identity and interests. It needs assurance that the larger side will not again attempt to intrude and dominate. A mature asymmetric relationship can result from an exchange of deference for autonomy. The tributary system is, thus, a ritualized version of an exchange of deference

---

[130] A. Watson, *The Evolution of International Society* (Routledge, 1992), p. 291.

(coming to Beijing with tribute) for autonomy (granting seals of office and titles).'[131]

The greatest navigator of his time Admiral Zheng He (1371-1433) had made his seven overseas missions to the territories that today are Indonesia, Malaysia, India, countries of the Arabian Sea and reached Hormuz on the Persian Gulf as well as the Eastern African coast. Yet, under the Emperors Hongxi and Xuande of the Ming Dynasty such voyages were halted, and the gigantic ships of the great fleet were either burned or allowed to rot. Whether it was the need to concentrate forces to face the northern marauding nomadic hordes or Emperors' belief in self-sufficiency of Chinese economy (or the combination of these factors), this self-isolation of China played a role in the fall of the Chinese influence in Asia and eventually contributed to its semi-colonisation and humiliation by European powers in the nineteenth century. For whatever reasons, but China refused to extend its dominance while it was able to do that. However, this is rather an exception confirming the general rule explained by Adam Watson.

French politician and academician Alain Peyrefitte already in the 1970s warned against insulting China by spreading ideas (fake news) about the 'yellow peril' coming from the East. He wrote: 'If the Chinese have any claim to superiority, it is due to their belongingness to the nation that has never tried to conquer the world. During their four-thousand-year history they have never ventured beyond the natural limits of their civilisation.'[132] In illustration of Western policies vis-à-vis China, Peyrefitte quotes Kaiser William II, who, while sending German troops to China in 1900, had stated: 'Beijing has to be raised to the ground. This is the battle of Asia against the whole Europe that you must protect. No mercy, take no prisoners.'[133] The Chinese haven't forgotten that. The West needs to be reminded it, so as not to repeat the same mistakes.

It is only my guess, but it may indeed be so that current Chinese leadership, including President Xi Jinping, has learned lessons from this sad for China experience.

---

[131] B. Womack, Asymmetry and China's Tributary System, *The Chinese Journal of International Politics*, Volume 5, Issue 1, Spring 2012, Pages 37–54, https://doi.org/10.1093/cjip/pos003.
[132] A. Peyrefitte, Quand la Chine s'eveillera … le monde tremblera, Fayard, 1973, p. 447.
[133] Ibid.

Chinese Empire can be blamed for the destruction of the Dzhungar Khanate (also known as Oirats) that existed in the 17th and 18th centuries in the territories that today belong to the Chinese Xinjiang Autonomous Region, Kazakhstan and Kyrgyzstan. Dzhungars, waging constant wars both in the North-West against the Kazakh and Kyrgyz tribes and in the South-East against Qing's China, were finally destroyed by the Chinese onslaught in 1758.[134] Peter Perdue calls Qing China's policy towards Dzhungars 'genocide', though he adds that 'the use of massacre for ethnic extermination was also atypical of Qing policy either before or after this time.'[135]

In contradistinction to messianic and proselytising religions such as Christianity and Islam, Chinese religions – be it Confucianism (if it is a religion?) or Buddhism don't try to convert those with whom China interacts into their religion or ideology. Today's China is rather pragmatically taking care of its economic interests, especially through its new One Belt, One Road (OBOR) Initiative, using investments not only in Asia, but much further away, especially in Africa. Never, since the fifteenth century Ming dynasty's admiral Zheng He's navigations to far-away places, has Beijing been so active, not only in Asia but also on other continents.[136] And though China has mainly been interested in the mineral, agricultural and energy resources of those far-away places, Beijing is also participating in post-conflict reconstruction in African countries, helping them build infrastructure objects as well as special trade and economic cooperation zones, and China's terms of loans tend to be better than those from Western companies.[137] As Deborah Brautigam concludes, while 'Westerners support government and democracy; the Chinese build roads and dams. In so doing, China may wind up supporting some dictatorial and corrupt regimes, but – and this is an inconvenient truth – the West also supports such regimes when it advances its interests. And given the limits of the West's success in promoting development in Africa so far, perhaps Westerners should be less judgmental and more open-minded in assessing China's initiatives there.'[138] Zambian economist

---

[134] M.H. Abuseitova et al., *A History of Kazakhstan and Central Asia* (in Russian), Almaty, 2001, p. 302.
[135] P. Perdue, *China Marches West. The Qing Conquest of Central Eurasia*, The Belknap Press of Harvard University Press, 2005, p. 285.
[136] See, e.g., C. Aleden, Zhang Chun, B. Mariani, S. Large, 'China's Growing Role in African Post-Conflict Reconstruction,' Global Review (SIIS), 2012, No. 1; R.Baker, Zhixing Zhang, 'The Paradox of China's Naval Strategy,' Stratfor, 17 July 2012.
[137] D. Brautigam, 'Africa's Eastern Promise,' *Foreign Affairs online*, 5 January, 2010.
[138] *Ibid.*

and writer Dambisa Moyo observes: 'In 2009, China became Africa's largest trading partner. Chinese foreign direct investment (FDI) is also steadily increasing. In 2010, China's FDI in Zambia topped $1bn, creating 15,000 jobs, and estimates for 2011 have the figure above $2,4bn. In exchange for copper and other resources, China is providing Zambia with much needed capital investment, jobs, and infrastructure.'[139] Dr Moyo emphasises her first-hand experience of the positive impact that Chinese investment has had on her country, and she is astonished that Chinese investments in Africa have garnered so much criticism in Western media. As she points out, Chinese investments in Africa stand favourably against the Washington led invasions of other resource rich countries, such as Afghanistan and Iraq, in a bid to gain dominion over scarce resources.[140]

China's policies in the East and South China seas are not primarily economic, though this aspect is naturally present, but geopolitical – namely the 'access denial' strategies *vis-à-vis* the United States, whose 'pivot to Asia' is guided primarily by geopolitical considerations and aimed at the containment of China. Beijing's claims and actions in the South China Sea are not principally aimed at its overseas neighbours (Philippines, Vietnam, Brunei or Indonesia), and China does not intend to impede the freedom of navigation (it would only natural that it should be China, not the United States, that would guarantee this freedom in the South China Sea). The main objective behind Chinese claims in these seas and islets is to counter American military presence close to the Chinese mainland, which has the potential of becoming an existential threat for Beijing in case Washington tries to militarily contain China's rise that is not, and cannot be, limited to economic matters.

Without a global geopolitical approach to the study of the conflicting claims and developments in the South China Sea, it would indeed seem that at the core of these tensions are bilateral disputes between China and its South Asian neighbours. In such a scenario Washington may appear as an impartial mediator, concerned primarily with the peaceful resolution of these tensions and upholding the norms of the law of the sea, including the freedom of navigation. And Washington would very much like the situation to be seen in such a light. Yet, only by looking at the bigger picture can we see that the main contradiction,

---

[139] D. Moyo, 'If I Ruled the World: We need a global framework that follows China's lead,' *Prospect*, 12 July 2012, p. 6.
[140] *Ibid.*

though indeed bilateral, is not between China and its smaller neighbours, but between the rising China and the United States that is trying to contain and control this rise. The Chinese policy and activities in the South China Sea, such as militarising existing islands and creating new ones by dredging up sediments and dumping them upon the submerged shoals, thus turning them into islands which could then be claimed by China, is a response to the threatening presence of the American 7th Fleet close to the Chinese coastlines.

Jean-Yves Le Drian, the French Minister of Defence under François Hollande and the Foreign Minister under President Macron, writes that the 'denial of access' policy is one of those landmark evolutions that mark a change in the effectiveness of military power – change that favours non-Western countries *vis-à-vis* the militarily superior West. He writes: 'It is so already in the Baltic Sea and the Black Sea and in the seas surrounding the mainland of China, where local powers install sophisticated systems in order to make for Western countries the cost of the deployment of their forces, in case of crisis, prohibitively high.'[141] This observation is correct, but what can be wrong with the policies of 'access denial'? These are defensive measures in response to NATO's expansion to the borders of Russia and Washington's policy of containment of China, which are aimed at the perpetuation of American hegemony, especially if we also take account of the fact that in December 2019, at its Summit in London, the North Atlantic Alliance for the first time identified China as challenge to NATO. Be that as it may with the Washington's stance *vis-à-vis* Beijing and its recklessness of the dual containment of Russia and China, but Europeans have certainly better things to do than joining Washington's new crusade, this time against China. Can NATO's pivot to Asia be an answer to the rise of China? How can such a turn to Asia be even thinkable for the American allies in Europe? Are they ready to sacrifice their own interests for the sake of Washington's vain attempts to perpetuate its hegemony in the world? As if European nations haven't already enough suffered from the Washington led confrontation with Russia?

Beyond the situation in the South China Sea and Taiwan, China has other problems and vulnerabilities that Washington may exploit, or is already exploiting, in its efforts to slow down China's rise. As American experts Graham Fuller and Frederick Starr have written, 'it would be unrealistic to rule out categorically American willingness to play the "Uighur card" as a means of

---

[141] J-Y. Le Drian, *Qui est l'Ennemi?*, (Les éditions du Cerf, 2016) p. 379.

exerting pressure on China in the event of some future crisis or confrontation.'[142] Charles Horner also believes that, 'China's problems in Xingjian cannot but become a temptation for the United States if a future deterioration in Sino-American relations focuses attention on China's most deeply-seated structural weaknesses,'[143] And Washington has already yielded to this temptation by playing the Uighur card against China. However, by encouraging radical Islamist Uighurs in their separatist activities in Xinjiang province, Washington is committing the same mistake it did when supporting Islamists, fighting the Soviets in Afghanistan or the Assad government in Syria. From this support emerged Oussama bin Laden and Al Qaida. Today, there are thousands of Uighur fighters[144], under the banner of East Turkestan Islamic Movement (ETIM) or Turkestan Islamic Party in the ranks of the Islamic State in Syria (ISIS), who have 'pledged to return to China and "shed blood like rivers".'[145]

Claims that these are the Chinese authorities that are to be blamed for the Uighur terrorist attacks because of the repressions against the Muslims in Xinjian province of China, are reminiscent of allegations made by quite a few Muslims after the 9/11 attacks against the United States. They claimed that it was Washington, which had called the terror attacks upon themselves. Of course, counter-terrorism strategies may be, and often have been, ineffective or even counter-productive, but they are not the main cause of terrorism. The sweeping and indiscriminate criticism of Chinese counter-terrorist policies in Xinjiang targeting mostly Uighurs, are particularly inappropriate in the light of the inadequacy of Western anti-terrorist measures. The wars in Afghanistan, Iraq and Libya have fuelled, not quelled, terrorism and recent terror attacks in London, Amsterdam and particularly in France show that so far nobody has come up with an ideal anti-terrorist strategy. Why not, instead of always pointing at the speck in the Chinese or Russian eye while ignoring the beam in its own? Why

---

[142] Graham E. Fuller and S. Frederick Starr, *The Xingjian Problem, Central Asia-Caucasus Institute*, Paul H. Nitze School of Advanced International Studies, Silk Road Paper January 1, 2003, The Johns Hopkins University, p. 46.
[143] C. Horner, 'The Other Orientalisms. China's Islamist Problem,' The National Interest, No.67, Spring 2002, p. 45.
[144] See more in Colin P. Clarke, Paul Rexton Kan, 'Uighur Foreign Fighters: An Underexamined Jihadist Challenge,' International Centre for Counter-Terrorism, The Hague (DOI: 10.19165/2017.2.05).
[145] J. Moore, 'ISIS Fighters From China's Uighur Minority Vow to 'Shed Blood' at Home' https://www.newsweek.com/isis-fighters-chinas-uighur-minority-vow-shed-blood-home-562948.

not to coordinate anti-terrorist measures and to learn from each other, including from each other's mistakes?

I can say much less about Chinese domestic politics, economy and culture, since I must confess that I don't speak Chinese. Moreover, even if a foreigner speaks the language of a country, it doesn't yet mean that he understands its society, especially if it is China with its thousands of years of history, with the biggest population in the world and rapid changes that I have seen with my own eyes when from time-to-time visiting China. For example, if during my first visit to Xi'an twelve years earlier, it was necessary to fly from Beijing to the ancient capital of China, now there a comfortable bullet train that took me from Xi'an to the capital city. In 2007 there was no underground in Xi'an; today there are four comfortable lines open and new ones are on their way. Travelling by train from Xi'an to Yan'an, that is famous as the wartime stronghold of the Chinese communists from the mid-1930s until 1949, took seven hours in 2007; in 2019 – my journey to the same area lasted slightly more than two hours. China is visibly changing and for the better. Moreover, and most importantly, Chinese people are optimistic about their future that is a rare commodity in today's world. This is what I see and feel. However, I would comment on an aspect that is more familiar for me and that could be called 'comparative studies of democracy.'

Bulgarian political scientist and one of the prominent European intellectuals, Ivan Krastev in 2013 published an article with an intriguing and provocative title: '*Is China more democratic than Russia?*'[146] His general conclusion was that notwithstanding the presence of most formal attributes of democracy in Russia and their virtual absence in China's political system, in substance the latter was nevertheless more democratic. In coming to such a conclusion Krastev relies on five criteria – power rotation, listening to the people, tolerance of opposition and dissent, recruitment of elites, and experimentation. It is necessary to note that Krastev's article was written and published just shortly after Xi Jinping had come to power. Therefore, it may be that today he would review some of his arguments and conclusions. So, in the 2019 book *The Light that Failed*, co-authored by Ivan Krastev and Stephen Holmes, we may read about 'the Chinese economic miracle, orchestrated by a political leadership that is unapologetically neither liberal nor democratic.'[147]

---

[146] I. Krastev, 'Is China more democratic than Russia,' *Open Democracy*, 12 March 2013.
[147] I. Krastev, S. Holmes, *The Light that Failed: Reckoning,* Penguin, 2019, p. 1.

In the West, Xi Jinping's ascent has been associated with the increase of authoritarian tendencies inside the country and assertiveness in its foreign policy. Chinese foreign policy, especially its activities in the South China Sea, differs from Deng's 'keeping the low profile,' though not abandoning the other maxim 'crossing the river by feeling the stones.' Most importantly and in contradistinction with other great or even not so great powers, China is not involved in any military adventure abroad. It is natural that together with the considerable rise of Chinese economy, its foreign policy is also becoming more active or proactive. What in the West is seen as rising authoritarianism, in the country is accepted, at least by most of the people, as the fight against corruption and the increase of the discipline. I have personally experienced these changes. First, the traffic that a decade ago was chaotic in all big cities, has become much more orderly. Drivers stop at zebra crossings to let the pedestrians through; the practice almost unheard of a decade ago. Lavish dinners offered by heads of universities or think tanks, that I also enjoyed a few times during my first longer stay in China, have gone. Moreover, bureaucrats have become more effective and polite. Although too much paperwork may be still needed to have things done, they are now done much quicker than before. Most Chinese I have spoken to are content that things are done quicker and better; the middle-class Chinese like to have bigger apartments, better cars (all university teachers have their own cars, often more than one in the family) and try to give the best available education to their children. Yes, there is no freedom of expression in China and there is a significant minority of Chinese, who are suffering because of that. Is it necessary to have the freedom of expression curbed in order to increase discipline and high economic growth? In Estonia, France or Great Britain certainly not and it would be counter-productive and even difficult to do. About China, I am not so sure. Even the brutal suppression of the peaceful manifestation of students in 1989 on Tiananmen Square in Beijing was not only, or maybe even not so much, about democracy *versus* authoritarianism, as about possible chaos (what the authorities are most afraid of, due to the Chinese historical experience) *versus* the continuation of economic reforms. China is not the only society where the choice is not limited to these two opposites – liberal democracy or authoritarianism. Chaos, anarchy, civil war or Islamic fundamentalism are plausible outcomes for quite a few of them.

Ivan Krastev's writings are often witty and imaginative. This also applies to the article, I mentioned above. It contains some original and true ideas as well as insightful observations. However, there is, in my opinion, also a deep underlying paradigmatic, what I would call a Hegelian-Marxist-Fukuyamian (in the sense of his end of history and last man concept), fallacy in his reasoning. His comparison of perspectives of democracy in China and Russia is based on the premise that the whole world and each country is, at least potentially, evolving in the same direction, passing through more or less the same stages towards the inevitable triumph of liberal democracy (for Marxists it was the ultimate victory of communism). As Marx said: 'The country that is more developed industrially only shows, to the less developed, the image of its own future.' [148] This observation is only partly true.

The basic assumption of Krastev's arguments is that the more democratic is a society, the more it corresponds to the Western liberal-democratic ideal, the more advanced it is and the better it is for the people. If in many cases such an assumption is true, in other situations it reflects wishful thinking with serious negative consequences, if attempts are made to act upon such thinking. A comparison of China and Russia in terms of their conformity to Western liberal democratic standards shows the inadequacy of such a general yardstick. As I will try to explain below, in some cases (e.g., China) such a yardstick may not be at all adequate, while in different situations (e.g., Russia), attempts to quickly squeeze societies that are not (yet) ready for the realisation of such standards result in inevitable backlashes.

In comparing China and Russia, Krastev found that notwithstanding the presence of many formal signs of democracy in Russia (regular multiparty elections, the existence of opposition media etc.), in substance China 'is arguably more democratic than Russia' since the ruling Chinese Communist Party (CCP) better understands, cares more and more effectively responds to what people want (fortunately, Krastev does not add to that, as is almost invariably done in the West, that this responsiveness is only due to the desire of the CCP to stay indefinitely in power), though 'neither country can satisfy the minimalist definition of democracy, i.e. competitive elections with uncertain outcomes.' However, already here we see a contradiction that cannot be resolved within the chosen paradigm. If neither China nor Russia satisfy even a minimalist definition

---

[148] *Karl Marx (2007). 'Capital: A Critique of Political Economy - The Process of Capitalist Production,' p.13, Cosimo, Inc. Author's prefaces to the First Edition. - Das Kapital (Buch I) (1867)*

of democracy, is it at all possible to assert that one of them is more democratic than the other?

China and Russia, notwithstanding comparable sizes of their territories and their common communist pasts, have very different societies and therefore it would be wrong to gauge them with the same general measurements (of course, it is possible to measure their respective GDP growths and other specific quantifiable details). Or to put it otherwise, such yardsticks have to be so general that their usefulness becomes questionable. To put it briefly and therefore also a bit simplistically, Russia is a European country, even if we add the qualification 'sort of', since due to her history, the great power status and even geography, Russia may not easily fit into a concept of Europe based mostly on the relatively recent evolution of the Western part of the continent. China is not simply an Asian country (it is obvious that Asian societies are rather different); China is, using Professor Weiwei Zhang's characterization, a civilizational state, governance of which 'can only be based mainly on its own methods shaped by its own traditions and culture.'[149] And as Professor Zhang emphasises: 'It is unimaginable that most Chinese would ever accept the so-called multi-party democratic system with a change of central government every four years.'[150] Of course, never say never, but looking from outside (even while being inside) I cannot imagine the political system of China even remotely resembling, say, that of France or Finland. Assuming impossible that somebody would try to impose, whether from outside or even from inside, something like that on China, then today's Brexit or even the collapse of the Soviet Union in 1991 would seem as relatively insignificant events. Negative impacts of such a foolhardy attempt would be felt all over the world.

However, the world is not devoid of self-righteous do-gooders or simpletons that may believe that everything is possible. Georges Malbrunot, a French journalist, in an article on Iran, quotes an anonymous Iranian intellectual, who deplores that, unfortunately, President Rohani of Iran 'is not Iranian Gorbachev; at best he could become our Deng Xiaoping.'[151] There is something disturbingly distorted in the idea that Michael Gorbachev had been a more successful reformer than China's Deng Xiaoping. One need only to compare today's China and Russia, and their respective economies and influences in the world (especially if we take also into account also their respective

---

[149] Zhang Weiwei, *The China Wave. The Rise of a Civilizational State*, World Century Publishing Corporation, 2012, p. 59.
[150] *Ibid.*, p. 60.
[151] G. Malbrunot, 'En Iran, Hassan Rohani sous pression,' *Le Figaro*, 26 November 2015.

starting positions). Such a mind-set goes against simple logic, to say nothing of a deeper comparative analysis of Deng's and Gorbachev's reforms and, specifically, their results. Such a myopia may be explained by the dominant narrative, mostly Anglo-American in origin, which claims that there is only one correct way of life, one adequate political and economic system – liberal democracy and free markets.

The last quarter of the twentieth century produced two leaders – Deng Xiaoping of China and Michael Gorbachev of the Soviet Union, whose policies not only changed the history of their countries, but also transformed geopolitical structures of the whole world. The West did wholeheartedly welcome Gorbachev, whose policies led to the collapse of the "evil empire." At the same time, it is becoming increasingly worried about Deng's legacy, which has made China an economic superpower claiming now an adequate place under the Sun. So, one of the August 2018 issues of *The Economist*, which was mostly devoted to China's rise and its Belt and Road Initiative (BRI), considered this initiative, if not yet 'a frontal challenge,' then at least a test to the Western-led 'rules-based liberal order.'[152] Why such a strange welcoming of reforms that failed, while being worried about those that have succeeded beyond expectations? Maybe the answer is hidden in the words 'beyond expectation'?

Of course, to change a society to such an extent that it also has global effects, one needs not only an extraordinary (not necessarily always in a positive sense of the word) man or woman at the helm of the State but also a big enough country to experiment with. It seems that recently it may have been the presidency of Donald Trump in the USA that has shaken the country and the world. Although American economy under him was doing fine, the growth rates were much higher than in Europe and the jobless numbers were also much lower than in the Old Continent (until the COVID-19 hit the world), benefitting from it were mainly those who have always been better off. However, the coming to power of Donald Trump, a person extraordinary mainly in his extravagance, has done a good job in exposing the controversies and antagonisms of the American society. The fact that something like that is also happening in Europe, shows that Donald Trump was not so much a cause of the current turmoil but rather a catalyst that accelerated the coming of the unavoidable crisis that may be followed by recovery. It is the controversy and antagonism between liberal elites and conservatives, of which much more in following chapters.

---

[152] *The Economist, July 28th – August 3d 2018.*

Trump has indeed deeply disturbed the anthill of American domestic as well as international politics so that not only Democrats but also many Republicans openly rebelled against their President. What such an infight has revealed is, first, that there have never been significant differences between Democratic and Republican elites. Hillary Clinton, epitomising the corrupt politics of the Democrats, lost the 2016 presidential elections not because of some foreign interference but because the rift between the political elite and the American people had become all too obvious. Externally, she has been a perfect example of those 'liberal interventionists' who differ too little from the 'neocons' who were running the show under the Republican presidency of George W. Bush. Therefore, the enlightened worldview of Barack Obama and basic instincts of Donald Trump on foreign affairs are on many issues (though not on all) closer than foreign policy preferences of those like Hillary Clinton. Equally, or even more, Trump's unpredictable and erratic foreign policy steps made it clear to some American allies that blindly following the self-proclaimed leader of the 'free world' is not necessarily good for them. His politically incorrect tweets and statements forced those who fight him either on Capitol Hill or in the liberal media to leave behind their own political correctness, which has, like Orwell's doublespeak, so far rather effectively covered the true face of American elites.

Is it possible that Trump's presidency could be a blip in the American history and things would return to 'business as usual'? Hardly so. Although Trump's presidency did not extend for more than the four years allocated to him by the voters, his legacy could be felt for many years ahead. In that respect, one would wonder what Henry Kissinger had in mind when in the summer 2018 interview to *The Financial Times* he somewhat enigmatically opined: 'I think Trump may be one of those figures in history who appears from time to time to mark the end of an era and to force it to give up its old pretences. It doesn't necessarily mean that he knows this, or that he is considering any great alternative. It could just be an accident.'[153] These words of the grand consigliere of American diplomacy could lead one to reflect on whether Donald Trump would be an American Deng or an American Gorbachev.

Donald Trump, or rather his role and legacy in history, notwithstanding all their personal differences, may be rather like that of Gorbachev, not at all that of Deng Xiaoping. Both Deng and Gorbachev at some point understood that 'business as usual' would be disastrous to their respective countries. Professor

---

[153] *The Financial Times*, 20 July 2018.

Weiwei Zhang of Fudan University, who used to be Deng Xiaoping's interpreter, told me that after the May 1989 meeting in Beijing with Michael Gorbachev, the Chinese paramount leader had, in the circle of his advisers, characterised the Soviet leader as naïve and weak. With hindsight, I tend to agree with this characterisation. Gorbachev understood that the Soviet political and economic model was not viable and had to be reformed. In that he bears a resemblance to Deng Xiaoping, who had come a decade earlier to a similar conclusion about the Chinese system. But here the similarities end.

Deng knew what he wanted and slowly but surely, sometimes using ruthless means and methods (e.g., pitilessly suppressing the 1989 Tiananmen Square protests), moved towards the goal of making China great again. Although the desire of the Tiananmen Square protestors for democracy and liberties may have been quite genuine, it was also naïve. Even if the authorities wouldn't have crashed the demonstration, even if they had tried to satisfy all the demands of the students, the chances of having liberal democracy in China would have equalled to zero. However, one thing would have been certain: it would have heralded the end of the economic growth of China.

Gorbachev, on the contrary, rather naively believed in the possibility of the Swedish-style socialism in the Soviet Union and in the sincerity of American promises not to move NATO an inch to the East. Gorbachev's nemesis Boris Yeltsin continued, in the 1990s, his predecessor's policies in the diminished borders of the Russian Federation, creating a country ruled by oligarchs, where the majority of people had become even poorer than they had been under the Soviet system.

Trump, being a ruthless, wily and ruse businessman, was nevertheless rather naïve in politics and ignorant in the world affairs. And this, notwithstanding his some rather good instincts that could be due, at least partly, to the very fact of being a novice in politics, particularly in the world affairs. What is NATO for, if the Cold War had been declared to be over; why to continue seeing Russia as an existential threat, while it is China that is threatening the American dominance the world; aren't uncontrolled migration and the rise of Islamist extremism becoming global problems? Of course, foreign policy based on personal instincts has necessarily its flip side. In international relations it is expressed, for example, in the US withdrawal from the Paris climate agreement as well from the Joint Comprehensive Plan of Action (JCPOA), signed by the five permanent members of the Security Council plus Germany with Iran.

If these were only the erratic decisions and tweets of the 45th President of the United States that disturb the American as well as the whole Western mainstream, Trump's impact would not be so great. Trump's acts and utterances were amplified by the feverish hostility of his opponents in the Congress and mainstream media. They had learned nothing from their failure to continue business as usual, expressed, *inter alia,* in the 2016 presidential elections. If Trump has turned the country, and to some extent even the world, upside down, his opponents, to get rid of their hated enemy, have been ready to tear down their own house. Moreover, in their frenzy they did not care about endangering international peace. As American political scientist Micah Zenko wrote in the article *Democrats Will Regret Becoming the Anti-Russia Party*: 'When a political party increases its animus towards a foreign country – believing that this will enhance its own popularity – it introduces second-order effects that can manifest themselves years later. It creates a voting bloc of Americans who become socialised to hate a foreign government and, by extension, its citizens. It reduces the motivations and complexities of that government to a simplified caricature of anti-Americanism or just plain evil. More broadly, it engenders hostility between the United States and foreign countries, which makes cooperation over shared problems difficult and rapprochement unimaginable.'[154] Hopefully, this dangerous infight may clear the ground for new people, who may be able to adopt policies, both for the country as well as in international relations, that differ from those of Donald Trump as well as from those of his fieriest opponents amongst the American political and media elites.

Therefore, Trump, like Gorbachev, can, using the insight of Henry Kissinger, 'mark the end of an era and to force it to give up its old pretences.' Like Gorbachev, he had no vision and no time for building something new that would correspond to the requirements of the American society that indeed has great potential. Like Gorbachev, Trump did not know what he was doing and what his legacy would be. Repeating what the clear-minded and great American elderly statesman, quoted above, said: 'It doesn't necessarily mean that he knows this, or that he is considering any great alternative. It could just be an accident.'

Of course, whatever Trump's legacy, the United States will not disintegrate as the Soviet Union did. USSR's collapse had much deeper causes than Gorbachev's naivety. However, as Gorbachev, not intending what he achieved,

---

[154] M. Zenco, 'Democrats Will Regret Becoming the Anti-Russia Party,' *Foreign Policy,* July 24, 2018.

cleared the way for the rebirth of Russia and re-configurated the geopolitical map of the world that had outlived its 'use by' date, so may Trump's policies accelerate the coming of a world, where a balance between different centres – America, China, Europe, Russia and potentially some others – will, sooner rather than later, replace the historical anomaly where one centre tries to control the whole world. Below, I will return to the geopolitical role of Europe. Here I would like to emphasise that a world without China or Russia is impossible, while a world against China or Russia is suicidal.

In my opinion, 'the minimalist definition of democracy,' about which Ivan Krastev writes, has nothing to do with China. While the European standards of liberal democracy could be *mutatis mutandis* applicable in Russia, they may be completely inadequate in measuring China's progress or lack of it. China is not more democratic than Russia, especially if one uses Western standards of liberal democracy for measurement, but China is better governed, she has made incomparable progress in boosting the betterment of the lives of the Chinese people, and notwithstanding all her problems, the Chinese people look to the future more optimistically than many other nations. As one of my former Chinese students in London, who is now professor back in China, recently told me: 'We have many problems, but the Chinese people have never lived so well as they live today.'

Ivan Krastev correctly, in my opinion, puts China above Russia on such criteria as recruitment of elites or power rotation, but these criteria have very little, if anything, to do with democracy. They are elements of meritocratic governance based on the Chinese Confucian legacy. 'In China,' write Nicolas Berggruen and Nathan Gardels, 'the idea of "elevating the worthy" to positions of power despite pedigree can be traced back to the Warring states period of 453-221 BC.'[155] Yan Xuetong, analysing writings of pre-Qin dynasty (i.e. the Spring and Autumn and the Warring states period) classics, concludes that 'competition for talent is not a phenomenon peculiar for the knowledge economy but rather is the essence of competition among great powers.'[156] In that respect China is different not only from Russia but also, from, say, the United States of America or European liberal democracies. This is not to say that China is better than the US or the US is better than China in terms of their respective governances. They

---

[155] N. Berggruen, N. Gardles, *Intelligent Governance for the 21st Century. A Middle Way between West and East*, Polity, 2013.

[156] Yan Xuetong, *Ancient Chinese Thought, Modern Chinese Power*, Princeton University Press, 2011, p. 66.

simply represent different models of societal development, and though their respective effectiveness can be compared (in a dynamic perspective this comparison favours China), it would be wrong for the US to try to imitate China or for China to try to resemble to the United States, though certain 'borrowing' from one another may be advisable and shouldn't be a one-way – from the West to the East - street. To prosper China may well become, in some important respects (more market and personal freedoms, less governmental control), more like the US while the latter may well have to borrow from the Chinese experience to deal with acute problems such as short-termism, populism and money-based influence of special interest groups. Moreover, due to the legalised role of money in the politics of even some highly developed liberal democracies (huge election contributions, lobbing and revolving door practices), their political systems are not less corrupt than those of some non-democracies. As Berggruen and Gardels observe: 'Western democracy is no more self-correcting than China's system. In a mirror image of China's challenge, one-person-one-vote electoral democracy embedded in a consumer culture of immediate gratification is also headed for terminal decay unless it reforms.'[157]

Therefore, it doesn't make much sense to compare Russia's social and political systems to those of China. It would be more useful to compare Russia – a European country – to other European states. In that respect we could indeed speak of a democracy deficit in Russia, as well as the presence of formal democratic institutions without much substance. These are also the conclusions drawn by Ivan Krastev, since he uses Western, not Chinese, criteria when comparing Russia and China. In my opinion, one would be justified in defining Russia either as a fledgling democracy or democracy with authoritarian tendencies or as an authoritarian state with elements of democracy. Of course, Russia is much more liberal than China and this, once again, has little to do with the fact that Russia is also more democratic.

On a more general note, one should be cautioned against asserting that phenomena such as liberalism and democracy carry the same universal value always and everywhere, or that they could be used as a common yardstick to measure progress or the lack of it in hugely differing societies. Equally, it is important to caution against confusing these values with different phenomena that are quite opposite to both liberalism and democracy, though they may have some superficial similarities to them – those of chaos and anarchy. Richard

---

[157] Berggruen, Gardels, *op.cit.*, p. 9.

Sakwa has made a pertinent comment on attempts to assess levels of democracy in Russia by comparing the incomparable: 'This regime inspection reached the height of absurdity with the annual Freedom House "Freedom in the World" survey, which in the 2007 version judged Russia to be as unfree as the Congo, ignoring entirely the social and political context in which the various freedoms operate and vastly differing levels of effective governance.'[158]Trying to find out whether the Democratic Republic of Congo is more democratic, less democratic or as democratic as Russia simply doesn't make any sense.

If we want to have a more general, more universal criterion for ranking states, measuring their progress or regress, it shouldn't be democracy but rather governance or governability, i.e. the yardstick should be good governance. In that respect China is indeed ahead of Russia and many other countries, quite a few of which could be considered democratic, or even liberal-democratic. Yu Keping argues that 'good governance will be the most important source of political legitimacy for human society in the twenty-first century.'[159] Such a prediction seems quite reasonable. Of course, good governance is not opposed to democracy. On the contrary, in many societies it is an important element or feature of a well-governed society, an important element of governmental legitimacy. But efficiency, stability and the rule of law are even more important characteristics, since they are more substantial criteria in comparison with 'the minimalist definition of democracy.' It is also important to note that in the West it was the rule of law that preceded democracy and served to make the latter sustainable. Today, in many non-Western societies we see how imported superficial features of democracy acquire distorted, even ugly forms that do not, and in my opinion even cannot, lead to the emergence of the rule of law. If democracy is mainly a procedural characterization of society's status, good governance, whose important aspect and element is the rule of law, is a much more substantial and richer criterion. Or to put is differently, without being underpinned by the rule of law, efficient governance and social stability, formal democratic institutions, which may be relatively easily imported, not only remain formal but they are not sustainable either. Having stayed in China for rather long periods, I can feel that China is considerably more collectivistic that Russia or other European countries. I believe that the famous Chinese hotpot, where

---

[158] R. Sakwa, 'New Cold War' or twenty years of crisis? Russia and international politics, 253 *International Affairs* 84: 2 (2008) 241-267.
[159]Yu Keping, 'Good Governance and Legitimacy,' in *China's Search for Good Governance* (Deng Zhenglai, Sujian Guo eds.), Palgrave Macmillan, 2011, p. 16.

different dishes are shared around a big table among many eaters and cooked in the same big pot on the table, being quite different from Western restaurants, where everybody orders his own dishes, well characterises distinctions between Chinese and Western societies.

When at the end of the 1980s, the Soviet Union as a whole and its biggest part – Russia embarked on the perestroika and glasnost reforms, Soviet intellectuals, as the main opinion-formers, being essentially European in their outlook, would not have backed a politically authoritarian model of economic modernisation. In China, on the contrary, intellectuals were supportive of Deng Xiaoping's model of economic modernisation under the leadership of the Chinese Communist Party. One of the important differences between China's and the Soviet Union's reforms and factors contributing to their respective success and failure has been analysed by Allen Lynch of the University of Virginia. At the end of his insightful article on the comparison of Deng's and Gorby's reforms, Lynch proposes an interesting, and in my opinion, useful counterfactual thought-experiment that may be of more general interest.[160] What would have happened had Yuri Andropov, a former long-time KGB chief, who became the Secretary General of the Soviet Communist Party after Brezhnev's death in 1982, been in better health and hadn't died after less than two years in office (Lynch is probably right that had Deng Xiaoping died soon after he started his reforms, China today wouldn't have been today's China). Lynch correctly, in my opinion, assumes that Andropov, in contradistinction to Gorbachev, would not have relinquished the leading role of the Communist Party, and would not have initialised political liberalisation of Soviet society. Lynch is also right that Andropov garnered more authority not only among the political and military elite, but also among Soviet society at large (the clear exception being a substantial part of the Soviet intelligencia) than Gorbachev. And Andropov certainly was enough of a realist; having been for a long time at the head of the KGB, he certainly knew the real situation in the country better than most in the Soviet leadership, and certainly better than most world leaders. Therefore, it is quite possible that Andropov's economic reforms would have borne some fruit, and the Soviet Union could have existed far longer than it did under Gorbachev.

However, I am sure that the Soviet Union under Andropov would not have been the same success story as China has been under Deng and his successors.

---

[160] A. C. Lynch, 'Deng's and Gorbachev's Reform Strategies Compared,' *Russia in Global Affairs*, 24 June 2012.

The reasons for such a conclusion, once again, lie mainly in the differences between the Chinese and Soviet societies (the USSR and Russia as its biggest part – a European country, China – an Asian nation with millennia of continuous statehood; China – a more or less homogeneous society, the USSR – a multi-ethnic, multi-religious country; the USSR – an urbanised, industrially developed society, China at the end of the 1970s – basically a rural, agricultural society etc.) as well as the differences between the personalities of the two men. If Deng was a visionary pragmatist who well understood his people and society, Yuri Andropov was an ideologue, though cleverer, more knowledgeable and personally less corrupt than most of his colleagues, but for him the colour of the cat was even more important than its ability to catch the mice. He was an ideologue who believed in the eventual superiority of the communist system, whose worldview was not shaken, but on the contrary, strengthened as a result of the Soviet suppression of the Hungarian revolt of 1956 against the communist rule and the Soviet domination, when Andropov was the Soviet Ambassador to Budapest.

Boris Yeltsin, in August of 1991, standing firm against the putschists, later used the proper lexicon necessary to be liked by many in the West. However, it was not so much democracy that emerged under President Yeltsin (though elements of it were of course present) as the oligarchisation of society, and a process of plundering Russia's wealth.[161] That is why what is often described in the West as a backlash against democracy under President Putin has to be seen in the context of what happened in Russia under Yeltsin, and to a great extent as a reaction to these processes. Nor have Western policies towards Russia helped the latter become more liberal and democratic. On the contrary, Russia's turn towards more conservative values is partly due to the Western policies *vis-à-vis* Russia, Western attempts to 'civilise' Russia, to make it follow the American lead.

There are signs that the developing China is also becoming more democratic. However, this doesn't at all mean either that she will evolve towards a Western style liberal-democracy or that she will become more accommodating to Western interests; China's democracy would certainly be democracy with Chinese characteristics. Russia, on the contrary, should give much more substance to her

---

[161] The process of the pillaging of Russia has been well documented in Pavel Khlebnikov's book *Godfather of the Kremlin and the History of Pillage of Russia*, which in English translation carries the title *Godfather of the Kremlin: The Decline of Russia in the Age of Gangster Capitalism* (Harvest Books, 2001).

formal democratic institutions, i.e. her progress could indeed be measured using benchmarks of Western style liberal democracy, although here a caveat is necessary. In carrying out her reforms, Russia should try to avoid the shortcomings of Western style democracy that have become especially obvious in the light of the on-going financial and economic crisis, and particularly in comparison with the efficiency of the Chinese responses to contemporary challenges. As Frances Fukuyama, who has been able and courageous enough to learn from the recent history and has left behind his simplistic in substance, though sophisticated in form, ideas of the 1990s observes: 'Many people currently admire the Chinese system not just for its economic record but also because it can make large, complex decisions quickly, compared with the agonizing policy paralysis that has struck both the United States and Europe in the past few years.'[162] Hence, Russia should learn from China too, though not necessarily from its democracy with Chinese characteristics.

---

[162] F. Fukuyama, 'The Future of History. Can Liberal Democracy Survive the Decline of the Middle Class,' *Foreign Affairs,* January/February 2012.

15- On Contemporary Revolutionary Situations in the World

At the end of the 1980s, together with Professor Lori Damrosch of Columbia University, I led a group of American and Soviet international lawyers to work on a joint project to bridge gaps between the US and Soviet approaches to international law. Being then young and enthusiastic, we chose only those scholars from both countries, who had not been tainted by the Cold War rhetoric. Our project ended with a book entitled *Beyond Confrontation: International Law for the Post-Cold War Era* (Westview Press, Bolder, 1995). We really believed in the end of confrontation and were ready to offer our small contribution to the cause that the Cold War would never raise its ugly head and that international law, instead of power-politics, would prevail in relations between states. Why the hopes for a world without great-power confrontations did not realise, why is there a new cold war brewing?

My shortest and the most general answer to this question is that since the end of the 1980s the world is passing through two interrelated revolutionary situations. Such situations, by definition, put strains on all kinds of normative systems, including law and morality, since, as being *normative* phenomena, they function well in circumstances that could be called *normal*. In revolutionary periods in any society – be it, say, in France at the end of the Eighteenth century, or in Russia at the beginning of the Twentieth, when normalcy was an exception and expediency ruled, law always broke down and even morality lost its guiding force. In that respect, the international society is not an exception.

The first revolutionary change is geopolitical. Starting from about the end of the 1980s the world entered into a period of radical geopolitical transformation. It started with the collapse of the rather stable bipolar system, going then through a unipolar moment of the 1990s and is moving today towards some kind of multipolarity. Until the 'revolutionary dust' settles down, one way or other, and new 'normalcy' emerges (*or the old* returns, though much less plausible scenario) it is difficult to expect that international law could function 'normally.'

The second revolutionary transformation, not unrelated to the first, is the crisis of liberal democracy that was meant to triumph after the failure, at the end of the 1980s, of its main ideological rival. After the collapse of the Soviet Union and the bi-polar world, it seemed to many that it was exactly liberal democracy that had triumphed and would continue to flourish until the whole world would become the same. However, the disappearance of the main enemy started revealing, though not immediately, internal contradictions of liberal democracy. As it usually happens, rare early warnings remained unheard. It was more than twenty years ago when Richard Rorty published a small book *Achieving our Country*, where he wrote that the American liberal left, concentrating on the rights of ethnic, racial, religious, cultural and sexual minorities, had neglected the widening gap between the rich and the poor. At some point, Rorty warned, 'something will crack. The nonsuburban electorate will decide that the system has failed and start looking around for a strongman to vote for—someone willing to assure them that, once he is elected, the smug bureaucrats, tricky lawyers, overpaid bond salesmen, and postmodern professors will no longer be calling the shots.'[163] Sounds eerily familiar and up to date, doesn't it? Rorty considered himself to belong to the category of liberal left, though as one of the brightest representatives of American pragmatism, he couldn't be branded a post-modern professor. And differently from many, if not from most, he did not ridicule, deplore or detest those who were different, but tried to understand them.

What happened in November 2016 across the Atlantic should have been enlightening also for Europe, not only for America. However, it seems that the American liberal left, like their ilk in Europe, hasn't learned much after the victory of Donald Trump. Indicative in that respect is an article in the French left-leaning *Libération*, published after President Trump's 2018 *The State of the Union Address*. The correspondent of the newspaper was listening to Trump's speech in Berkeley's bingo – the stronghold of American liberalism. He sympathised with the liberal crowd in this watering hole that found Trump's speech 'shameful, sad and disheartening.' They were all laughing and toasting with bottoms up every phrase they found particularly objectionable or idiotic. The French paper highlights the words of Berkeley's scientist – certain Alex – who, in his words, had come to this bingo to 'laugh with likeminded rather than

---

[163] R. Rorty, *Achieving Our Country*, (Harvard University Press, 1997), 90.

cry alone at home.'[164] These words reminded me the famous maxim of Baruch Spinoza: 'non ridere, non lugere, neque detestere, sed intelligere' (don't ridicule, don't deplore, don't detest, but try to understand). Although I too found many things in Trump's 2018 Address (like his many other statements or acts) objectionable, especially on matters of international relations and geopolitics, laughing or deploring won't help. And particularly important for those in America, who are critical of, even hysterical about, Donald Trump, would be to understand that it was mainly due to them that Trump won, not so much thanks to those 'losers and ill-informed' or much advertised Russian interference in the American 2016 presidential elections. Spending months trying to impeach Trump, his domestic adversaries only weakened the political system of the country. Moreover, trying to divert attention from deep structural divides in American society and accusing Russia of meddling into American elections, Trump's distractors are also jeopardising peace and security in the world.

Globalisation that was welcomed not only as a *conditio sine qua non* for the worldwide economic growth, but also as vehicle for the spread of ideas and practices of liberal democracy, started, soon after the collapse of the Soviet Union, showing its less attractive side. The invention and the spread of the Internet, worldwide web and the assent of social media, that were all meant to undermine authoritarian regimes, soon turned against liberal elites that had had dominant positions in the so-called traditional media – radio, TV and mainstream newspapers and journals. The globalisation, from which liberal elites in Western democracies benefited and who therefore wholeheartedly welcomed it, soon revealed its negative aspects. Those masses that hadn't reaped benefits of globalisation and were left behind, found in social media that was not controlled by liberal elites, an outlet through which to reveal their grievances and mobilise. Their cause was immediately picked up by those who became known as populist leaders, like Donald Trump, Boris Johnson, Marine Le Pen or Matteo Salvini. Probably, these two phenomena – the globalisation of economy and financial markets and the rise of information technology – are the two sides of the same coin, contributing to the crisis of liberal democracy and turning against their progenitors.

The first of these revolutionary changes – the shift in the balance of power – started at the end of the 1980s with the changes in the Soviet Union. Since then,

---

[164] R. Duchesness, 'Discours sur l'état de l'Union de Trump : « Honteux, triste, décourageant »', *Libération*, 31 janvier, 2018.

it has already passed through several stages and is far from over. This is a period that may be compared, say, with the end of the Roman Empire and emergence of the medieval European international system of multi-layered authority where the Pope in Rome (or in Avignon), the Emperor of the Holy Roman Empire of the German Nation (all the wrong nouns and adjectives, but nevertheless something tangible) and various kings, dukes and minor princes vied for the better place under the Sun, the period that ended with the conclusion of the Westphalian peace of 1648, thereby marking an end of the religious wars in Europe and leading to the emergence the European system of sovereign states, and also of international law as it is understood, in its main features, until today. However, as historical processes have significantly accelerated since those bygone years, today's revolutionary changes also happen much faster.

Until 1989, for those who believe that the fall of the Berlin Wall was the most seminal event, or until the end of the 1991, for those who consider the collapse of the Soviet Union to be the greatest landmark and the most important symbol of the beginning of the new era, we all lived in the relatively stable bipolar world. The period of the end of the 1980s and beginning of the 1990s was like a socio-political earthquake that shook the whole world. It seemed that Francis Fukuyama, who had declared the end of history, had been right after all. Even many of those, who were rather critical of Fukuyama and his quite convoluted, if not Marxist then at least Hegelian, methodology, were themselves nevertheless covert Fukuyamians. So, in their otherwise interesting, balanced and forward-looking article two American professors, Daniel Deudney and G. John Ikenberry, observed that 'Just as the Nazis envisioned a "new order" for Europe and the Soviet Union designed an interstate economic and political order, so, too, did the liberal West.' So far, so good and it is true that liberal democratic thought and Marxist ideas are both of Western origin. However, using also the same method that the Marxists had used, these two American professors came to the optimistic conclusion that, '[T]he foreign policy of the liberal states should continue to be based on the broad assumption that there is ultimately *one path to modernity* [emphasis added] – and that it is essentially liberal in character,' and that 'liberal states should not assume that history has ended, but they can still be certain that it is on their side.'[165] This is only a slightly modified and moderated

---

[165] D. Deudney and G. John Ikenberry, 'The Myth of the Autocratic Revival. Why Liberal Democracy Will Prevail,' *Foreign Affairs*, January–February 2009.

version of the deterministic, unilineal and unidirectional Hegelian, Marxian and Fukuyamian end of the history way of thinking.

Like Marxists had tried to accelerate the coming of the promised land of socialism and communism, so did liberal democrats. Like Ernesto Che Guevara was trying to foment a leftist rebellion in the jungles of Bolivia (I am using particularly this example since in parallel with writing I am also reading a book *Fille de la révolutionaires* by Laurence Debray – the daughter of Régis Debray and Elisabeth Burgos; Régis Debray – today a member of *L'Academie française* – was Che's main theoretician), liberal democrats have attempted to expand democracy and liberalism in Afghanistan, Iraq, Syria and other places, that are particularly hostile for the acceptance of these ideas.

In that respect, let us take, for instance, Afghanistan and let me refer to my fellow countryman – the former Estonian Ambassador to Afghanistan, as quoted in the book by the former British Ambassador to the same country. In November 2008, Ambassador Harri Tiido was being given a tour of Helmand province. Estonians were stationed in Nawzad, which had once been a town of 30,000 people, but was then deserted, 'with the two sides dug into first world war-type trenches with their lines 300 yards apart.' After receiving the usual PowerPoint briefing, Tiido was asked by his British hosts if he had any questions: 'I have only one,' he replayed: 'What the fuck are we doing here?'[166] I read about this episode some years ago in a book by Sherard Cowper-Coles, the former British Ambassador to Afghanistan, who was haunted by the same question. However, the Americans and its NATO allies are still there and therefore the question – what 'the most successful Alliance in history,' to use the terminology of the December 2019 NATO Summit's Declaration, is doing there – remains. The negotiations between the US and the Taliban that are underway while I am writing these lines, may indeed bear fruit and put and to the war in this long-suffering country, and this would be the right thing to do. However, this also shows the futility of all the efforts during those nineteen years to radically change the country. The cost of erroneous policies, both in human lives lost and resources thrown to the wind, have been enormous.

However, it was not only because of the mistakes that were made by all American administrations – both Democratic and Republican, since the end of

---

[166] S. Cowper-Coles, *Cables from Kabul: The Inside Story of the West's Campaign*, Harper Press, 2011; see also Christina Lamb, *Farewell to Kabul: From Afghanistan to a More Dangerous World*, William Collins, 2016.

the bi-polar world such as the alienation of Russia, protracted unwinnable war in Afghanistan, the invasion of Iraq in 2003 and the support of the so-called 'Arab spring' that quickly and predictably turned into autumn and winter in most Middle Eastern countries, especially in Libya and Syria, that made this unipolar world so short. There is a more general reason for that: the world is simply too big, complex and diverse to have its rich tapestry to be flattened into a carpet where one pattern, be it of a Judeo-Christian, Anglo-Saxon, Confucian, Muslim or even secular liberal-democratic pattern, dominates.

16- Balance of Powers
A Precondition for International Law and Relatively Peaceful World

The pessimistic Report prepared for the February 2017 Munich Security Conference was alarmingly entitled *Post-Truth, Post-West, Post-Order*.[167] The Report was full of anxieties that the world may be, 'on the brink of a post-Western age, one in which non-Western actors are shaping international affairs, often in parallel or even to the detriment of precisely those multilateral frameworks that have formed the bedrock of the liberal international order since 1945.' The Report questions: 'Are we entering a post-order world?' The 2020 Report, entitled *Westlessness*[168], continues in the same spirit. Written from the Western perspective and moaning about bygone days when the West dominated the world, the Report is adding a name-calling to its earlier documents. So, those guilty of this 'westlessness' of the world, have acquired new names: China has become the Meddle Kingdom while Russia is renamed as the Putemkin's State. Such meaningless smirking and playing with words are signs of the lack of adequate ideas in the face of new serious challenges.

However, there is no need to be so pessimistic. Indeed, the world, and particularly liberal democracies, have certainly benefited from the liberal international order. But no order, be it international or national, is forever. And this liberal international order was not so liberal after all. Rather, it was an order where liberal states, ruling the world, were attempting also to widen the circle of liberal societies (especially after the collapse of the USSR), while ostracising or even destroying those that did not want to, or could not, become liberal. An international order that we see today rising – a multi-polar, balance of powers

---

[167] https://www.securityconference.de/en/news/article/post-truth-post-west-post-order-preview-of-the-msc-2017-in-berlin/
[168] https://securityconference.org/en/publications/munich-security-report-2020/

and concert of powers world – may indeed not be liberal in that sense, but it would be much more democratic to an extent and in the sense that these notions – liberalism and democracy – are at all applicable in international relations. It would accept differences not only within societies, as liberal orders in principle do, but also between them. In that respect, it could be even more liberal than the post-1945 international order. These would be challenging times in many parts of the world. However, there is no need to become despondent. What is needed is the correct and frank diagnosis of current crises. And the remedies needed to face these challenges may differ depending on regions and societies. There is no end of history, or rather the end of history would mark also the end of the humankind, but it is often so that only through a crisis the recovery becomes possible. As Winston Churchill had once put it: 'Never waste a good crisis.' It is true in politics; it is also true in personal lives. A crisis that doesn't kill a patient usually opens the way to the recovery.

Above I generalised that the main reason why our expectations of the world where international law would play increasingly important role didn't materialise, is the fact that the world has entered into the period of revolutionary changes. Until this period ends and a new order would hopefully emerge and become recognised, if not by all then at least by the majority of most important players, international law simply cannot properly perform its functions.

After the collapse of the Soviet Union and the end of the bipolar international system the existing balance between the two powers also disappeared. Most Western politicians and experts, forgetful of lessons of history and believing in its end, welcomed this turn. In the 1990s there was, indeed, only one centre of power – Washington whose dominance was welcomed by its allies and no counter-balancers were seen on the horizon.

Just as in societies organised as states, power in international society has also the tendency to concentrate more and more in one or more centres. The phenomenon of power concentration, be it in economics (the tendency toward monopolisation, absent regulation) or in politics, seems to be a general rule of societal life. Even in academia we can see that some universities, think tanks or labs that have become successful are trying to impose their schools of thought, while supressing and marginalising dissenting views and opinions. Such tendencies of concentration of power, if allowed to continue, usually lead to negative consequences. That is why developed societies adopt antimonopoly legislation, provide for separation of powers with its check and balances in politics, and encourage different schools of thought in academia.

This all is true also in international relations. Swiss politician and journalist Guy Mettan is right in observing that 'a power when becoming hegemonic, as the Great Britain was after the Napoleonic wars, tends to establish permanent supremacy, trying to destroy any rivalry until there is somebody who would bring it to its senses.' And he emphasises:

> 'Any power without counter-power tends to become absolute whether this takes place within a state or outside, if there is no other power (powers) that would be able restrain it; law in itself is not the sufficient guarantee against such tendencies. A candidate for a dictatorship can always change the constitution in his favour if there is nobody strong enough to challenge him and a power that is dominant internationally is able to 'interpret' or re-write international law in accordance with its own interest, if there is no other power able to resist. And law becomes simply a façade that is called to conceal the pure relations of power.'[169]

If concentration of power within a society evolves towards totalitarianism, in globalised world it leads, if not counterbalanced, towards the emergence of a world-wide empire, where instead of international law an imperial law (under the name a world law) applies. However, super-concentration of power usually ends in a Big Bang, similar to the explosion of black holes in the universe leading to the emergence of new galaxies. While totalitarian societies explode in rebellions of those who have nothing to lose but their chains, in international relations, as the world history testifies, there always emerge those who start counter-balancing against the imperial centre.

Any balance of power presumes, by definition, the existence of more than one centre of power, just as the separation of powers domestically presumes the existence of at least legislative, executive and judicial branches, between whom a certain equilibrium should exist. The concentration of power by Washington in the 1990s, that according to Hubert Védrine had become a hyper-power, was unheard of in the history of the world. Even the greatest empires of the past such as those of Alexander the Great or Genghis Khan, including the British Empire,

---

[169] G. Mettan, *Russia-Occident. Une Guerre de Mille Ans: La Russophobie de Charlemagne à la Crise Ukrainienne* (Éditions des Syrtes, 2015), p. 239.

on which the sun never sat, controlled only parts of the Planet Earth. After the end of the bipolar world the United States considered the whole world as the sphere of its vital interest, where no rival power could be allowed to rise. Such an anomalous situation, being an historical aberration, couldn't last for long.

If the multipolarity in the international system is an obvious necessity due to sheer scale of the world and its social, cultural and developmental diversity, it is also necessary condition (*conditio sine qua non*) for the very existence of international law. This was well understood already by Swiss international lawyer Emerich de Vattel, who in 1758 in his celebrated *The Law of Peoples* wrote about the foundation of international law: 'This is the famous idea of the political balance or equilibrium of power. We have in mind a situation where no power is able to dominate absolutely, to make laws for others.'[170] In 1861, Sir Travers Twiss, a prominent English jurist, Queen's Advocate-General, and also my distant predecessor as Professor of International Law at King's College, London, wrote that 'the concept of general balance designed by the treaty-systems [he had in mind particularly the Utrecht peace treaty of 1713 that had put an end to the wars of the Spanish succession and treaties adopted by the Congress of Vienna of 1815] would guarantee particularly the existence of the sovereignty of less powerful nations against the more powerful states.'[171] Without a balancing power (or powers), there would develop an imperial system where there is no place for independent entities. This is why Lassa Oppenheim wrote in the first edition (1905) of his famous treatise on international law: 'Law of Nations can exist only if there is equilibrium, a balance of power, between the members of the Family of Nations.'[172] In that respect the world has not changed. Even today the arrogance of one superpower can be controlled and tamed by the might of another superpower (or coalition of powers); international law can be helpful and play its role in this process, but without such a balance it not only becomes helpless, it simply disappears, opening way to the emergence of imperial law.

International law as such, in contradistinction, for example, to the imperial legal systems or the current EU law, cannot exist in a system with one dominant centre. International law as a more or less coherent system of rules and principles,

---

[170] Emerich de Vattel, *Le Droits des Gens*, & 47-48, Chapitre III.
[171] T. Twiss, *The Law of Nations Considered as Independent Political Communities: On the Rights and Duties of Nations in Time of Peace* (Oxford, 1861), p. 140.
[172] L.F.L. Oppenheim, *International Law: A Treatise, vol. I, Peace* (London, 1905), p. 73.

that is, as a legal system, started developing after the Westphalian peace of 1648, which had concluded the devastating Thirty Years War in Europe. Before that period there had existed in Europe a political system of multi-layered authority, where the Papacy, the Emperor of the Holy Roman Empire and a multitude of kings, counts, earls and dukes competed for a place under the Sun.[173]

The Westphalian international society, i.e. society of sovereign states, that emerged in the aftermath of the Thirty Years War was a regional international society, which at the end managed to extend itself, as well as its characteristics and principles, to the rest of the world. Adam Watson writes: 'The European society of states evolved out of the struggle between the forces trending towards a hegemonial order and those which succeeded in pushing the new Europe towards the independences end of our spectrum... The Westphalian settlement was the charter of a Europe permanently organised on an antihegemonial principle.'[174]

Only with the emergence of relatively equal centralised nation-states could modern international law (then often called the 'international law of civilised nations,' i.e. European international law), with its concepts of sovereign equality, non-interference in internal affairs and non-use of military force take shape. Of course, not all states were equal, and there was a constant struggle for dominance and attempts to either ignore international law, to re-interpret it in accordance with one's interests or to instrumentalise it for one's own purposes. However, with the exception of the relatively brief period of Napoleonic Europe, no power had been able to dominate the whole continent. Hitler tried but was defeated. And it was exactly for that reason, after Napoleon Bonaparte had disturbed the existing power balance to its very roots and established an almost continental-wide empire, that, in 1815 in Vienna, the victorious powers consciously and conscientiously created a continental international system that became known as the European Concert. It guaranteed the longest peaceful period the Old continent had ever known. Importantly, it was not only the *de facto* balance that was restored after Napoleon had been defeated; it was also the recognition, in Vienna of 1815, of the necessity of this balance for the European security (i.e., practice plus *opinio juris*). Notably, it was also the inclusion of France in the concert of powers, notwithstanding the efforts of some to humiliate the defeated

---

[173] See H. Bull, *Anarchical Society: A Study of Order in World Politics* (Macmillan, 1977).
[174] Watson, *The Evolution of International Society*, Routledge, 1992, p. 182.

enemy, to add insult to injury. Unfortunately, neither the winners of the First World War nor those of the Cold War were as wise as Alexander I, Viscount Castlereagh and Clemens von Metternich had been in Vienna in 1815.

The post-Cold War unipolar moment also led to attempts to transform existing international law into a unipolar normative system controlled from the single centre, where there should be no room for counterbalancing. For a while, it seemed that international law would indeed evolve in that direction. The widespread use of military force for humanitarian purposes, both authorised by the UN Security Council (therefore lawful, though not always necessarily legitimate) or bypassing the Council (illegal, but for some states and experts, legitimate); the rapid evolution of international criminal law and jurisdiction and high expectations that this could change the world for the better. Downgrading the role of state sovereignty and almost complete neglect of the principle of non-interference in domestic affairs, were also among the signs of such a tendency. But from the onset of the twenty-first century, not only have the 'usual suspects', China and Russia, begun counterbalancing, but other regional powers have also started to force multipolar elements into the emerging international system. However, such a trend has not been to Washington's liking, and through its containment and roll-back policies, either unilaterally or through NATO and even the European Union, the United States is targeting Russia and China in an attempt to perpetuate the unilateral moment of the 1990s.

Many influential authors even prophesised the demise of nation-states that have always been the main and indispensable subjects of international law. So, Japanese economist, businessman and public intellectual Kenishi Ohmae and Frenchman Jean-Marie Guehenno, the former UN Under-Secretary General for peace-keeping operations, until recently the President and CEO of International Crisis Group, both published books with identical titles *The End of the Nation-State*.[175] In parallel with forecasting the death of nation-states, there emerged great enthusiasm for humanitarian interventions, i.e. the use of military force to save lives in foreign countries and narrowing to the minimum the scope of domestic affairs. International law, based on fundamental principles such as sovereign equality of states, non-use of force and non-interference in internal affairs of states, would be gradually replaced by law made at the image of the

---

[175] See, Kenichi Ohmae, *The End of the Nation State: How Regional Economics Will Soon Reshape the World*, Simon & Schuster, 1995; Jean-Marie Guehenno, *The End of the Nation-State*, University of Minnesota Press, 2000.

law of the European Union since in the globalising world the Euro-governance was seen by many as the antechamber of the global governance.[176]

Although not the most important sign of this tendency, but nevertheless rather emblematic, was the welcomed rise in importance of the role of international criminal law and especially international criminal jurisdiction. The creation of the two interlinked *ad hoc* international tribunals – the International Criminal Tribunal for the Former Yugoslavia (ICTY), in 1993, and a year later the International Criminal Tribunal for Rwanda (ICTR), as well as the adoption in 1998 the Rome Statute, founding the permanent International Criminal Court (ICC), were seen as heralding the beginning of the new era in international law and relations.

It so happened that in the early 1990s, I taught international criminal law at the London School of Economics and Political Science (LSE). If at the 1992-1993 academic year my master's degree (LLM) class was composed of no more than ten students, the following year I had already more than hundred. The enthusiasm was boundless, though unjustified.

International criminal law has, of course, a role to play in international relations, but quite a modest one, since international relations are, by definition, political relations because states, as main subjects of international law and politics, are *per se* political entities. In politics, however, it is constitutional law that governs relations within states, while public international law plays the important role in relations between them; the role of criminal law in international relations is secondary due to their inherently political nature.

These were not criminal tribunals in The Hague, but political and military means, which brought relative peace to the Balkans and to Rwanda. The International Criminal Court is also in trouble. The major states have not ratified its Statute, most defendants before the Court have been so far African politicians and some states that had earlier ratified the Statute, are already denouncing their acceptance. Threats of the Trump administration to undertake sanctions against the ICC in case it tries to prosecute American military personnel for crimes committed in Afghanistan or Israelis for acts against Palestinians, though being Trump-specific in form (i.e. rude and thoughtless), reflect nevertheless the general attitude of great powers to international criminal jurisdiction.

The normative effect of all these developments has been that while in most sensitive areas the existing norms of international law have become undermined,

---

[176] See, J. Rabkin, *Law without Nations?*, Princeton University Press, 2005, p. 130-157.

new ones have not been able, and in the foreseeable future will not be able, to crystallise. Consequently, today we live in an atmosphere of increased normative uncertainty. The way to remedy the situation is not to further undermine states' sovereignty or to act unilaterally. It is necessary to take collective actions through multilateral mechanisms based on balance of power, transforming the existing ones (first of all, the UN Security Council) into effective instruments of crises management, instead of using them as propaganda fora, and creating, where necessary, new ones.

Due to the multiple crises, the world, including the Old Continent, cannot go on as usual. Need for change seems to be obvious. However, the need for change, even if there were conditions favouring it – that is not the case – is not in itself enough to make it happen. The third element is the advent of inspiring strong personalities. The launch of the European project in the 1950s was genuinely a visionary endeavour. But once launched and well underway, there followed within European and in Western societies generally a relatively smooth and prosperous period of evolution that brought to the surface a class of managerial politicians. There was rarely a need or quest for visionaries. The rule of the thumb was: if it works, don't touch it. Today, however, it no longer works.

In January 2018, at Sandhurst, the British Royal Military Academy, President Macron of France gave an interview to the BBC's Andrew Marr who asked him: what had the President meant by saying that he liked to be a Jupiter-like President? Macron's somewhat evasive response was: 'when you preside, you preside and that is different from governing,' It seems that Emmanuel Macron understands that not only France, but also Europe and the entire world is in need of different kinds of policies, which in turn calls for politicians with vision and even charisma. Whether Macron is a person who can act upon such an understanding is a different and a more difficult question. At least, he seems to be trying.

Throughout human history, be it in the history of a single country or in the world history, there have been revolutionary periods that have called for strong visionary leaders. Like, say, Franklin Delano Roosevelt, introducing the New Deal when the Great Depression had hit America and the world, and standing firm and wise during the war against Nazism; Winston Churchill before and when WWII broke out; General de Gaulle throughout crucial periods of French history. Even Jacques Chirac and Gerhard Schroeder showed the wisdom and courage when in 2003 they stood up against George W. Bush's disastrous Iraqi invasion. Such a person was Yitzhak Rabin, whose murder put an end to the possibility of resolving the Israeli-Palestinian conflict in the form of a two-states solution, or Deng Xiaoping without whom the Chinese miracle would have been impossible, Lee Kuan Yew, who ruled Singapore for more than thirty years, or Nelson Mandela without whom South Africa may have succumbed into a bloody conflict. I am sorry if I hurt the sensibilities of many liberal democrats, but I would add to this list also President Vladimir Putin of Russia, President Xi Jinping of China and President Narendra Modi of India. They seem to belong to the category of politicians who have a vision for their respective states, for the place of their countries in the world and consequently also for the world, though one has to admit that the jury is still out. Visionary politicians may also be wrong and make mistakes, but political managers are not able to find solutions in revolutionary situations, and even less able to carry them through. They dare not to think, let alone act, beyond the box.

One of the serious problems of democratic politics is its short-termism – from election to election. Additionally, the qualities needed to be elected rarely correspond to those necessary to get the things done once elected. As the French international relations scholar Dominique Moïsi has observed: 'To be able to debate well on TV or to tweet on social network, to be able to use short key words and phrases – all this doesn't imply that such a person has the courage to take difficult but necessary decisions and have what the Latins called the gravitas, i.e. the mixture of seriousness and experience.'[177] I would put it a bit differently: today there is a need for leadership, a quest for personalities who have both brain and spine and happen to be at the right time in the right place.

---

[177] D. Moïsi, *La Geopolitique des Series ou le triomphe de la peur* (Stock, 2016), 596.

17- Nation-State – A Cradle of Democracy

The 1990s and first years of the 2000s, as I wrote in the previous chapter, saw the publication of dozens of books and many more articles by well-known authors, all promising the withering away of nation-states, whose disappearance would have marked also an end of international law. If a century earlier these were mainly Marxists who had prophesised the death of the state under the world-wide communism, now these were free-market liberal democrats, coming up with similar predictions. This time, however, it would not be the solidarity of working classes of different countries (Proletarians of all Countries – Unite), but the greed of capitalists not recognising national boundaries, which should have led to the demise of the state. Like the communist utopia, promising a world-wide peace in a stateless world, the extinction of national borders as a result of world-wide triumph of liberal democracy and capitalism, would also lead to the ascension of universal democratic peace.[178] Although capitalists' greed is, certainly, a much more concrete and tangible item than the working-class solidarity, it is not leading to a better world. As history should have taught us, good intentions do not always pave the way to the paradise.

Democracy in the post-feudal Europe emerged hand in hand with, and was conditioned by, the advent of so-called nation-states. The core political idea of nationalism that a nation must have, or deserves to have, a state (or *vice versa* that a state should be based on a nation) inspired politicians and thinkers, who fashioned and consolidated statehood in England, France, the Netherlands and other parts of Western Europe. This idea, and practices founded on it (or the practices, followed by *ex post facto* ideological justifications?), were opposed,

---

[178] See, a critique of theories of 'democratic peace' in R. Müllerson, *Regime Change: From Democratic Peace Theories to Forcible Regime Change,* Martinus Nijhoff Publishers, 2013.

on the one hand, to the feudal fragmentation of Europe, and one the other, to the imperial dominance. Nation-states consolidated their positions and their sovereignty (both internal and external aspects of it) in parallel with the weakening of the supremacy of the Holy Roman Empire and later in the process of struggle against the dominance of the Austro-Hungarian and the Ottoman Empires. Democratic institutes such as parliaments and local authorities of self-governance emerged within these nation-states. John Stewart Mill, in the middle of the nineteenth century, summarising the practices of such institutions, wrote that it was, 'a necessary condition of free institutions that the boundaries of government should coincide in the main with those of nationalities,' and that, 'among a people without fellow-feeling, especially if they read and speak different languages, the united public opinion necessary to the workings of representative institutions cannot exist.'[179] However, more than two centuries later, and contrary to Mill, Daniel Cohn-Bendit, the 1968 students' movement leader, reflecting about the continuing effect of the 1968 events, believed that 1968 opened the way to the diversity paradigm (*paradigme diversitaire*). He wrote: 'For me, this was the opening of thoughts to the acceptance of differences as a unifying factor. The recognition of differences may unite us and give additional strength to the society.'[180]

Certainly, today's European societies have radically changed in comparison with the times of John Stewart Mill; there is greater diversity and its wider acceptance as well. However, there are also differences that make the integration of society impossible and lead to the parallel existence of incompatible sub-cultures within one and the same society that, at the end of the day, may even lose its societal characteristics.

Globalisation with its tendency to homogenise the world and heterogenise individual societies is already creating problems that in their aggregate may soon become insurmountable even without artificial attempts to accelerate these processes. For example, immigrants have indeed brought various, especially economic, benefits for quite a few countries. However, the uncontrolled massive and rapid migration of people, especially if their cultural, religious or ethical backgrounds considerably differ from those dominant in receiving countries, may lead to ghettoisation, well exemplified by Molenbeek in the centre of

---

[179] J.S. Mill, *Utilitarianism. On Liberty, Considerations of Representative Government*, Basil and Blackwell, 1993, pp. 392, 394.
[180] D. Cohn-Bendit, *Forget 68*, Éditions de l'aube, 2008, p. 36.

Brussels. Two Belgian journalists Christophe Lamfalussy and Jean-Pierre Martin write in their book entitled *Jihad in Molenbeek*: 'Walk just two hundred meters from Grande Place in the centre of Brussels and you are in Saudi Arabia.'[181] In this district bruxellois of six square kilometres, there are 41 places of worship, of which 25 are mosques. Out of around 500 Belgian jihadists who have fought or are still fighting in Syria, 79 are of Molenbeek origin. Even if Molenbeek may be a rather extreme example of the difficulties on the road of integration, the parallel existence of hugely differing communities in many European cities is not an exception.

Supporting and promoting diversity within societies have, as a corollary, the elimination of diversity between societies organised as states. While some societies, especially in the West, have become so diverse that the societal bonds holding them together are breaking down, in others, particularly in the East and South, the implantation of societal models that have worked in the West leads to the collapse of traditional societies. Melting pot policies could have worked within a society of immigrants, like that of the United States or Australia, where indigenous peoples were either eliminated or confined to reservations. Such policies are failing in Europe, where they are leading to the rise of populism and nationalism as a reaction to efforts to put into practice the idea of making all of us Europeans instead of Estonians, French, Dutch or Italians. I am cautioning against such policies notwithstanding the fact that due to the vagaries of the fate I have become a cosmopolitan, who feels almost at home in many places in the world.

Historically, the emergence and development of democracy was, if not conditioned, then at least facilitated by the homogenous nature of societies. If they were not homogenous enough, they had to be made such. As the Italian novelist and politician Massimo Taparelli d'Azeglio famously put it in 1861: 'We have created Italy. Now all we have to do is to create Italians.'[182] To put it otherwise, without certain degree of homogeneity, d'Azeglio believed, the

---

[181] C. Lamfalussy, J.-P. Martin, *Molenbeek-sur-Djihad*, Grasset (Paris), 2017.
[182] See, S. Tharoor, E Pluribus, India: Is Indian Modernity Working?' *Foreign Affairs*, 1998, vol. 77, No. 1, p. 128. India seems to be a considerable exception to the requirement of homogeneity for democracy to be sustainable. That is why Robert Dahl called India a 'improbable democracy' (R.A. Dahl, *On Democracy*, Yale University Press, 1998, p. 159.), while Amartya Sen spent pages explaining why democracy, notwithstanding all 'non-facilitators', has nevertheless survived in India (A. Sen, *The Argumentative Indian. Writings on Indian History, Culture and Identity*, Allen Lane, 2005).

country would not stay together. British diplomat and theorist of international relations Adam Watson was right in stating that, 'the self-assertion of the middle class in Europe took two forms: the demand for participation in government, and nationalism,' and that, 'the ideas of nationalism and democracy were related.'[183] Nationalism, the formation of nation-states and development of democracy in Europe went, indeed, hand in hand. Without nationalism there wouldn't have been nation-states, without nation-states there would not have been democracy, at least in its current form.

A dark side of these processes of nation-state formation was that most of them came into existence and consolidated their societies through policies and practices that today would be defined as 'ethnic cleansing' or even crimes against humanity. American historian Charles Tilly wrote that, 'almost all European governments eventually took steps that homogenised their populations: the adoption of state religions, exclusion of minorities like the Moors and the Jews, institution of a national language, eventually the organisation of mass public instruction. The tolerance of states of South- Eastern Europe for linguistic, cultural, and religious diversity stood in sharp contrast to the intolerance of their North-Western brethren, and surely stood in the way of effective state making. The failure to homogenise increased the likelihood that a state existing at a given point of time would fragment into its cultural subdivisions at some time in the future.'[184] My only, but significant, correction to Tilly's otherwise insightful comment would be that South-Eastern nation-states, as such, didn't yet exist at the time when Western European states consolidated their statehood and developed democratic institutions. At best, these nations were struggling to break away from either the Austro-Hungarian, Russian or the Ottoman Empire. Both of these nationalisms – Eastern European and Western European were exclusionary. While the first was anti-imperial aiming at the creation of nation-states, i.e., excluding themselves from wider entities, the Western European nationalism tried to erase existing differences by excluding or assimilating those who differed. The Eastern European late comers to the European family of nation-states are even today keener about the homogeneity of their societies and independence of their newly found statehood than those in the Western part of the continent. Having forgotten the bloody history of their own state-building,

---

[183] A. Watson, *The Evolution of International Society*, Routledge, 1992, p. 244.
[184] C. Tilly, 'Western State-making and Theories of Political Transformation,' in Tilly (ed.) *The Formation of National states in Europe*, Princeton University Press, 1975, p. 28.

Western European political elites are today rather critical of their Eastern European counter-parts when the latter use even much milder methods of consolidation in their nation-building.

We see that already at the beginning of the emergence of contemporary representative democracy and the formation of nation-states their relationship contained controversial aspects: no democracy without a triumphant nationalism, but at the same time, exclusion and suppression of differences and repression of those who were the carriers of those differences. Nationalism that played a positive role in helping democracy rise and liberate people from imperial dependency, today shows both of these sides. Most states in the world have remained, notwithstanding all the efforts of homogenisation, or have become even more multi-ethnic or multi-confessional due to the waves of migration. Therefore, today nationalism, instead of consolidating societies, has become one of the sources of conflicts in quite a few of them. The crucial question remains and is exacerbated by the negative aspects of globalisation (or hyper-globalisation): can democracy flourish and even exist 'without a fellow-feeling' among people, without and beyond the boundaries of nation-states? I have serious doubts about it. And is it correct, in such a case, to define the sum of those communities existing in parallel with their own mores, habits and ways of life as society? Paraphrasing the old Latin maxim *ubi societas, ibi ius* (where there is society, there is law) we can say that if there is no integrated society, there is neither rule of law nor democracy.

Empires have indeed often been more tolerant towards ethnic and/or religious diversity than nation-states. They simply didn't have a choice. Even homogenisation of nation-states, integrating (assimilating) of people of different ethnic, linguistic and religious background, has been a Herculean task. Homogenisation of empires, apart from co-opting and integrating elites of various of imperial peripheries, has always turned out to be impossible. For example, amongst the highest nobility of the Russian Empire and its highest officials were widely represented Tatars (Prince Felix Yussupov, who is remembered mostly for his participation in the murder of Grigory Rasputin), Georgians (General Piotr Bagration, a hero of the 1812 war against Napoleon), Baltic Germans (Count Vladimir Lamsdorf and Count Karl Robert Nesselrode were Czarist Foreign Ministers) and other minorities. Among the Bolshevik leaders of the Soviet Russia in 1917 ethnic Russians were in minority. Genghis Khan cared even less about the ethnic origin or religion of his batyrs (baghaturs), though it is appropriate to note that European empires with overseas colonies were indeed also quite racist. So, British historian Denis Judd observes that higher than usual rate of homosexuals among British males was partly due to the racism of colonial officials who instead of looking for sexual partners among local females, whom they considered as not deserving their attention, preferred their male colleagues.[185] Or that, 'concern about racial amalgamation tended if anything to encourage same-sex sex.'[186] Ann Laura Stoler writes that in the Dutch case, at least, 'concubinage between European men and native women was considered an alternative, albeit an unattractive one, to homosexuality, among the ranks.'[187]

Even if usually more tolerant *vis-à-vis* ethnic diversity than the nation-state, especially during the stages of the formation of the latter, the imperial rule has never been democratic. Even if the imperial centre, as was the case of Great Britain, was a liberal democracy, its rule even over its last colonial possession – Hong Kong, though liberal, lacked any vestiges of democracy. At the same time, empires of the past took care also of so-called common goods. So, Genghis Khan's empire for a quite a while and the Tamerlane's for a shorter period both guaranteed relative peace and prosperity on the ancient Silk Road. When their imperial power waned, local chieftains felt free to rob the caravans travelling between China and Europe thereby putting an end, at least for long, to one of the lengthiest terrestrial trade-routes.

Today the terms 'empire' and 'imperialism' have become so discredited that no entity would claim to have imperial status (Jean-Bédel Bokassa of Central Africa seems to have been the last proud emperor). However, if the time for formal empires may indeed be over, there are some political arrangements that may be defined, with some justification, as 'informal' empires. There is a centre and there is a periphery; there is also a relationship of dominance and submission where a dominant centre guarantees certain common goods (e.g., security or economic benefits) demanding in return unwavering obedience and punishing disobedience.

In a very interesting, though controversial (more often than not these two adjectives go hand in hand) book with a provocative title *The Virtue of*

---

[185] See, D. Judd, *Empire: The British Imperial Experience from 1765 to the Present*, HarperCollins, 1996.
[186] R. Aldrich, *Colonialism and Homosexuality*, Routledge, 2013.
[187] See, A. L. Stoler, *Race and Education of Desire: Foucault's History of Sexuality and the Colonial Order of Things*, Duke University Press, 1995.

Nationalism, Israeli author Yoram Hazony writes that when the struggle against communism ended, 'the Western minds became preoccupied with two great imperialist projects: the European Union, which has progressively relieved member nations of many of the powers usually associated with political independence; and the project of establishing an American "world order", in which nations that do not abide by international law will be coerced into doing so, principally by means of American military might. These are imperialist projects, even though their proponents do not like to call them like that.'[188] In defence of international law it should be said that it is not this rather noble normative system, which willy-nilly worked even during the Cold War, that Washington tries to impose by its military might, but so-called 'rules-based liberal international order,' i.e. the order based on rules determined mostly by Washington and its allies that often have very little to do with international law. And it is not accidental that the only aspiring global empire is accusing those opposing its imperial ambitions, especially China and Russia, of either building or restoring their own empires.

However, there is not only undemocratic (or authoritarian) liberalism on the rise, of which more below, but already for some time we are facing liberal imperialism[189], euphemistically described as 'liberal international order', giving additional impetus to the rise of nationalistic populism, of which also below. Liberal imperialism, i.e. attempts to impose liberal values, either by persuasion or by force, as universal values to all and everybody, is a wake-up call for those for whom, say, collectivistic values, historical traditions, stability or national independence are more, or at least not less, important than individual liberties. Many influential liberal authors, be they philosophers or economists, have been campaigners for liberal imperial order. Friedrich Hayek, one of the most important theoreticians of liberalism of the last century, believed that the idea of interstate federation would be 'the consistent development of liberal point of view'[190], while Ludwig von Mises advocated the end of nation-states and creation of a 'world super-state.'[191] Yoram Hazony is right when asserting that: 'For all their bickering, proponents of the liberal construction are united in

---

[188] Y. Hazony, *The Virtue of Nationalism*, Basic Books, 2018, pp.3-4.
[189] See, R. Müllerson, A Critic of Liberal Imperialism, https://valdaiclub.com/a/highlights/liberal-imperialism/ 30 December 2018.
[190] F. Hayek, *The Economic Conditions of Interstate Federalism* (https://fee.org/articles/the-economic-conditions-of-interstate-federalism).
[191] L. von Mises, *Liberalism in the Classical Tradition*, Cobden Press, 1985, p. 150.

endorsing a single imperialist vision: They wish to see a world in which liberal principles are codified as universal law and imposed on the nations, if necessary by force. This, they agree, is what will bring us universal peace and prosperity.'[192]

It is unfair, in my opinion, to accuse the European Union of being an imperial project, though one may agree that promising (and acting on this promise) to create an 'ever-closer union', a kind of federal Europe, European political elites have gradually become more and more detached from the aspirations of their peoples. It is becoming increasingly obvious that European societies, in contradistinction to political elites, are not (not yet, at least) ready to throw the nation-state into the dustbin of history. These are not only those losers in the hyper-globalised world, who care about where and with whom they live. Many highly intelligent, successful and multi-lingual persons treasure their ethnic, religious or cultural origins, are patriots of their countries and cherish their roots.

Benedict Anderson was not completely wrong when he defined nations as 'imagined communities'[193], since historical myths and purposeful efforts of political leaders to make a nation out of diverse communities have always played a role in nation-building. However, there is also something much more tangible, even primordial, without which nations would not and could not emerge. Shared history, cultural and religious traditions, common language and even territorial closeness - are all factors that have played a role in the formation of nations. Today, more than decades ago, more and more Europeans, being afraid of becoming strangers at home, in their own country, city or even village, are in search of their historic roots. Both the liberal lefts and the conservative rights have become concerned about their identity. If the first try to find their identity in the belongingness to a multitude of small, often marginalised, groups (depending on sexual orientation, specific interests or ways of life), the second usually try to find or restore their affinity with bigger communities, like nations, nation-states or traditional religions.

Current population movements, also a part of the process of globalisation, have moved migration problems to the centre-stage of domestic politics of practically all European countries. Not only individual member-states but also the European Union have failed to find solutions to the problem of uncontrolled

---

[192] Y. Hazony, *The Virtue of Nationalism*, Basic Books, 2018, p.45.
[193] B. Anderson, *Imagined Communities: Reflections on the Origin and Spread of Nationalism*, Verso, 1983.

migration. Many European societies have economically benefitted from, and even encouraged, previous migrations. It would be difficult to imagine, for instance, the United Kingdom without doctors and pharmacists from the Indian subcontinent. British public health system (NHS), and not only that, would collapse without migrants. However, on the flipside of the mass migration is not only and not even so much that 'they-take-our-jobs'. There is a real concern among the local people about the loss of their identity. Although there are those who can be anywhere (borrowing from David Goodhart), there are still many more who want to be somewhere, i.e. they care about their roots, traditions, religion and other values that they have inherited from their ancestors.

In his book *Demeure*[194], Francois-Xavier Bellamy, a philosopher and a French member of the European parliament, well depicts and explains one of the important modern (or post-modern, if you prefer) predicaments: when everybody and everything has to be on the move, when more and more goods must be produced, traded and consumed as quickly as possible, when change and innovation are required from everybody and there is no time for contemplation, lest left behind, many people start thinking about the meaning of such runaway lifestyle. It is not only that not every innovation or change is not necessarily for the better. Humankind is standing on the shoulders of the past giants. Therefore, only learning and inheriting from our past can we understand directions of the change and innovation. Only knowing where we come from can we chart the way ahead. Therefore, the conservatism *à la* Bellamy, if not necessarily progressive (and it is not supposed to be), is humane. It calls for the preservation of everything valuable from the past of our different societies.

Both progressiveness and conservatism have their place and value as well as their flipsides. Not every change or innovation is for the better, not every tradition needs to be preserved. However, if without change and innovation we would still live in caves, by squandering our inheritance we lose our humanity. We may well disagree with Plato on the value of democracy or with Aristoteles on the understanding of slavery, but without them and many others Western civilisation wouldn't exist, as it would be much poorer without Lev Tolstoy, Fyodor Dostoyevsky, Anton Chekhov or Piotr Tchaikovsky. I am mentioning particularly these Russian intellectual and spiritual giants not only because they too belong to the European cultural heritage, but also because, as I will try to

---

[194] F.-X. Bellamy, *Demeure: pour échapper à l'ère du mouvement perpétuel*, Grasset, 2019.

explain below, one of the European quandaries needs for its resolution a helping hand of Russia.

One of the values most peoples, including in Europe, treasure is independent statehood. Both UN 1966 Covenants on human rights confirm the right of peoples to self-determination. This principle was used by colonial peoples in Africa, Asia and elsewhere to claim their independent statehood. Even the constituent republics in the USSR (with the exceptions of the Baltic nations, who considered themselves to be occupied by the Soviet Union in 1940 and therefore wanted to put an end to this occupation) fought for their independence under the banner of self-determination. The idea that human rights, including the right to democracy, cannot exist without independent statehood guided those who in the 1950s and 1960s fought against colonialism. This idea not only remains valid today, but excesses of globalisation have even increased its attractiveness. Of course, today it is not the British Empire or the Soviet Union, which deny sovereignty to colonial peoples or nations in the USSR, but it is more than anything else 'the invisible hand' of global capitalism, which makes democracy hollow and meaningless. These are the global financial markets and multinationals, led by GAFAs, that are *de facto* more 'sovereign' than most nation-states. This 'invisible hand' favours, needs and encourages global movement of people and freedom of migration, while people in many parts of the world try to find rescue from the excesses of such globalisation, or as the French say, from *la mondialisation malheureuse* (unhappy globalisation), in the restoration of sovereignty of their nation-states. Unrestrained global markets and democracy seem to be incompatible. Of course, there may still be free and fair elections, but those who are elected are bound not by the mandate of their electorate but by impersonal and invisible hand of global markets. There is no world-wide democracy or democracy in international relations. A worldwide democracy, like the idea of the world government, is a utopia like the idea of the worldwide communism accompanied by the withering away of states.

As European elites, or at least a considerable part of them, consider the concept of state sovereignty as somewhat outdated and prefer to speak instead of European sovereignty (read, e.g., Emmanuel Macron), the issue of sovereignty of European states has become a European-wide bone of contention. Although nowadays no European leader is openly calling for the establishment of the 'ever closer union' (today, it is replaced by the phrase 'we need more Europe, not less'), there is still a dominant trend towards federalisation of Europe that has, however, become counterbalanced by calls for the union of nation-states instead. Member-states of the European Union, are not in a hurry to get rid of their sovereignty. It is difficult to imagine France, even under Europhile President Macron, giving up its permanent seat with the veto power in the UN Security Council to make place for EU's membership.

Mathieu Bock-Coté is right when he observes that, 'when one attacks national sovereignty and historical identity of the people, its cultural heritage or civilisational roots of the Western world, one undermines knowingly or inadvertently what has helped democracy survive. The men and women fought against totalitarianisms not only to save their rights but also to save their country, their culture and their civilisation.'[195] Around the competition of these two trends – a further federalisation of the Union *versus* retaining or even strengthening the sovereignty of its member-states – there is a host of more specific problems: the criticism of widening the Union (i.e., extending it to the Central and Eastern Europe, including the Baltic states) instead of deepening the integration of the historical core of the Union; the issue of a multi-speed Union; difficulties with the Schengen zone etc. Attempts to resolve this bundle of controversial topics indeed amount to the Herculean (or rather Archimedean) task of squaring the circle.

On the one hand, Europe indeed needs more unity (not only economic but also political and strategic) to adequately face contemporary global challenges. Even biggest European states are too small to adequately play (or wrestle) in the weight-category of China or the United States, to say nothing of smaller countries. Strategically Europe has, since the end of the Second World War, been wholly dependent on the United States. If during the Cold War such a dependence was understandable, with the disappearance of the Soviet Union and the end of the bi-polar world it has lost its *raison d'être*, at least for Europe, if not for the United States. With the advent of the Trump administration, that took off the velvet gloves from Washington's iron fists even *vis-à-vis* its European allies, many Europeans feel, to put it mildly, uncomfortable, even humiliated.

To become one of the poles in world politics that would correspond to its economic weight and potential, Europe must transform itself into an even more integrated entity, especially on such important matters such as fiscal policies or defence. It ought to become a kind of federal Europe. However, many, if not

---

[195] M. Bock-Coté, *Le multiculturalisme comme une religion politique*, Les Editions du Serf, 2019, p. 326.

most European peoples are not ready for that, they don't want it. This is, in my opinion, one of the main obstacles on the path of Europe becoming a powerful pole in a multi-polar world that is emerging (or has already emerged). The political and strategic weight of Europe in the world is well below its economic potential. To protect and develop economic potential in competition with other poles, Europe must have also a political weight equalling that of the US, China, Russia or India.

Trump's withdrawal from the Iranian nuclear deal and Washington's use of its extraterritorial legislation *vis-à-vis* its allies and sanctioning them have brought home for many Europeans the need to lessen Europe's dependency from Washington's whims. Hence, the need for strategic consolidation against America's dominance. Equally, the economic rise of China is not only benefitting, but also worrying Europeans, lest the Continent become too dependent not only on Washington but also on Beijing. Once again, there is a need for more unity. However, as we have seen above, European peoples still value the sovereignty of their states and are not ready to sacrifice it on the altar of a 'ever close union' even if it is called 'more Europe, not less'. This is indeed a problem of squaring the circle.

If the squaring this circle is impossible, at least for the foreseeable future, the European Union may still increase its weight and strategic autonomy, especially *vis-à-vis* Washington and Beijing by considerably improving relations with Moscow. If Washington, in the attempt to perpetuate its global domination, may indeed be interested in the simultaneous containment of both China and Russia (though a dangerous and probably even counter-productive endeavour), Europe is suffering from its poor relations with Moscow not less than Russia. There is no benefit whatsoever for Europe of demonising Russia and its political leadership. Having at least normal relationships with Russia would not only be economically beneficial for Europe; it would also widen the space of strategic manoeuvring for Europe even without creating a European super-state. As Caroline Galactéros, a French political scientist, incisively puts it, 'strategic rapprochement of the EU with Russia would add additional value to Europe in new geopolitical games.'[196] This is also understood by some European leaders. So, President Macron is absolutely right when he declares that 'we have to build a new architecture of confidence and security in Europe, because the European

---

[196] C. Galactéros, 'Un nouveau partage du monde est en train de se structurer,' *Figaro Vox*, 9 novembre 2019.

continent will never be stable, will never feel secure if we will not have peaceful relations with Russia.'[197] Yet, often right things are easier said than done, especially as there are those, not only in America but also in Europe, who believe that American interests are better served, using the words of the first Secretary-General of NATO Lord Ismay, by 'keeping Russia out' of Europe, even if it this would force Russia to become closer to China. However, the rational policy transformation, proposed by President Macron, need not be oriented against the United States or China. This would only mean that Europe would considerably lessen its strategic dependency from Washington and have at the same time also a stronger bargaining positions *vis-à-vis* Beijing.

The fact that the relations of Europe with two centres of power, Washington and Moscow, are skewed in favour the United States disfavour not only Russia but also Europe. Since the beginning of the 2000s, when Jacques Chirac was the President of France and Gerhard Schroeder Chancellor of Germany, Europe has completely outsourced its decision-making on strategic issues to Washington. Such subordination of European interests to the American vision of the world has greatly contributed to the worsening of European – Russian relations. The crisis in and around Ukraine, which has multiple contributing factors, is detrimental to European as well as Russian interests, while it may be beneficial for Washington's strategic vision of the world, as it was described in uncertain terms (with President Trump's finger- or footprints all over) in the National Security Strategy of the United States, revealed in December 2017. Thierry de Montbrial, the President and founder of IFRI (The French Institute of International Relations) warns: 'If Europe and Russia will not find during a reasonable period of time a ground for a strong mutual understanding, both will run the risk of finding themselves as objects of a great-power competition, which is already unfolding between the United States and China for the future domination of the Eurasian continent.'[198] I am less certain about the Chinese desire or ability to dominate the Eurasian continent, but the American hegemony over the Western part of the continent (under a usual pretext of protecting it), is becoming more and more dangerous for the Old Continent. Going on as usual, i.e. muddling through, is not any more a rational choice. New approaches are needed. However, even the greatest of ideas remain only ideas if they don't result

---

[197] *Discours du Président de la République à la conférence des ambassadeurs.* L'Élisée, 27 août 2019.
[198] T. de Montbrial, *Vivre le Temps des Troubles*, Albin Michel, 2017, p. 140.

from collective frank discussions of all European peoples, discussions that are not anesthetised by rules of political correctness, ideological clichés and demonisation of those who think differently. And of course, no good idea can be put into practice without political leaders with brain, and even more importantly, with spine, who happen to be at the right time in the right place.

Hazony, exaggerating imperial ambitions of the European Union, is however right about the American liberal imperial project. Almost immediately after the end of the Cold War, notwithstanding some rather vague ideas about a 'new world order' that would unite majority of humankind against common threats, like the climate change or terrorism, the 'deep state' in Washington already started preparing for the 'American century'. There were those who prophesised conflict and prepped the American psyche for the coming clash with those who may oppose the American imperial project. So, an influential report published in 1998 by the RAND Corporation and written by Zalmay Khalilzad, who later became the US Ambassador to the United Nations, Afghanistan and Iraq, and Ian Lesser, conjured four scenarios for the coming century: the 'great game', the 'clash of civilisations', the 'coming anarchy' and the 'end of history.'[199] The authors considered the last two scenarios less probable than the first two; they foresaw the great-game theory as the most plausible, which would pitch the West (i.e. Washington) against China and Russia in a new great-power game. The Islamist threat was not seen as the most serious challenge to the United States. 9/11 may have altered these priorities, but – as it turned out – only for a while.

Today we see that Washington, confronting Russia in Europe and trying to contain China in East Asia and Pacific is doing exactly what was said to be Henry Kissinger's nightmare – containing two superpowers at the same time and thereby pushing them closer to each other. Dimitri Simes observes that 'since Nixon administration directed America's foreign affairs, it has been the policy of the United States to strive for better relations with China and Russia than the two powers with one other. Yet, America's current policy seems to amount to a simultaneous frontal assault on both countries, at least as they see it.'[200] Simes sees such a policy of Washington as counterproductive and dangerous even for America and writes that 'there is no path to responsible policymaking that does

---

[199] Z. Khalilzad, I. Lesser, *Sources of Conflict in the 21st Century: Regional Futures and U.S. Strategy* (RAND Corporation, 1998).
[200] D. Simes, 'Dangerous Liaisons,' *The National Interest*, 16 December 2018.

not begin with understanding and accounting for the unintended consequences of confronting two great powers simultaneously.'

Although the dual containment of Russia and China may indeed be short-sighted, but it is what the power braced for the world-wide dominance may be trapped into. It seems that while during the 2016 Presidential election campaign Donald Trump instinctively (and correctly, in my opinion) saw rising China as the main threat to the primacy of the United States in the world, Trump's domestic opponents, accusing him of collusion with President Putin, have concentrated their fire-power on Russia. As to the so-called Russian interference in the 2016 US Presidential elections, even if all, what the Mueller inquiry found, were true, Russia was only giving the US a taste of its own medicine, since Washington has a long tradition of interfering in political processes of other countries, including Russia. It is of interest to note that already during the May 1968 students' demonstrations and riots in America and in Western Europe, there were those, who saw in them a long arm of the world communist movement directed from the Kremlin. So, Michel Debré, who was the first Prime Minister of the Fifth Republic under Charles de Gaulle, wrote: 'Whatever they tell me, I cannot believe that there is no political manipulation behind these unrests; that is to say, no desire of certain groups or circles to weaken the state.'[201] Similarly, American Democrats simply couldn't believe that they had lost the elections without simple-minded Americans being manipulated from abroad.

Until recently most politicians and experts in the West have called people not to believe in various conspiracy theories, especially those spread via social media, there is a category of such theories that are, however, hailed and widely circulated over the mainstream Western media. One of the most incredible claims that Russia is meddling in democratic processes in the West – the Benjamin Griveaux affair in France – prompted French journalist Ingrid Riocreux to publish an article entitled *Russian interference – an authorised conspiracy theory.*'[202] She writes that no conspiracy theory is far-fetched and implausible when it concerns Russia. This case involved eccentric Piotr Pavlenski, considered by some to be an artist, who became famous (infamous) by sewing his lips shut, nailing his scrotum to the pavement on the Red Square and setting fire to the doors of the Lubyanka building in Moscow, before moving to France where he also set fire to the windows of the Bank of France in Paris.

---

[201] M. Debré, *Mémoires : gouverner autrement*, Albin Michel, 1993, p. 24.
[202] I. Riocreaux, 'Ingérences russes : le complotisme autorisé,' *Causeur*, 19 février 2020.

However, when Pavlenski – an ethnic Russian – circulated on the Internet compromising images of Benjamin Griveaux, who was running for the post of the mayor of Paris, Western media immediately saw Russian, particularly Putin's, hand behind this affair. This notwithstanding that chances of Griveaux, though running from Macron's *La République en Marche (REM)*, to win the race were considered by opinion polls to be relatively low and the post of the mayor of Paris, though important for the millions of Parisians and tourists, seems to be far from President Putin's concerns. Nevertheless, *The Irish Times* even published an article entitled 'Griveaux sex scandal threatens to reshape France's relationship with Russia'[203], where it was held against Russia that its authorities had been 'surprisingly lenient with Pavlenski' (I imagine what would have been Western media's reaction had Russian authorities been less 'lenient'!) and that Pavlenski's lawyer had 'heard that Putin laughed when Pavlenski left Russia.' However, as a lawyer, he added a caveat: he didn't know whether that was true or not. And such idiotism is spread not through social media, but published in newspapers once considered respectable!

---

[203] *The Irish Times*, 17 February 2020.

18- Revolution in the Western World: Democracy v. Liberalism

Besides a revolutionary situation in international relations, where the existing balance of powers was broken and the two main competing geopolitical visions of the future – a unipolarity with one centre of power and refashioned multipolarity with different centres of power – are competing, there is also a revolutionary situation in countries that have been most stable and have served as examples for others. This is the crisis of liberal democracy that is also related to, and conditioned by, processes of globalisation.

Modern democracy, originating in Western European societies, has had from its inception dialectical (i.e. where different phenomena, depending on concrete circumstances, have a kind of friend-enemy relationships) relationships with three other phenomena that have, on the one hand, supported democracy's emergence and growth while also putting limits on its expansion and deepening. These three phenomena are nationalism, capitalism and liberalism. As in the post-WWII world the last two have been considered almost inseparable (i.e. individual liberties and market freedoms have been often seen as two sides of the same coin), the controversial (i.e. dialectical) relationship of democracy with capitalism and liberalism can be dealt with as one dialectical controversy, notwithstanding that there have been societies where, and periods when, free market has coexisted (or still coexists) with conservative and anti-liberal social policies (like Chile under General Pinochet or South Korea under the military rulers) or that economically liberal societies may not be so liberal socially and vice versa. As I have already discussed the controversial relationship between democracy and nationalism in the previous chapter, where I dwelled upon the role of nationalism the nation-state in history and in today's world, here I will concentrate on the dialectical relationship between democracy and liberalism.

At the beginning of the twenty first century, the positive aspects of the relationships between democracy and liberalism, which for decades had prevailed in the post-Second World War West, have become overwhelmed by negative features. Democracy and liberalism, which had rather peacefully and with mutual benefits coexisted for many decades, are more and more undermining each other's potentials in the globalised world. The main reason for such a turnaround lies in the negative aspects or consequences of the processes of globalisation. As Harvard economist Dani Rodrik has argued, there is a fundamental incompatibility between hyper-globalisation, on the one hand, and democracy and national sovereignty, on the other.[204] One cannot have all of them at the same time.

The spread of market economy and democracy – the concepts that are considered by many to be the goods as obvious as God, motherhood and apple-pie – have in practice turned out to be a mixed blessing. If the planned economy of the Soviet type left everybody, and society as a whole, poor and market freedoms may indeed be one of the preconditions for political freedoms and personal liberties – the shock introduction of markets, especially unbridled markets, make a few extremely rich while many become even poorer than they were under the previous system. As one of the central tenets of democracy (with some important qualifications of course) is that the many count more than the few, it should be clear that economic 'shock therapy' and political democracy are incompatible and one either has a shock or democracy; not both. Cambridge economist Ha-Joon Chang goes even further writing that 'Free market and democracy are not natural partners'[205], though it must be emphasised that Professor Chang is speaking rather of 'unbridled markets', as advocated by Milton Friedman and his followers.

One of the most persistent market-friendly advocates of political freedoms, Karl Popper, already half a century ago incisively observed that: 'Even if the state protects its citizens from being bullied by physical violence (as it does in principle, under the system of unrestrained capitalism), it may defeat our ends by its failure to protect them from the misuse of economic power. In such a state, the economically strong is still free to bully one who is economically weak, and to rob of his freedom. Under these circumstances, unlimited economic freedom

---

[204] D. Rodrik, 'The inescapable trilemma of the world economy,' 27 June 2007 (https://rodrik.typepad.com/dani_rodriks_weblog/2007/06/the-inescapable.html).
[205] H.-J. Chang, *Bad Samaritans. Rich Nations, Poor Policies & the Threat to the Developing World*, Random House Business Books, 2007, p. 18.

can be just as self-defeating as unlimited physical freedom, and economic power may be nearly as dangerous as physical violence.'[206]

Free market (capitalism) and liberal democracy, phenomena that on the one hand presume each other, have always been in constant rivalry. The freer is a market, the greater is the economic inequality; the greater inequality, the less would there be democracy, and *vice versa*. Strong democracy attained by curbing inequality almost inevitably also bridles market freedoms. Economic inequality *de facto* and inevitably also increases political inequality, while political equality puts breaks on the widening economic inequality. Democracy tries to make a society more equal, while unbridled market increases inequality. In the post-Second World War Western world, there was a more or less successful balancing between liberalism and democracy, between liberties and equality, though at the end of the day it was liberalism that gained an upper hand.

John Dunn observes that within the liberal democratic movement 'the partisans of the order of egoism', i.e. capitalists, have defeated 'the partisans of equality'[207], i.e. democrats. One of the important causes of equality's defeat in the hands of economic egoism has been that in the long run the uncompromising instruments for attempting to realise equality and the rigidities inherent in its pursuit have blunted equality's appeal as a goal.[208] Both the French and especially the Russian revolutions, where contrary to the American revolution, the aim was not, as Hannah Arendt wrote, the 'freedom from oppression' but 'freedom from want', and one of the main requirements therefore was *egalité* (equality), have contributed to such a balance within today's understanding of democracy. She writes that 'the inescapable fact was that liberation from tyranny spelled freedom only for the few and was hardly felt by the many who remained loaded down by their misery. These had to be liberated once more and compared to this liberation from the yoke of necessity, the original liberation from tyranny must have looked like child's play.'[209]

The process of globalisation has revealed and accentuated not only the contradiction between democracy and nationalism, whose ideal had become enshrined in the concept of the nation-state and where modern democracy

---

[206] K. Popper, *The Open Society and Its Enemies*, Volume 2. Hegel & Marx, Routledge, 1996, p. 124.
[207] J. Dunn, *Setting the People Free. The Story of Democracy*, Atlantic Books, 2005, p. 134
[208] Ibid., p. 129
[209] H. Arendt, *On Revolution*, Penguin Books, 1965, p. 74.

emerged and evolved (the nation-state and democracy as twin brothers), but also between democracy and liberalism – both economic and social. Economic liberalism boosted by global uncontrolled world-wide financial markets, together with social liberalism, putting the primacy of the individual with her interests and desires above the interests of society, are destroying social bonds that have helped hold societies together, and are, as a result, also undermining nation-states – the cradles of democracy.

This dialectical controversy between democracy and liberalism has been like a ticking bomb (*une bombe à retardement*) waiting for its time to explode. Though these two phenomena – liberalism and democracy – have often been supportive of each other, there has also been, as if by necessity, a constant balancing necessary between them. Most Western, especially Western European, societies have until recently managed this controversy relatively well. In some, democracy has had an upper hand (e.g., in Scandinavian social democracies), while in others liberalism has prevailed (e.g., in the United States), but there has not been an open conflict between these phenomena. However, already for decades, due, first, to the rapid globalisation of the world and later also to the changing balance of power in the international system, this controversial friend-enemy relationship between democracy and liberalism has become less friendly and more inimical. It is reflected, *inter alia*, in the fact that liberal elites in most Western countries have started labelling those democrats whose policies and ideas (or/and personalities) they do not like as populists (let us recall that Ralf Dahrendorf has noted that, '*one man's populism* is another's *democracy*, and vice versa,' though he has also qualified this statement by claiming that 'while populism is simple, democracy is complicated'[210]). At the same time, democrats (or populists) have started considering liberals to be arrogant elitists who have become alienated from the people, from their needs and ways of thinking, believing them to be losers and ill-informed (let's recall Hillary Clinton's characterisation, though later hypocritically retracted, of Donald Trump's supporters as 'racist, sexist, homophobic deplorables').

The dialectical contradiction between liberalism and democracy must be carefully and wisely handled, lest it blow up in the face. This is what is happening today in quite a few Western countries. While liberal ideas are prevalent among

---

[210] R. Dahrendorf, 'Acht Anmerkungen zum Populismus,' 156 *Transit-Europäische Revue* 25 (2003).

European elites, values of democracy are today often expressed by populist parties and movements.

One of the most visible results of the defeat of democracy by liberalism has been indeed the rise of populism as a popular reaction to the rule of cosmopolitan elites. Already in 2008, in my lectures at The Hague Academy of International Law, I analysed the dialectical contradictions between nationalism, liberalism and democracy. However, then these contradictions hadn't yet reached today's acuteness, while populism was still a marginal phenomenon, not worthy even mentioning. Those, who were accused of being populists where primarily leftist leaders of some third-world countries like Hugo Chavez of Venezuela or Rafael Correa of Ecuador.

Today's populism is mostly a Western and right-wing phenomenon. French writer and journalist Alexandre Devecchio writes that notwithstanding variations between populisms in different societies there is something important in common in them: 'a desire to defend national sovereignty and identity against globalisation, to significantly limit immigration, certain hostility towards multiculturalism and support of programmes of social protection that benefit only citizens of the country.'[211] This is indeed that unites politicians such as Donald Trump, Boris Johnson, Matteo Salvini, Victor Orban, Marine Le Pen and others. One more important thing in common between populisms is that differently from so-called (self-defined) progressists, who, like President Emmanuel Macron of France, are leaders of cosmopolitan political, economic and intellectual elites, populist leaders find support mainly among those, though not only, who are left behind or have suffered because of the processes of globalisation.

The rise of populism, besides the negative effects of globalisation, has been boosted also by the revolution in information technology. Alexander Devecchio compares the effect of the spread of the Internet to that of the invention of the printing press by Gutenberg, in 1454. The latter undermined the power and position of the Roman Church and the clergy, which had enjoyed the monopoly in controlling peoples' hearts and minds, and led to the emergence of the Protestantism, as well as religious wars. Devecchio asks: 'But if the invention of the Web is going to provoke a similar fracture? This time not between Catholics and Protestants, but between traditional elites, who are in the process of losing

---

[211] A. Devecchio, *Recomposition : Le nouveau monde populiste*, Les éditions du Serf, 2019, Loc. 724.

their monopoly, which they have so far had over the mass media and the spread of information, and a new elite that can convey their populist message through the non-traditional means of communication.'[212] Yascha Mounk also believes that, 'the social media networks have closed the gap between the people and the elites, between those who have the power and those who don't.'[213]

Traditional media has been considered, already for some time and with some justification, as the 'fourth power' of the state, together with legislative, executive and judicial powers, though somewhat independent, but nevertheless in the service of the economic, political and intellectual elites, similar to the other three powers. For decades this separation of powers has been relative, all of them serving interests and reflected the values of economic, political and intellectual elites.

British author David Goodhart, in his book *The Road to Somewhere*[214], distinguishes between those Europeans whom he calls *anywheres* and those who according to him are *somewheres*. If the members of the first category (no more than 20-25% of the population in the West and much less in the Rest) belong to the cosmopolitan elite that has profited from globalisation and feels at home in different places in the world, the majority (more than 50% in the West) feels a need to maintain solid links to their country, to its history, traditions and language. To the latter category belong, naturally, not only those who believe that globalisation has by-passed them.

Tensions between solidarity and diversity, between the welfare state and mass migration have worsened, giving way to a growing divide between the 'people of anywhere' and 'people of somewhere' or as Alexander Devecchio puts it, between 'sedentaries' and 'nomads'.[215] It is a conflict between those who care for their 'rootedness' and entrenchment in a definitive place, be it a local village, a town or a nation-state, and cosmopolitans, i.e., those who feel at home in different places. There have always been a minority those who see the whole world, or Europe as the case may be, as their home, and a majority of those who feel at home only there, where they were born and among those who speak the same language and profess the same religion. For centuries, the first category

---

[212] A. Devecchio, *Ibid.*, Loc. 1581.
[213] Y. Mounk, *The People vs. Democracy: Why our Freedom is in Danger and How to Save It*, Harvard University Press, 2018, p.
[214] D. Goodhart, *The Road to Somewhere: The New Tribes Shaping British Politics*, Penguin, 2017.
[215] A. Devecchio, *Recomposition*, Loc. 1798.

was a relatively small minority, while most of the people were born, lived and died in the same place, except for mass movements of population that have several times occurred in the history of humankind.

Disturbing, in my opinion, but optimistic from the point of the authors, scenario was depicted in the joint article by Anne Hidalgo – the mayor of Paris, and Sadiq Khan – the mayor of London, published in *Le Parisien* and *The Financial Times*. Complaining about the lethargy of nation-states (in that respect they were right), they predicted the emergence in the twenty first century of the world of cities, instead of nineteenth century world of empires and the twentieth century world of nation-states.[216] These would be London, Paris, New York, Tokyo and other conglomerates that would lead the world instead of nations organised as states. Although it is often said with a lot of truth that, say, Moscow is not Russia, New York is not America, and Paris is not France, further concentration of elites in big cities, while neglecting the periphery, is the surest way to further divide people. Besides, big cities face no less acute problems than nation-states, which have, indeed, began to wake up from their lethargy.

The current conflict between liberal elites and masses of people is not the first standoff of that kind, though earlier ones were geographically much more limited. In her recent excellent study with an emblematic title *Il faut s'adapter* (*It is Necessary to Adapt*)[217] French philosopher Barbara Stiegler has shown how, at the beginning of the twentieth century, two prominent American thinkers Walter Lippmann and John Dewey were offering different answers to the question of the adaptability to the rapid societal change caused by the industrial revolution. There are significant parallels between what was happening then and current challenges. Stiegler writes:

'For the first time in the evolution of life and living beings, one species – our human species – finds itself in the situation, where it is not adapted to the new environment. For Lippmann, it was the situation where there was a huge gap between the natural inclination of the human species to remain as they were, inherited from the long and slow history of biological and societal evolution, and the demands of the rapid adaptability to the new environment, brutally imposed by the industrial revolution. Hence, the central theme of

---

[216] S. Khan & A. Hidalgo, 'London and Paris are leading the charge to shape the 21st century' *The Financial Times*, 27 June 2016.
[217] B. Stiegler, *Il faut s'adapter : sur un nouvel impératif politique*, Gallimard, 2019.

Lippmann's political studies: how to adapt human species to constantly and rapidly changing environment.... The fundamental question for Lippmann was how to avoid that this tension between the change and stasis, openness and closing, do not lead the masses to choose nationalism, fascism and generally all forms of isolationisms, in their effort to oppose to the rapid change, to restore the stasis and isolation.'[218]

Hence, it was this abyss between slow historical and biological evolution of human species and the rapidly changing physical environment, caused by the industrial revolution that worried Walter Lippmann. If at the turn of the twentieth century it was the industrial revolution, also combined with economic globalisation, at the turn of the twenty first century it is the revolution in information technology and whipped up globalisation of economic and financial markets that have, once again, uprooted masses of people in different countries, where only those who are adaptable to the change can survive. This is a bio-social experiment of the survival of the fittest and the fittest are the rationally thinking experts and managers and impartial judges using rational laws, who know in which direction the humankind must and will evolve. The masses should be taught to suppress their irrational impulses and follow the lead of enlightened experts, who have been able to adapt and readapt to the constantly changing environment. One of the main aims of public education should be 'the manufacture of the consent' of the masses with the policies contrived by the experts. As to the role of politicians, Lippmann writes that, 'though he (the statesman) cannot himself keep the life of the nation as a whole in his mind, he can at least make sure that he is taking counsel from those who know.'[219] A politician has to be only an expert in the choice of experts.

While Lippmann, and the neoliberals after him, saw the solution to the gap between rapidly changing environment and the inability of the masses to adapt to the new environment, in the combination of expertise of specialists, application of rational laws and 'manufacturing' the consent of the masses (i.e. indoctrinating them), Dewey would rely more on the collective intelligence of masses. Dewey was also the foremost detractor of neoliberal thinking. He wrote:

---

[218] *Ibid.*, p. 14.
[219] W. Lippmann, *A Preface to Politics*, p. 98.

'A class of experts is inevitably cut off from the common interests to such an extent that it becomes a class with its own private interests. Every governance by experts where masses are unable to inform the experts of their needs cannot be anything else than an oligarchy that rules in the interest of some. And enlightened information has to force the specialists to take account of the needs of masses. The world has suffered more from leaders and authorities than from masses.'[220]

We see that this almost a century old intellectual confrontation that has influenced policies of Western governments, has acquired the new acuteness. It is a conflict between elites and masses, between self-proclaimed progressives and those who are denigrated as populists.

In the globalised world these are not only authoritarian regimes that constitute a threat to democracy in their countries. The spread and liberalisation of global, particularly financial, markets are curbing democracy all over the world. Increasing the overall GDP of many countries, unbridled liberal markets make a few extremely rich while the majority of people are left behind. The wealth gaps are increasing practically in all countries. If in autocracies people are powerless *vis-à-vis* their rulers, in the globalised world people are powerless *vis-à-vis* global markets, even if they live in so-called liberal democracies. This is how economic liberalism is undermining democracy. At the same time, the rise in importance of individual rights and rights of a multitude of minorities, who aggressively promote their – often newly-found – identity, are undermining social cohesion and common values. This is how social liberalism undermines democracy. Societies that become 'atomised', to use the English title of Michel Houllebecq's novel *Les Particules élémentaires*, become non-societies, where there is no place for democracy. That is why today liberalism and democracy have become more antagonistic than supportive of each other.

Decades ago, those who fought against colonialism and colonial empires in Africa or elsewhere were considered and revered as freedom-fighters, though it would be more correct to qualify them as independence-fighters. Many of these leaders of national liberation movements were populists and quite a few of them (e.g., Gamal Abdel Nasser, Fidel Castro and Robert Mugabe) ended up as dictators. However, when they fought against imperial forces, they were seen by

---

[220] J. Dewey, *The Public and Its Problems* in *The Later Works of John Dewey 1925-1953*, vol. 2, Southern Illinois University Press, 1984, pp. 364-365.

many, particularly in countries which they led to independence, as genuine heroes, though in imperial capitals they were all regarded as mutineers and criminals. Today's populists are considered by cosmopolitan elites (and not only by those in their own countries since one of the characteristics of current elites is that they are generally cosmopolitan) to be narrow-minded, inward-looking protectionists, at best, and xenophobic nationalists, at worst. Yet, aren't the effects of the forces, today's populists are against, similar or sometimes even identical to the forces the anticolonial freedom-fighters were struggling against. Globalisation, global markets, particularly financial markets, deprive peoples of any say in their future. These impersonal forces, having become uncontrollable, make democratic decision-making meaningless. These are not only masses of people in small or underdeveloped countries, who are voiceless. Therefore, populists can be seen as freedom fighters against excesses of globalisation, against the rules established, say, by GAFAs and those who serve their interests. This tendency exists almost everywhere. Only those belonging to cosmopolitan elites benefit from surfing on the waves of globalisation, though quite a few of them also fall and drown in the process.

Globalisation and the current migration tide, as one of its manifestations, are exacerbating today's crisis of the European Union, where those who can be *anywhere* do not understand those who want to be *somewhere*. Those who can be *anywhere,* being dominant in politics, economy and media, are behaving like liberal autocrats *vis-à-vis* those whom they consider belonging to the mob. Without resolving this contradiction between the aspiration of European peoples to be somewhere (to feel at home in France, in Germany, in Italy, in Estonia, in Hungary) and the ambition of transnational elites to be anywhere, Europe will not come out unscathed from the current crisis.

Populists are accused of dividing societies with their criticism of democratically elected governments and by-passing traditional media, which has been and remain generally supportive of authorities, being critical only of some aspects or excesses of the authorities. But this is confusing the cause and the effect. The populist parties and leaders have become prominent namely because Western societies have become more and more unequal and divided.

Besides the chasm between 'somewheres' and 'anywheres', David Goodhart has drawn attention to different, though related to the previous one, aspect of a dangerous societal divide – between those with higher education aiming at cognitive professions and those who do manual jobs or take care of young, elderly, disabled and sick. He calls them as representing Head, Hand and Heart professions, respectively. If jobs of the first category (Head) are highly respected and usually also well paid, the other two enjoy lower remuneration and considerably lesser social prestige. And this notwithstanding of the fact that due to the spread of mass higher education, leading to the overall devaluation of university diplomas, there is an overproduction of people with diplomas but unable to perform highly paid cognitive jobs. Moreover, due to the advancement of artificial intellect (AI), the number of such jobs is diminishing, at least percentagewise. Goodhart is right also in pointing out that:

> 'It is also the case that a significant proportion of jobs that require quite high levels of academic qualification are demonstrably less useful and productive than many low-qualification jobs. Can we really argue that the work of a junior account manager in a City PR firm is more useful than that of a bus driver or an adult care worker? Moreover, many jobs in law, finance and other highly remunerated professions are often zero-sum: one individual or corporation wins and another loses. Public welfare has not been enhanced. A successful society must balance the tension between the inequality of esteem that arises from relatively open competition for highly rewarded jobs and the ethos of equality of esteem that flows from democratic citizenship. It is a tension that pits economic inequality against political equality. That means a democratic society that wants to avoid a powerful undercurrent of resentment must sufficiently value and reward a broad range of achievement embracing both cognitive and non-cognitive aptitudes and must provide meaning and respect for people who cannot – or do not want to – achieve in the examination room and professional career market.'[221]

If current elites, no matter whether they are represented by left-of-the-centre or right-of-the-centre political parties, don't want to give way to populists, they should pay attention to this widening divide between those with higher education and those, who belong to the category of people working mainly with hands or hearts.

There is quite a lot of truth in mutual criticism from both sides – from the side of self-declared progressists as well as from the side of those whom their

---

[221] D. Goodhart, *Head Hand Heart*, Penguin Books Ltd., 2020, p. 9.

critics call populists. In a way and simplifying a bit, both Brexit and Trump's victory in 2016 have been triumphs of populism over elitism (or if you like, democracy over liberalism). Personally, I don't have much sympathy for Boris Johnson because of his rude manners and being too often, even for a politician, economical with the truth; as an Estonian national living in London with my family, who are all Estonian passport holders, I am a bit apprehensive of Brexit too. Yet, this doesn't mean that I cannot see genuine concerns of Brexiteers.

The minicab driver, who took me from my home in Blackheath in South-East London to Heathrow in the North West of the city, helping me catch my September 2019 flight to Xi'an, in the Chinese heartland, told me that he had voted, in 2016, for Brexit. He also emphasised that if Britain would fail to exit the European Union, he would never participate in any future election. In his opinion, this would be one more sign that that the voice of the people doesn't count at all. I didn't argue with him, but I thought that here I was – a non-Brit, having lived for long in Britain, being obviously one of those who feels at home, if not everywhere, then at least in different places, including London, and here he was – a Brit, who had been born and had lived his whole life in Kidbrooke of South London, being one of those, who wanted to live there where he had been born and brought up. He had also travelled quite a lot, he told me, though the purposes of his trips had been quite different from reasons of my frequent voyages. For example, in summer 2018 he had been to Russia to support the English national team in their World Cup efforts. He was looking forward to his next flight to Japan to support there the English rugby team. And almost throughout our trip from Blackheath to Heathrow, he listened to the radio transmission of the cricket match between England and Australia that was going on at the Oval stadium, which we were passing on our way. Our chance encounter that lasted less than two hours revealed for me, at the very personal level, conflicts of interests and perceptions that exist in the country, and even beyond. This was my personal experience, easily generalisable.

David Goodhart was right when he said in his interview to *Le Figaro Vox* that the Brexit mess was not necessarily a sign of the end of democracy, but a conflict between two visions of democracy – representative and direct democracy expressed, *inter alia*, through referenda.[222] Both of them have their advantages as well as serious shortcomings. If representative democracy has led

---

[222] D. Goodhart, 'Après le Brexit, le Royaume-Uni ne va pas couler en mer' *Le Figaro Vox*, 4 octobre 2019.

to the alienation of elites from the people, direct democracy may contain seeds of authoritarianism. However, Brexit has been a mess not because of the use of a referendum as an element of direct democracy, but because the deep divisions in society and alienation of elites from the majority of the people. London is not Britain and the City of London is not even the whole London.

While writing my memoires, which are more about the times I have lived through and issues I have dealt with, than my own personality and life-experiences, I understood better than before that our ideas and approaches are more influenced by our personal histories than by what may be called 'objective' reality. I hadn't much thought and never written anything about populism – a phenomenon that has always existed, sometimes commented[223], but that sprang into prominence only recently. I have become, through hazards and ambition, someone whose profession and lifestyle are, *par excellence*, cosmopolitan, even at home I speak different languages with different members of my family. Having held professorships in most prestigious universities, and worked on various diplomatic posts, I probably also belong to a kind of cosmopolitan elite, whose wealth, if any, is mostly intellectual with a meagre material component. However, having been brought up by a single mom as well as by my grandparents in a remote Estonian village and having dropped out of the school at the age of 15, starting making my own living, I feel strong affinity with many of those who vote for populist parties. I would even say that while I sympathise with the populist electorate, I have much less respect for those who this electorate brings to power. I understand the minicab driver, who took me from Blackheath to Heathrow and was a strong Brexiteer, and what moral right do I – a cosmopolitan Estonian – have to tell a London-born mini-cab driver which way would be more rational to cast a vote on the referendum on the future of his country. I also sympathise with my relatives in the Southern Estonia, the majority of whom voted for EKRE – the party whose populist leaders are, to put it mildly, unsympathetic for me. However, as Canadian essayist Mathieu Bock-Coté writes, 'there are, no doubt, among populist politicians extreme rights who nurture crazy and repulsive ideas, but it would be wrong to confuse ideological obsessions of such politicians and those real issues that form the basis of a significant part of the electorate and public concerns that have been censured by the dominant

---

[223] Guy Hermet observes that the term 'populism' was mentioned in French dictionaries for the first time only in 1929 (G. Hermet, Narodniki, boulangisme, People's Party: trois populismes fondateurs du XIX ciècle, in *Le Retour des Populismes : Etat du Monde 2019* (Bertrand Badie, Dominique Vidal eds.), 2018, Loc. 345.

ideology.'[224] These are mainly the faults of so-called mainstream political parties, be they of centre-right or centre-left, which have neglected these real issues. Populist leaders can exploit only what is exploitable.

After Fareed Zakaria published, more than twenty years ago, an article on 'illiberal democracy'[225], the term has become firmly anchored in both academic as well as political discourse. Agreeing with Zakaria that there are democracies where liberal values are not in high esteem, I wondered whether the reverse can be also true? Could there exist political regimes that may be defined as liberal but undemocratic, i.e. nondemocratic liberalism? Now I am sure that such regimes not only can, but in reality, exist.

If in illiberal democracy it is democracy that trumps liberalism, under undemocratic (or authoritarian) liberalism it is liberalism that has the upper hand and puts constraints on democracy. There are, political regimes that may be defined as 'liberal', but which have serious deficit of democracy. It is not to say that the emergence of such regimes is the only cause of the current rise of populism or that liberalism trumping democracy can be necessarily cured by populist remedies. However, there is certainly a causal link between populism and the deficit of democracy in Western liberal societies. Undemocratic liberalism is a political regime, where out of the triptych – the government of the people, by the people and for the people – only the first still stands, i.e. where the participation of the people in the governance is both formal and ineffective and where the governance is exercised not in the interest of the majority of the people. Today many, if not most, Western societies have been infested with the germ of 'undemocratic liberalism'. French philosopher Chantal Delsol was right when she wrote that 'The populists, contrary to what some may be say, are really democrats, but they are not liberals. At the same time, universalist elites, like those in Brussels, are really liberals, who are not any more democrats since they don't like when people vote to limit some liberties.'[226]

Populist parties of movements may face setbacks in coming elections and their popularity ratings may suffer. However, the phenomenon is not going away, as its sources persist. Moreover, so-called mainstream parties are more and more

---

[224] M. Bock-Coté, *Le Multiculturalisme comme Religion Politique*, Cerf, 2019, pp. 291-292.
[225] F. Zakaria, The Rise of Illiberal Democracy, *Foreign Affairs* (November–December 1997).
[226] C. Delsol, 'Populiste, c'est un adjectif pour injurier ses adversaires,' *Le Figaro Vox*, 6 septembre 2018.

using populist slogans and policies. The clearest example of this tendency is the metamorphoses of the British Tories, who under Boris Johnson are not any more a traditional conservative party, as we had known it. Having used some traditional Labour Party precepts as well as Nigel Farage's Brexit Party ideas, luring voters from both of them, the Tories have become a populist party – partly left-wing, partly right-wing.

19- Instead of Conclusions: Is E Pluribus Unum Indeed Replacing Ex Uno Plures?

When working for the UN in Central Asia, I spent my summer vacation on the shores of one of the most beautiful, also one of the deepest, lakes in the world – Issyk Kul in the Tian Shan Mountains in eastern Kyrgyzstan. My wife Irina and son George joined me for this wonderful trip, where we also met Musurkul Kabylbekov, a former journalist, PhD in philosophy and a devout Muslim, praying five times a day, and not tolerating any of my jokes, when they even remotely touched upon Islam. Nevertheless, during those two weeks when we were together, we became and still remain friends notwithstanding all the differences in our views and lifestyles. Therefore, once riding on horseback high in the Tian Shan Mountains, I said to Musurkul that Rudyard Kipling was, probably, wrong when he wrote: 'Oh East is East, and West is West, and never the Twain shall meet, Till Earth and Sky stand presently at God's great Judgement Seat.' Our friendship has showed that we, representing respectively the East and the West, having met by chance, could very much enjoy each other's company, even if disagreeing on many important issues. To my remark Musurkul reminded me that I had stopped, as most of those who know Kipling superficially, short of reading the next phrase of the poem: 'But there is neither east nor west, Border, nor Breed, nor Birth, When two strong men stand face to face, though' they come from the ends of the earth!'

Naturally for Musurkul, and I believe for Kipling too, only when two strong men meet, not strong women – an obvious oxymoron from their point of view – there will be neither east nor west. In that respect, too, our differences remained. While I believe in the possibility of giving a modern, not a fundamentalist or literal, interpretation to Kipling's *The Ballad of East and West*. 'There is neither east nor west, Border, nor Breed, nor Birth' for all men and women (maybe even those who are gender fluid) who are strong enough to overcome their religious, racial, ethnic or other prejudices and associate themselves not only with their tribe or faith but also with the whole humankind, for Musurkul such a reinterpretation of Kipling – changing the meaning depending on the context and time (called *ijtihad* in Islam) contains seeds of heresy. It would be a slippery slope: one who starts modifying and modernising Kipling, dragging him out of his historical context, may well end up re-interpreting also the Holy Book. So, when I once expressed my doubts about the righteousness of the first four Caliphs, who succeeded Muhammad and are called in the Sunni Islam Righteous Caliphs, Musurkul politely but firmly asked me not to go further. Unlike Charlie Hebdo cartoonists I chose not to insist.

In the shores of Issyk Kul and in the Tian Shan mountains, drinking *kumys* (fermented mare's milk) in a *yurta* (a tent of nomadic peoples of Central Asia), I vividly understood how different we are due to our belongingness to human societies, which for millennia had evolved miles away from each other and become hugely different, but being still able, if we want and if we make an effort, to understand each other as human beings, while retaining our differences. Of course, what we need is a common language. In Central Asia we were lucky that we had Russian as our *lingua franca*. Once again, I discovered that empires have had some positive effects as well. Common languages, spoken by many, is one of them. No need to discard them by throwing the baby out with the bath water. Spread of languages and studying different languages make the world also a bit more homogeneous. But where have our differences come from? What do we have in common? Can we overcome our differences and is it, indeed, necessary to overcome them? And here my personal experience, particularly on the shores of the lake Issyk Kul and surrounding it Tian Shan mountains, led me to the reflections on the evolution of humankind that have a bearing on current conflicts of which I wrote above.

The American motto *E Pluribus Unum*, written on the American dollar in Latin, reads in plain English: 'out of many – one'. It symbolises not only the union between the thirteen states forming the Federation, but also the melting pot idea of the American political system, aimed at making Americans out of various migrants of European, mostly Anglo-Saxon, extraction. Now, more than two centuries later, the Washington is in the vanguard of spreading American way of life, including the melting pot experience, all over the world. To understand what it means for the humanity and for various societies one needs to step back to see the whole picture since as Russian poet Sergei Yesenin wrote: 'Face to face you can't see the features. You need distance to see what is great.'

In this big picture we see that tens of thousands of years before anybody used Latin, or any other known language for that matter, another, an opposite process had begun that could be called 'out of one – many' (*Ex Uno Plures* in Latin). It began (allegedly, since new discoveries may further change the dates and locations) more than 50,000 years ago when the Homo Sapiens started their journey from an East African village to all over the world. During that journey, our forefathers and foremothers, who at the beginning of this migration did not differ much from each other as to the colour of their skin, slant of their eyes or the ways in which they communicated between themselves, acquired visible physical and profound cultural differences, though remaining members of the same species of Homo Sapiens. This process of the colonisation of the planet Earth, during which 'out of one emerged many', was slow; it took tens of thousands of years until foot-and fingerprints of Homo Sapiens could be found in all hospitable, and today even inhospitable, places on Earth. Being always genetically very similar, humans became visibly, i.e. superficially, rather different (some blue-eyed, others dark-eyed, some tall while others much shorter and so on). However, groups of Homo Sapiens, gradually forming tribes, ethnic groups, nations and civilisations, became profoundly different from each other in terms of their cultures, religions, mores and languages spoken. As American philosopher Michael Walzer once aptly put it: 'Every human society is universal because it is human, particular because it is a society.'[227] Cultural differences between peoples, be they historical, religious or ethical, that may or may not be immediately visible, became huge over the millennia and they still remain profound. As physical or biological beings we are rather similar, as social animals we may be worlds apart.

American social psychologist Jonathan Haidt has persuasively demonstrated that even in today's world there still coexist at least three different categories of societies: those with the ethics of autonomy, those with the ethics of community and those with the ethics of divinity. In the first category, the individual with her wants, needs and preferences runs prime; in the second, concepts such as duty, hierarchy, respect, reputation and patriotism are predominant, while in the third prevails the idea that people are, first and foremost, only temporary vessels

---

[227] M. Walzer, *Thick and Thin: Moral Argument at Home and Abroad* (University of Notre Dame Press, 1994), p. 8.

within which a divine soul has been implanted.[228] Professor Haidt concludes his essay with a warning against moral monists: 'Beware of anyone who insists that there is one true morality for all people, times, and places – particularly if that morality is founded upon a single moral foundation.' [229] However, notwithstanding such learned voices and warnings, there have been, and still are, those who in their provincial ignorance of the complexities and societal differences existing in the world try not only to unify the world but also make it uniform; for example, either communist, liberal democratic or Muslim. Such worldviews have their roots in the Judeo-Christian and the Enlightenment belief in a universal history and in a linear progress leading inexorably towards some specific goal where history ends. Those who don't recognise this truth, it is argued, are 'on the wrong side of history.' If the communist experiment of the realisation of universal history has, at least for the time being, miserably failed, then liberal democratic projects for the whole world are, notwithstanding all the red rights blinkering here and there, still actively promoted. Even Islamists have joined the ranks of such 'practical utopians' by their attempts to islamise the globe, beginning with the Middle East. All these movements contain a mixture of determinism and voluntarism; the belief in an unavoidable unilineal course of history and the burning desire to accelerate the coming of some inevitable bright future.

One may, of course, reasonably argue that the process of global heterogenisation, expressed in *Ex Uno Plures*, has by now ended. Indeed, there are many signs of global homogenisation, as articulated in the formula *E Pluribus Unum*. Within the general process of globalisation, we can distinguish global homogenisation combined with the heterogenisation within individual societies. To an extent, these are natural processes. It is to be expected that different societies interacting, rubbing shoulders and borrowing from those with whom they interact, may become, at least in some respects, more like each other. It may indeed be that instead of *Ex Uno Plures* humankind has already begun a reverse journey towards *E Pluribus Unum*. However, the processes of heterogenisation that went on for tens of thousands of years, cannot be undone within decades and probably even within centuries, if ever. Even if individuals from different societies can cross the boundaries of their cultural and ethical

---

[228] J. Haidt, *The Righteous Mind: Why Good People Are Divided by Politics and Religion* (Penguin, 2013), p. 116.
[229] *Ibid.*, p. 368.

communities, to step, so to say, outside of their 'moral matrix', or sometimes even straddle and enjoy more than one of them, communities themselves change much more slowly, and changes that are instigated and forced on them, either from above or from the outside, may have lasting negative effects. Yet, there are those who seek to artificially accelerate the processes of global homogenisation, using, *inter alia*, human rights discourse, exportation of democracy and liberal values, carrying out operations of regime change, sometimes using military force for that purpose. Such 'one size fits all' policies foreseeably spread chaos and destruction instead of democracy and human rights. The much advertised and enthusiastically welcomed by the West 'Arab spring' led to the collapse of statehood in Iraq, Libya, Syria and Yemen, while in other Middle East nations the authorities, to avoid likely implosion, returned to authoritarian rule. Even admitting that the process of 'out of one – many' has ended, and the tendency of 'out of many – one' is manifesting itself in the processes of globalisation, it would be irresponsible to try to artificially accelerate this movement. Moreover, the end of history, be it either à la Karl Marx or à la Francis Fukuyama, would also be the end of social experimentation. The uniformity of social, economic or political systems would also mark the end of societal progress. Diversity here is no less important than biodiversity or diversity within societies organised as states.

However, such a social diversity, existing worldwide, can hardly subsist and survive within the same society organised as a state without ripping it apart. I very much enjoy the company of my Muslim friend Musurkul when from time to time we meet. However, I doubt whether we could live so peacefully in the same apartment, house or even neighbourhood having so differing understandings and perceptions on many important as well as unimportant matters. Two strong men on horseback in Tian Shan Mountains may well enjoy each other's company and become enriched by their communion. However, when back to their families and communities where they live and work, they re-enter into different, more habitual for them, relationships – patriarchal, modern or post-modern. Their enjoyment of each other's company and their friendship remains strong as long as they live far from each other, as long as the societies from which they come don't intermingle in the same neighbourhood. Although for me it would be difficult to accept that 'good fences make good neighbours', greatly differing communities can well communicate and enrich each other when they do not become too close. Those individuals, whether they consider themselves as cosmopolitans or not, who want to step outside of their cultures and join different societies, should be ready to abandon parts of their identity in order to become integrated into their new homelands. Maybe at the end of the day the world will indeed become one without countries, borders or religions to die for but this day is still far away.